Historical Perspectives on Homosexuality

This volume is published in hardback as Volume 2 of the monograph series *Research on Homosexuality.*

Series Editor: John P. De Cecco, PhD, Director, Center for Homosexual Education, Evaluation & Research, San Francisco State University, and Editor, *Journal of Homosexuality.*

Volumes in this series include:

Homosexuality and the Law
(The Hardbound edition of Volume 5, Nos. 1/2 of the *Journal of Homosexuality.* Guest Editor: Donald C. Knutson, JD). Fall/Winter 1979/80.
Historical Perspectives on Homosexuality
(The hardbound edition of Volume 6, Nos. 1/2 of the *Journal of Homosexuality.* Guest Editors: Sal Licata, PhD and Robert Petersen, PhD Candidate). Fall/Winter 1980/81.
Nature and Causes of Homosexuality: A Philosophic and Scientific Inquiry
(The hardbound edition of Volume 6, No. 4 of the *Journal of Homosexuality.* Guest Editor: Noretta Koertge, PhD). Summer 1981.
Homosexuality and Psychotherapy
Editor: John Gonsiorek, PhD. Winter 1981.
Alcoholism and Homosexuality
(The hardbound edition of Volume 7, No. 4 of the *Journal of Homosexuality.* Guest Editors: Thomas O. Ziebold, PhD and John Mangeon). Summer 1982.
Homosexuality in Literature
Editor: Stuart Kellogg.

This series is published by The Haworth Press, Inc., under the editorial auspices of the Center for Homosexual Education, Evaluation & Research, San Francisco State University, and the *Journal of Homosexuality.*

Historical Perspectives on Homosexuality

Compiled and Edited by
Salvatore J. Licata, PhD and
Robert P. Petersen

Volume 6, Nos. 1/2, Fall/Winter 1980/81
Journal of Homosexuality

Co-published by The Haworth Press, Inc.,
and Stein and Day/Publishers/New York

The *Journal of Homosexuality* is published quarterly in Fall, Winter, Spring, and Summer. Volume 1 was published over a two-year period: Vol 1(1), Fall 1974; Vol. 1(2), Winter 1975-76; Vol. 1(3), Spring 1976; Vol. 1(4), Summer 1976. An index is included in the Summer issue of each volume.

Articles from the *Journal of Homosexuality* are selectively indexed or abstracted in the *ABS Guide to the Behavioral and Social Sciences, Abstracts for Social Workers, Abstracts in Anthropology, BioSciences Information Service of Biological Abstracts (BIOSIS), Le Bullétin Signalétique, Chicago Psychoanalytic Literature Index, College Student Personnel Abstracts, Criminal Justice Abstracts, Current Contents: Behavioral and Social Sciences, Excerpta Medica, Index Medicus, Index to Periodical Articles Related to Law, Pastoral Care and Counseling Abstracts, Selected List of Tables of Contents of Psychiatric Periodicals, Psychological Abstracts, Psychological Reader's Guide, Social Science Citation Index, Sociological Abstracts,* and *Women's Studies Abstracts.* Selected articles are also cited through *CERDIC* (France), *ERIC/CAPS, International Bibliography of the Social Sciences*, and the *National Criminal Justice Service (NCJRS) Index.*

MANUSCRIPTS may be submitted to John P. De Cecco, Editor, *Journal of Homosexuality,* Center for Homosexual Education, Evaluation and Research, San Francisco State University, San Francisco, CA 94132. Information concerning the preparation of manuscripts may be obtained from the Editor.

BUSINESS OFFICE. All subscription and advertising inquiries should be directed to The Haworth Press, 149 Fifth Avenue, New York, NY 10010. Telephone (212) 228-2800.

SUBSCRIPTIONS are on an academic year, per volume basis only. Payment must be made in U.S. or Canadian funds only. $28.00 individuals, $48.00 institutions, $65.00 libraries. Foreign orders: $28.00 individuals, $48.00 institutions, $70.00 libraries. Postage and handling: U.S. orders, add $5.00; Canadian orders, add $5.00 U.S. currency or $5.50 Canadian currency; foreign orders, add $10.00.

CHANGE OF ADDRESS. Please notify the Subscription Department, The Haworth Press, 149 Fifth Avenue, New York, NY 10010 of address changes. Please allow six weeks for processing; include old and new addresses, including zip codes.

Second-class postage paid at New York, NY and additional mailing offices.

ISSN: 0091-8369

Historical Perspectives on Homosexuality is a co-publication of The Haworth Press, Inc. and of Stein and Day Publishers, Scarborough House, Briarcliff Manor, New York 10510.

The Haworth Press, 149 Fifth Avenue, New York, New York 10010

Library of Congress Cataloging in Publication Data
Main entry under title:

Historical perspectives on homosexuality.

(Research on homosexuality, ISSN 0091-8369 ; v. 2)
(Journal of homosexuality ; v. 6. no. 1-2)
Includes bibliographical references and index.
1. Homosexuality, Male—History—Addresses, essays, lectures. I. Licata, Salvatore J. II. Petersen, Robert P. III. Series: Research on homosexuality ; v. 2. IV. Series: Journal of homosexuality ; v. 6, no. 1-2.
HQ75.J68 vol. 6, no. 1-2 (HQ76) 306.7'6'09 80-6262
ISBN 0-917724-27-5 (Haworth) AACR2
ISBN 0-8128-2810-0 (Stein and Day)

Printed in the United States of America

This volume is dedicated to the men and women
of the Center for Homosexual Education, Evaluation and Research,
San Francisco State University

The *Journal of Homosexuality* is devoted to empirical research, and its clinical implications, on lesbianism, male homosexuality, gender identity, and alternative sexual lifestyles. It was created to serve the allied professional groups represented by psychology, sociology, anthropology, medicine, and law. Its purposes are:

a) to bring together, within one contemporary periodical, rigorous empirical research on homosexuality and gender identity;
b) to provide scholarly research which, although not rooted in strict experimental methodology, has heuristic value for the understanding of homosexuality and gender identity; and
c) to show the implications of these findings for helping professionals in a wide variety of disciplines and settings.

ABOUT THE EDITORS

Salvatore J. Licata received his PhD in history from the University of Southern California. His dissertation explores the history of the American homosexual rights movement in the twentieth century. Dr. Licata has taught history courses on homosexuality at several universities and most recently was an Associate Researcher at the Center for Homosexual Education, Evaluation and Research, San Francisco State University, where he was instrumental in establishing an Archive on Homosexuality. Dr. Licata has been active in the homosexual rights movement since 1974 and serves on the national boards of the Gay Academic Union and the Institute for the Study of Human Resources. He currently resides in New York City.

Robert P. Petersen is Research Associate at the Center for Homosexual Education, Evaluation and Research, San Francisco State University.

HISTORICAL PERSPECTIVES ON HOMOSEXUALITY

A Special Double Issue of The Journal of Homosexuality

Compiled and Edited by Salvatore J. Licata, PhD, and Robert P. Petersen

Volume 6, Numbers 1/2, Fall/Winter 1980/81

Historical Perspectives on Homosexuality

FOREWORD

As movingly documented in this volume, the history of homosexuality is largely a chronicle of how society has made the homosexual option unbelievably difficult and dangerous for those who exercised it. Such treatment could not drive homosexuality away any more than fasting obliterates the desire for food. Persecution could and did remove homosexual behavior from ordinary public observation and discourse. These pages narrate an exciting, frightening story of institutional duplicity and oppression.

Historical Perspectives on Homosexuality is the second volume in the Research Monograph Series jointly sponsored by The Haworth Press and the Center for Homosexual Education, Evaluation and Research; it also composes the first two issues in the sixth volume of the *Journal of Homosexuality.* I wish to express my deepest appreciation to the guest editors, Salvatore Licata and Robert Petersen, for their conception of the project and most successful effort in recruiting a distinguished group of scholars. I congratulate the authors on their contributions. I also want to express my gratitude to Stuart Kellogg, who provided the editorial guidance for the project.

John P. De Cecco, PhD
Editor, *Journal of Homosexuality*

INTRODUCTION

Salvatore J. Licata, PhD
Robert P. Petersen

For nearly a century, homosexuality has been investigated by social scientists but has received almost no attention from historians. Professional researchers in history have neglected, overlooked, or been afraid to examine homosexuality because of the stigma attached to the topic. This stigma also has inhibited the preservation of sources that would allow historical research. Families of famous people often destroy or restrict the use of documents that refer to an ancestor's sexual orientation. Archives and libraries hide or, even worse, throw away as worthless materials that might shed some light on sexual nonconformity. As a result, histories dealing with homosexuality have been rare.

The situation is beginning to change. For at least a decade, historians have begun to pay more attention to the role of women and to areas of personal concern, such as the family and sexuality.[1] Homosexual history is also coming to be recognized as a viable area of historical research.

The essays in this volume have been prepared to stimulate thought and especially to further the work of the growing number of researchers studying sex and sexual orientation. This introduction, divided into three sections, begins with a discussion of the resources available, including research currently underway, and efforts undertaken to preserve historical source material. The second section is an overview of some of the major works that would best acquaint the reader with the subject matter. The introduction ends with suggestions for further research.

AVAILABLE RESOURCES

The present state of historical research on homosexuality in the United States includes local history projects, archives, courses, and conferences. The increased interest in open lifestyles and civil rights has inspired the formation of local organizations devoted to research. Many of the people who work on local history projects are not academics but simply those who want to know more about homosexuality in the past. Scholars, such as Alan Berubé of the San Francisco Lesbian and Gay History Project, have recorded historical profiles of in-

Journal of Homosexuality, Vol. 6(1/2), Fall/Winter 1980/81

dividuals and used this information in multimedia presentations. Similar projects are underway in Boston, Buffalo, Chicago, New York, and Washington, D.C. A primary goal of all these projects is to locate, preserve, and publish evidence of sexual nonconformity. Many of these groups are developing archives to facilitate their research.

Early efforts to preserve North American historical records grew with the development of the homosexual rights movement. In the early 1950s, ONE, Inc. began building an impressive collection of primary and secondary materials. The collection was divided in the mid-1960s between ONE, Inc. and the Homosexual Information Center, and both archives have continued to expand their collections. A third private archive in Los Angeles is the National Gay Archives, formerly the Western Gay Archive. In San Francisco, the archives of the Mattachine Society and the Daughters of Bilitis have been deposited in the Institute for the Advanced Study of Human Sexuality.

One of the oldest collections on the East Coast is the Institute for Sexual Ethics in Hartford, Connecticut, which has been collecting materials for decades. If opened and processed, these could prove to be a treasure of documents and rare printed material. In New York City, the former Mattachine library was bought at an auction by the Church of the Beloved Disciple, which now houses the collection in their church building. The Lesbian Herstory Archive, also in New York, is available to women researching lesbian history. The Archive recently initiated a national drive to collect photographs of lesbians. The Lesbian Heritage Archive in Washington, D.C. preserves materials for Washington women. Among other collections, the most notable are the library of the Institute for Sex Research at Indiana University in Bloomington; the Stonewall Library in Hollywood, Florida; and the archive of research data and reports at the Center for Homosexual Education, Evaluation, and Research (C.H.E.E.R.) at San Francisco State University.

In addition to these established archives and libraries, individuals and groups in many cities have special collections of secondary materials and limited amounts of unprocessed archival records. These records are scattered, unavailable, and vulnerable. Their quantity and quality are unknown. A survey would help to locate these records and preserve them for eventual deposit in archival centers.

Although nonacademic organizations have shown lively interest in the area, the development of research and teaching on homosexual history in academic institutions has been slow and limited. There are a number of reasons for the small number of courses dealing with homosexuality. At a time when enrollments are decreasing, history departments are cautious in offering new courses and reluctant to offer anything controversial. It has been argued that there are no scholarly materials suitable for class reading lists. The lack of professors qualified to teach courses in the history of homosexuality is cited as another problem. Over the past decade, only a few college classes have been offered, and of these only a handful were exclusively within the historical discipline. Most of the courses do include a historical introduction but then move on to the areas of greatest research: sociology, anthropology, and psychology. Times are changing, however, and research on homosexuality in history has begun to surface. There are increasing numbers of qualified professors, and there is sufficient reading material to stimulate teaching and further inquiry.

Historians involved in research on homosexuality have complained that professional conferences neglect this new area. Many say it is difficult to get panels accepted at the larger conferences and that panels that are approved are scheduled at the least desirable time slots. Smaller professional conferences and interdisciplinary conferences have been cited as being more supportive of historical research. Regional and national Gay Academic Union conferences and the Committee on Lesbian and Gay History also have offered supportive atmospheres for research.

MAJOR WORKS

Most historians of homosexuality rely on ecclesiastical records, legal documents, medical opinions, and artistic expressions. These sources were produced by the groups who maintained the status quo. When the groups under study are perceived as threatening to the dominant social and sexual norms, the reliance on records kept for an elite can bias historical judgment; nevertheless, a great deal can be learned by studying these documents. Several studies have made creative use of them to survey the changing attitudes toward homosexuality over long periods of time and in many societies. Among the best known is Vern Bullough's *Sexual Variance in Society and History.*[2] Although there is wide divergence of opinion among these books and their attitudes toward homosexual men and women, they do give overviews of the evolution of sexual norms and the methods used to prevent deviation.

Monographs that examine homosexuality are beginning to appear in larger numbers, for example, Kenneth J. Dover's *Greek Homosexuality* and Michael Goodich's *The Unmentionable Vice: Homosexuality in the Later Medieval Period.*[3] These provide greater depth and knowledge of particular places and shorter time frames than can the comprehensive studies.

Biographies of renowned homosexual individuals are one of the more popular forms of published research. The depth and scope of the biographies vary from surveys, such as works by A. L. Rowse and Noel I. Garde, to in-depth studies of individuals, such as Louis Crompton's forthcoming study of Lord Byron and Hyde's biography of Oscar Wilde. Autobiographic works, such as Del Martin and Phyllis Lyon's *Lesbian/Woman*, are occurring with increasing frequency.[4]

In the history of literature there are two major categories: studies of homosexual love as a literary topic and analyses of works by homosexual writers. Studies of the first type were pioneered in the United States by Jeannette Foster's *Sexual Variant Women in Literature.* Ian Young's *The Male Homosexual in Literature*, a bibliography with essays, continues this tradition. Of works representative of the second category, Roger Austen's *Playing the Game* and Robert K. Martin's *The Homosexual Tradition in American Poetry* analyze the prose and poetry of American homosexual authors.[5]

The homosexual rights movements have received increasing attention. Studies available in English have focused mainly on efforts in Germany, England, and the United States. Historical research on the German movement began with the writings of Magnus Hirschfeld and have continued with publications by James Steakley, John Lauritsen, and David Thorstad. English homosexual rights efforts have been analyzed by Jeffrey Weeks. Among the first historians of the American movement were movement activists, including James Kepner, Jr., Del Martin, and Phyllis Lyon. Recent academic studies have been authored by John D'Emilio and Salvatore Licata.[6]

There also have been attempts to examine the lives of ordinary homosexual men and women. The best-known collection of documents of this type is Jonathan Katz's *Gay American History.*[7] This is especially important in Western history, where an open homosexual presence is so recent that to limit historical study to movement leaders and openly homosexual individuals famous in their own right would restrict its time frame to the period since the mid-nineteenth century and its scope to biographical history.

SUGGESTIONS FOR FURTHER RESEARCH

Research on the history of homosexuality has just begun. Much of the work done so far has been devoted to demonstrating the severity of the treatment accorded homosexual men and women. Important areas still are unexplored. More attention could be given to the study of positive and negative attitudes as affected by changes in social structure, economic activity, political leaders, and ideas. Consideration of the interrelationship of social, intellectual, and economic factors with laws and their enforcement would give us a more complete picture of the sources of oppression and liberation.

Preoccupied with the enforcement of antihomosexual laws, scholars have tended to overlook the question of whether the official justifications for these laws were accepted by the general population. Historians have paid insufficient attention to the self-conceptions of homosexual men and women. Scholars such as George Rudé and E. P. Thompson have pioneered new ways to study groups that leave few records.[8] Census data have been used by Stephen Thernstrom to study social mobility patterns in individual municipalities.[9] Birth and death records, land records, and probate records identify concentrations of single-person residences and trace the disposition of estates. These records could be used to describe unmarried individuals and their occupations, race, ethnicity, age, and class. Combining these sources with diaries and newspaper records would allow historians to draw profiles of individuals who may have been homosexual, their social networks, and their institutions. Imaginative use of these materials could chart pre-movement life patterns and the homosexual social underground.

The studies of social scientists like Clellan S. Ford and Frank A. Beach have shown the tremendous range and scope of sexual expression in different cultures.[10] Following their example, historians of homosexuality should compare societies on the basis of economics, national and regional differences, demographics, and politics.

As in any new field, many new questions remain unanswered: Why, for example, did the Napoleonic Code decriminalize same-sex acts during a period of conservative reaction? Why did the homosexual rights movements appear when they did? Why did the first known protests against sodomy laws occur in Germany in the latter half of the nineteenth century? Why did the movement in the United States first take hold in the 1950s, after Henry Gerber's attempt had failed in the 1920s? To what degree is cultural homophobia related to erotophobia or to fear of immoral behavior? Same-sex occupations and education systems also require study, as do patterns of femininity and masculinity in the past.

Many studies of homosexuality ignore lesbianism. Although Oscar Wilde and his friendship circle have received considerable attention, Natalie Barney's Paris salon has not. Who were the prominent lesbians of the past and what was their role in society? How do lesbians compare with other sexual minorities in terms of treatment and self-conception? How does the treatment of all women compare with the treatment of lesbians?

In the last ten years, historians and political activists have opened the door to the study of sexuality and homosexality. The women's movement and the gay movement questioned women's roles, patterns of femininity and masculinity, traditional family arrangements, and abridgements of civil liberties. Historians, too, became interested in areas of personal concern. To family history, women's history, and psychological history, the historical profession now may be willing to add sexual history and homosexual history. More published work in these areas would afford everyone an opportunity to learn about the sexual past and, therefore, to understand their present condition.

NOTES

1. John C. Burnham was one of the first scholars to call for historical writing on sexuality. See "The Progressive Revolution in American Attitudes Toward Sex," *Journal of American History* 59, no. 4 (March 1973): 885-908, and "Early References to Homosexual Communities in American Medical Writings," *Medical Aspects of Human Sexuality* 7, no. 36 (August 1973): 40-49.

2. Vern L. Bullough, *Sexual Variance in Society and History* (New York: John Wiley & Sons, 1975).

3. Kenneth J. Dover, *Greek Homosexuality* (Cambridge: Harvard University Press, 1978); Michael Goodich, *The Unmentionable Vice: Homosexuality in the Late Medieval Period* (Santa Barbara, Calif.: ABC-Clio Press, 1979).

4. Alfred L. Rowse, *Homosexuals in History: Ambivalence in Society, Literature and the Arts* (New York: Macmillan, 1977); Noel I. Garde, *Jonathan to Gide: The Homosexual in History* (New York: Vantage Press, 1964); H. Montgomery Hyde, *Oscar Wilde: A Biography* (New York: Farrar, Strauss, Giroux, 1975); Del Martin and Phyllis Lyon, *Lesbian/Woman* (San Francisco: Glide Foundation, 1972).

5. Jeannette H. Foster, *Sex Variant Women in Literature: An Historical and Quantitative Survey,* 2nd ed. (New York: Vantage Press, 1956); Ian Young, *The Male Homosexual in Literature* (Metuchen, N.J.: Scarecrow Press, 1975); Roger Austen, *Playing the Game: The Homosexual Novel in America* (New York: Bobbs-Merrill, 1977); Robert K. Martin, *The Homosexual Tradition in American Poetry* (Austin and London: University of Texas Press, 1979).

6. James D. Steakley, *The Homosexual Emancipation Movement in Germany* (New York: Arno Press, 1975); John Lauritsen and David Thorstad, *The Early Homosexual Rights Movement (1864-1935)* (New York: Times Change Press, 1974); Jeffrey Weeks, *Coming Out: Homosexual Politics in Britain from the Nineteenth Century to the Present* (London: Quartet Books, 1977); James Kepner, "Who Founded America's Gay Movement?" *Entertainment West,* Summer 1974, pp. 3, 9-10; Martin and Lyon, *Lesbian/Woman*; John D'Emilio, "Dreams Deferred," Parts 1-3, *Body Politic,* November 1978, pp. 19-24, December 1978-January 1979, pp. 24-29, and February 1979, pp. 22-27; Salvatore Licata, "Gay Power: A History of the American Gay Movement, 1908-1974" (Ph.D. dissertation, University of Southern California, 1978); Salvatore Licata, "The Emerging Gay Presence," Parts 1-3, *The Advocate,* no. 245, July 12, 1978, pp. 7-8, 43, no. 246, July 26, 1978, pp. 7-8, and no. 247, August 9, 1978, pp. 17-18, 20.

7. Jonathan Katz, *Gay American History: Lesbians and Gay Men in the U.S.A.—A Documentary* (New York: Thomas Y. Crowell, 1976).

8. George Rudé, *The Crowd in History: A Study of Popular Disturbances in France and England, 1730-1848* (New York: John Wiley & Sons, 1964); Edward Palmer Thompson, *The Making of the English Working Class* (New York: Pantheon Books, 1964).

9. Stephen Thernstrom, *Poverty and Progress; Social Mobility in a Nineteenth-Century City* (Cambridge: Harvard University Press, 1964).

10. Clellan S. Ford and Frank A. Beach, *Patterns of Sexual Behavior* (New York: Harper, 1951).

THE MYTH OF LESBIAN IMPUNITY
CAPITAL LAWS from 1270 to 1791

Louis Crompton, PhD

ABSTRACT: The standard history of antihomosexual legislation states that lesbian acts were not punished by medieval or later laws. This essay challenges this view by documenting capital laws since 1270 in Europe and America. A major influence was Paul's condemnation in Romans I, 26. By 1400, the lex foedissimam, *an edict of the Emperors Diocletian and Maximianus, issued in 287, was interpreted to justify the death penalty. Executions took place in Germany, France, Italy, Switzerland, and Spain. A brief survey of presently known male deaths in Europe and the Americas, which number about 400, also is included. This study draws on canon law and the commentaries of such jurists as Cino da Pistoia, Saliceto, López, Gómez, Farinacio, Cotton, Carpzow, Sinistrari, de Vouglans, and Jousse. It also discusses the records of a German trial of 1721, published elsewhere in this issue, that also led to the execution of a woman.*

Little has been written about lesbianism and the law from a historical point of view. Indeed, I am not aware of a single modern essay on the subject, and even brief references are comparatively rare.[1] In 1955, Derrick Sherwin Bailey, in what is still the standard study of early antihomosexual legislation, wrote categorically that lesbian acts were "ignored by both medieval and modern law."[2] As we shall see, this statement is clearly wrong. In making it, Bailey was generalizing in an unwarranted fashion from the situation in England. It is true that England's traditional "buggery" statute, first enacted in 1533 under Henry VIII, used terminology (still in force until 1967) that was not interpreted as criminalizing relations between women. American legal tradition until the twentieth century tended to follow English standards, with one remarkable exception to be noted later. In Europe before the French revolution, however, notably in such countries as France, Spain, Italy, Germany, and Switzerland, lesbian acts were regarded as legally equivalent to acts of male sodomy and were, like them, punishable by the death penalty. On occasion, executions of women were carried out. The purpose of this paper is to illuminate

Dr. Crompton is in the Department of English, University of Nebraska, Lincoln, Nebraska 68588. *He wishes to express his gratitude to Dr. Stanley Vandersall for valuable help in translating several of the Latin sources.*

Journal of Homosexuality, Vol. 6(1/2), Fall/Winter 1980/81

this tradition of capital legislation, to trace its sources, and to document some of the deaths by hanging, burning, drowning, and beheading that did in fact take place. It also is intended to serve as an introduction to the records of a remarkable trial, conducted at Halberstadt, Germany, in 1721, which are translated into English for the first time by Brigitte Eriksson in this issue of the *Journal of Homosexuality.*

It is well known that the death penalty for male homosexuality can be traced back in Judeo-Christian tradition to Leviticus 20:13. The Jews of ancient times, however, do not seem to have looked on lesbianism as a serious offense. There is no reference to it as a crime in the Old Testament. In the Babylonian Talmud, Rabbi Huna (who died in 296 A.D.) is quoted as ruling that "Women who practice lewdness with one another are disqualified from marrying a priest." But even this mild sanction is rejected by the Talmud, which prefers the view of Rabbi Eleazar (circa 150 A.D.), who argued that such a relation was no bar to priestly marriage, since "the action is regarded as mere obscenity."[3]

One may legitimately ask why, when Judaism looked on male homosexuality with such deadly hatred, it was comparatively indifferent to lesbianism. The most likely explanation is that male homosexuality was a religious practice of the "holy men" *(kedeshim)* of the Canaanite cults which were competing with orthodox Jahwism, while the correspondent "holy women" *(kedeshoth)* of these cults were not lesbians but women who engaged in heterosexual relations as part of their religion. Thus, the King James translation of Deuteronomy 23:17 reads, significantly, "There shall be no whore *(kadeshah)* of the daughters of Israel, nor a sodomite *(kadesh)* of the sons of Israel." The result of this religious animosity seems to have been the proscription of male, but not female, homosexuality, and the incorporation of the death penalty into the Levitical code, probably during the sixth century B.C., in a form applicable only to men.[4]

In Romans I, 26, however, St. Paul condemns women "who did change the natural use into that which is against nature." Eventually, as time passed, this animadversion of Paul's was to have fateful consequences for the legal status of lesbians in Christendom. Nevertheless, the first Roman Christian Imperial laws explicitly penalizing homosexuality, the edicts of Constantine and Constans in 342 A.D. and of Theodosius in 390 A.D., use language that specifically threatens death to men only, though, as we shall see, the scope of the law of 342 A.D. (cum vir) was subsequently broadened by medieval jurists to cover women. Both these laws ultimately were incorporated in the *Codex Justinianus.* A later law, Justinian's Novella 77 of 538 A.D., criminalizes "acts contrary to nature;" but Novella 141, which was issued six years later, speaks only of "the defilement of males" (de stupro masculorum).[5] We do not know how Novella 77 was construed, but we have as yet no evidence that it was interpreted to include lesbianism.

The earliest secular law I am aware of that seems to make explicit reference to sexual relations between women appears in a French code called *Li Livres di jostice et de plet,* usually dated about 1270, which derives from the district of Orleans. This compilation contains the following penalties:

> 22. *He who has been proved to be a sodomite must lose his testicles. And if he does it a second time, he must lose his member. And if he does it a third time, he must be burned.*
> 23. *A woman who does this shall lose her member each time, and on the third must be burned. (Feme qui le fet doit a chescune foiz perdre membre et la tierce doit estre arsse.)*[6]

Conceivably, the formula "perdre membre" in 23 might refer to the loss of an arm or leg; however, it is identical with that used in 22, where the context indicates that the man's penis is meant. Apparently this law called for the infliction of a clitorectomy, but it is difficult to imagine how this operation could be performed twice. Rarely has a law aimed primarily at male offenders been more grotesquely adapted to women. Surprisingly, Bailey translates these laws but takes no note of their relevance to lesbians.

The idea of lesbianism as a capital crime had certainly taken root in the popular imagination by this time. This is attested by a French romance presumed to have been written before the early fourteenth century, in which two women are threatened with burning. It is the tale of Princess Ide, an extension of the *Huon of Bordeaux* legend. Because of her military exploits, the Princess Ide, who has fought disguised as a man, is commanded by the Emperor to marry his daughter. Though the women, in the words of the sixteenth-century English translation by Lord Berners, pass their time in nothing more than "clyppinge and kyssyinge," the Emperor, when he discovers Ide's true sex, "wold not suffre suche boggery to be vsed," and commands that "bothe you and my doughter shall be brent." Ide and her lover are saved from the flames only by a miracle of the Virgin, who transforms Ide into a man in response to her prayers.[7]

By this time the theory that lesbianism was a heinous crime, fully as evil as male homosexuality and equally deserving of the death penalty, obviously had replaced Jewish tolerance. How are we to account for this change of attitude? Basically, it seems to have occurred as a development in the logic of Christian moral theology, as a rationalized conception of natural law came to replace earlier cultic anxieties. The broader idea of crimes against nature, criminal because they provided sexual pleasure without procreation, superseded the earlier cultic offense of male sodomy. In extending the death penalty for sodomy to women, St. Paul's condemnation in Romans was, undoubtedly, of paramount importance. Though modern scholars have commented on the ambiguity of his language, which might conceivably refer to women who engaged in heterosexual sodomy,[8] a study of Paul's early commentators shows that they did, indeed, regard the women who "changed the natural use" as lesbians. For example, the most influential of the Greek Fathers, St. John Chrysostom, preaching on Romans I, 26, 27, at Antioch about 390 A.D., paraphrased the passage by declaring that, in Paul's day, "even women again abused women, and not men only. And the men stood against one another, and against the female sex, as happens in battle by night." So the devil went about "to destroy the human race."[9] A Latin commentary of the same period, attributed to St. Ambrose, says of Paul, "He testifies that, God being angry with the human race because of their idolatry, it came about that a woman would desire a woman for the use of foul lust."[10] Writing at the beginning of the twelfth century, St. Anselm of Canterbury explained Paul's sentence: "Thus women changed their natural use into that which is against nature, because the women themselves committed shameful deeds with women."[11] A few years later Peter Abelard glossed Paul's reference to women's acts against nature even more forcefully: "Against nature, that is, against the order of nature, which created women's genitals for the use of men, and conversely, and not so women could cohabit with women."[12] Most of the numerous explications of Paul's Epistles do not, of course, deal with the sexology of Romans I, 26; however, an extensive search through early commentaries has as yet yielded no examples of commentators who read the passage in other than a lesbian sense.[13]

It is not surprising, therefore, to find that lesbianism was singled out as a sin in some early penitentials, notably that of Theodore of Tarsus, Archbishop of Canterbury, which dates from about 670 A.D., and of the Venerable Bede, compiled before 734 A.D.[14] Two works that were to become definitive guides to Christian moral theology also set lesbianism morally on a par with male sodomy. Gratian's *Decretum* of 1140 remained a standard work of canon law until 1917. It incorporated a passage from the *Contra Jovinianam* ascribed to Augustine: "Acts contrary to nature are in truth always illicit, and without doubt more shameful and foul, which use the Holy Apostle has condemned both in women and in men, meaning them to be understood as more damnable than if they sinned through the natural use by adultery or fornication."[15] Though his language, like Paul's, is potentially ambiguous, it was undoubtedly construed, as was his, to refer to lesbianism. The other medieval authority, whose influence on Catholic moral thinking has remained paramount down to the present day, was St. Thomas Aquinas. The *Summa Theologica*, written in 1267-1273, describes four forms of "unnatural vice." The third of these is distinguished as "copulation with an undue sex, male with male, or female with female, as the Apostle states (Rom. I, 27): and this is called the vice of sodomy" (Pt. II-II, Qu. 154, Art. 11).[16] Thus Aquinas set his seal on the received interpretation of Paul and placed lesbianism unequivocally in the same moral category with male relations. Canon law and Catholic moral theology had a very considerable influence in shaping medieval secular law. Some Carolingian kings actually promulgated the canons of various church councils as laws of the realm.[17]

Another important influence in the Middle Ages was the revival of Roman law, which began in Bologna in the eleventh century. The writings of jurists who made it their study soon came to have weight throughout Europe. Two commentators of this school were regularly cited by later authorities to justify the punishment of lesbians. These were Cino da Pistoia, poet and friend of Dante, and Bartholomaeus of Saliceto, who taught at Bologna at the end of the fourteenth century. Cino, in the *Commentary* on the Code of Justinian which he published in 1314, interpreted an imperial edict of 287 A.D. as referring to lesbianism. This law, issued jointly by the Emperors Diocletian and Maximianus, was eventually incorporated as law 20 of the *lex Iulia de adulteriis* (book 9, title 9), the part of the Code dealing with sexual offenses. Diocletian and Maximianus made numerous additions to the *lex Iulia* that refine and delimit earlier laws. The *lex foedissimam*, as it was called from its opening word, appears to have been formulated to protect the rights of rape victims by removing them from the class of unchaste women (prostitutes, etc.) whom Romans of the upper ranks were legally forbidden to marry. It seems unlikely that the first part of the law, which is entirely vague in its reference to female sexual misconduct, was designed to create any new offenses or to be used in place of earlier statutes. Rather it merely seems to imply that older laws were not to be revoked, except for violated women. The language of the law suggests that a controversy over the rights of such women (or of the men who sought to marry them) had arisen in the courts and that the Emperors wished to confirm a decision in their favor. Since, however, this was the Roman statute that medieval jurists used to place lesbians in the shadow of the stake and the gallows for at least five centuries, its text is perhaps worth quoting in full:

The laws punish the most foul wickedness (foedissimam nequitiam) *of women who surrender their honor to the lusts of others, although not the blameless will of those who are defiled by violence, since it was properly decreed that they should be of inviolate reputation and that marriage to them should not be forbidden to others.*[18]

But whatever was intended in the third century, Cino's gloss on the *foedissimam* unambiguously interprets the law as applying to lesbians: "This law can be understood in two ways: first, when a woman suffers defilement by surrendering to a male; the other way is when a woman suffers defilement in surrendering to another woman. For there are certain women, inclined to foul wickedness, who exercise their lust on other women and pursue them like men."[19] Cino cites no prior authorities; only further research among the early glossators will show whether he was echoing an established tradition or inaugurating a new one.

Bartholomaeus de Saliceto, in his *Lectures* of 1400, refers to an earlier gloss on the *lex foedissimam* (which may well be Cino's) in applying the law to the defilement of women by women. He then goes a step further by definitely prescribing the death penalty, which he justifies by a cross-reference to *cum vir* (book 9, title 9, law 31), which provided that male homosexual acts be punished by the "avenging sword."[20] Saliceto's glosses on these edicts remained standard references until the eighteenth century. Since, according to the Roman tradition, the opinions of eminent jurists often had the force of law, it would have been possible, by using these dicta, to argue for the death penalty for lesbianism even in parts of the continent with no national or local legislation. In Italy the influence of Roman law was all-pervasive; in Spain the *Partidas* were largely based on it; in France the kings fostered its revival; and even in Germany, after 1500, and Scotland, after 1600, it enjoyed remarkable, if belated, triumphs.[21] Thus, throughout the continent, lawyers trained in Roman law and imbued with Levitical-Pauline principles were encouraged to write provisions for the killing of lesbians into the civic, regional, and imperial codes they drafted during the late Middle Ages and the Renaissance.

Were such executions carried out? Derrick Sherwin Bailey, writing in 1955, systematically minimized the effect of church-inspired capital laws for sodomy. More recently, in his otherwise admirable study, *Sexual Variance in Society and History*, Vern Bullough has uncritically followed Bailey's conclusion.[22] Evidence now has accumulated, however, to show that a significant number of executions of men and women did in fact take place. Henry Lea noted several dozen burnings of convicted men by the Inquisition in Spain.[23] G. Ruggiero has documented the execution of sixteen young noblemen in Venice in 1406-1407[24] and Clark Taylor has recorded fourteen burnings in Mexico City in 1658.[25] E. W. Monter's study of sixteenth and seventeenth century Switzerland records another twenty-eight deaths.[26] Drawing on an earlier study by Van Römer, I have published the names and occupations of sixty men executed in Holland in 1730 and 1731, and from statistical tables issued by the British government have established that an equal number of hangings took place in Britain during the years 1806-1835.[27] Arthur Gilbert, by examining records of courts martial, has added another forty-five hangings in the British navy from 1703 to 1829.[28] Claude Courouve's forthcoming *Archives de l'homosexualité* will document thirty executions in France from 1317 to 1783;[29] however, a new survey of unpublished appeal records shows seventy-seven death sentences confirmed by the Parliament of Paris during the years 1565-1640, about eight times the number of executions Courouve's studies of published sources have revealed for the period.[30] No studies I know of exist for Scandinavia, Russia, or for German or Italian city-states other than Venice and Ferrara. My research at present substantiates more than 400 deaths in eight countries but I do not doubt this will prove to be only a small fraction of the total.

The earliest execution I have been able to discover in Christian Europe is that of John de Wettre, "a maker of small knives," who was condemned at Ghent on September 8, 1292, and "burned at the pillory next to St. Peter's."[31] Executions of women, of course, are much rarer, but Rudolph His in *Das Strafrecht des deutschen Mittelalters* records the drowning of a girl at Speier in 1477 "for lesbian love."[32] In the sixteenth century, Antonio Gómez tells us that two Spanish nuns were burned for using "material instruments."[33] In France, Jean Papon describes the trial and torture of two women, Françoise de l'Etage and Catherine de la Manière, at Bordeaux in 1533. They were, however, acquitted for insufficient evidence.[34] Henri Estienne mentions a woman from Fontaines who disguised herself as a man, married another woman, and was burned alive about 1535 after the discovery of the "wickedness which she used to counterfeit the office of a husband."[35] Montaigne, in his *Diary* of a journey to Italy, tells the story of a hanging in the Marne district in 1580:

Seven or eight girls around Chaumont en Bussigni secretly agreed, some years ago, to dress themselves up as men, and so to continue their life in the world. One of them came to this place, Vitry, under the name of Marie, gaining her livelihood by being a weaver, a well-behaved young man who made friends with everybody. He engaged himself at the said Vitry to a woman who is still alive, but for some disagreement which arose between them, their bargain went no further. Afterwards, having to go to the said Monter-en-Der, still earning his livelihood at the said trade, he fell in love with a woman whom he married and lived four or five months with her, to her satisfaction, according to what they say, but, having been recognized by somebody from the said Chaumont, and the matter being brought before justice, she was condemned to be hanged, which she said she would rather endure than to return to the state of a girl; and was hanged on the charge of having, by illicit devices, supplied the defects of her sex.[36]

Hanging, or some other form of capital punishment, would have been sanctioned, as far as I have been able to determine, by the generality of the Renaissance jurists, and various codes of that period support this view. Section 116 of the Constitutions of the Holy Roman Emporer Charles V, issued in 1532, provided that "if anyone commits impurity with a beast, or a man with a man, or a woman with a woman, they have forfeited their lives and shall, after the common custom, be sentenced to death by burning."[37] Other European communities, less extensive than the domains of Charles, also adopted laws that made lesbianism explicitly an offense. An instance of this was a macabre provision in the statutes of the Italian town of Treviso, near Venice, which, taking both sexes into account, provided that

> *If any person (leaving the natural use) has sexual relations with another, that is, a man with a man if they are fourteen years old or more, or a woman with a woman if they are twelve or more, by committing the vice of sodomy—popularly known as "buzerones" or "fregatores"—and this has been revealed to the city magistrates, the detected person, if a male, must be stripped of all his clothes and fastened to a stake in the Street of the Locusts with a nail or rivet driven through his male member, and shall remain there all day and all night under a reliable guard, and the following day be burned outside the city. If, however, a woman commits this vice or sin against nature, she shall* [*also*] *be fastened naked to a stake in the Street of the Locusts and shall remain there all day and night under a reliable guard, and the following day shall be burned outside the city.*[38]

The Spanish seem to have been preeminent in Renaissance Europe as specialists on the subject of lesbianism and the law. The most important medieval Spanish law on sodomy was Title 21 of the last book of *Las Siete Partidas*, compiled under the direction of Alfonso X about 1265. Ley II of Title 21 prescribes the death penalty for men, but the standard gloss on the *Partidas*, prepared by Gregorio López for the Salamanca edition of 1555, argues at length that the law applied to women as well as men. López cites St. Paul, the gloss of the *lex foedissimam*, Saliceto, and Angelico de Aretino: "Women sinning in this way are punished by burning according to the law *(pragmatica)* of their Catholic Majesties which orders that this crime against nature be punished with such a penalty, especially since the said law is not restricted to men, but refers to any person of whatever condition who has unnatural intercourse."[39] López, however, notes the minority opinion of Abulensis,[40] according to which lesbian acts were not as heinous as acts of male sodomy since women were by nature more passionately responsive than men. Moreover, male couples "perfect" the act and "defile the image of God," whereas women, though they may suffer from disordered wills, cannot "pollute" each other, presumably because they were not capable of penetration and emission. On these grounds, Abulensis held that lesbian acts might sometimes be punished with penalties short of death. This view seems to have influenced López's contemporary, Antonio Gómez, who was much cited in later continental sources. Gómez lays down the principle that "if any woman act the part of a man with another woman . . . both are said to commit the crime of Sodom against nature and must be punished with the prescribed penalty."[41] Gómez cites both Romans I, 26 and St. Thomas II-II, Qu. 154, Art. 11 as authorities for this position. He then distinguishes two possibilities. First, "if a woman has relations with another woman by means of any material instrument," they must be burned. Second, "if a woman has relations with any woman without an instrument," a lighter penalty is permissable. He tells us of such a prosecution in Granada where the women were whipped and sent to the galleys.

Russian legal tradition was also severe. Gregory Karpovich Kotoshikhin, summarizing capital crimes in his *On Russia in the Reign of Alexis Mikailovich* (i.e., shortly after 1645), records that "females are put to death as follows: for blasphemy and church robbery and sodomy they are burned alive."[42]

Catholic and Orthodox Europe, however, were not the only parts of the continent that favored severe punishment. Though lesbianism was ignored by English law, this was not the tradition in other protestant countries, such as Germany and the Calvinist cantons of Switzerland. E. W. Monter notes that the executions which followed the triumph of the Calvinist party in Geneva in 1555 included the case of a woman who was put to death in 1568. The woman originally had been arrested for fornication, a charge which she denied in a fashion her judges found blasphemous. Later she confessed that she had indulged in sapphism at an earlier date. She was convicted of all three crimes and drowned. Monter mentions also a woman named J. Cuasset who was tried on September 10, 1635, at Fribourg. Her fate, however, is unknown since the sentences meted out at the Fribourg trials apparently have not survived.

The same Puritanism that animated the Swiss in the sixteenth and seventeenth centuries had effects elsewhere. When settlers in New England drew up their first code of law, they seriously considered breaking with English tradition by making lesbianism a capital crime. In 1636 the Rev. John Cotton presented to the General Court of Massachusetts a body of laws, article 20 of which provided that "unnatural filthiness [is] to be punished with death, whether sodomy, which is a carnal fellowship of man with man, or woman with woman, or buggery, which is a carnal fellowship of man or woman with beasts or fowls."[43] It appears that these laws never were formally adopted by the court. In New Haven, however, a very elaborate and unusual law passed in 1655 provided that "If any man lyeth with mankinde, as a man lyeth with a woman, both of them have committed abomination, they both shall surely be put to death. Levit 20.13. And if any woman change the naturall use into that which is against nature, as Rom. I, 26, she shall be liable to the same sentence, and punishment."[44]

This law was superseded a few years later when New Haven became part of Connecticut, and no record has yet come to light of any rigorous penalties being applied to women in America. The one episode noted so far resulted in a lenient sentence.[45] The records of the General Court of New Plymouth for March 8, 1648/49, describe the arraignment of "the wife of Hugh Norman, and Mary Hammon, both of Yarmouth, for luede behauior each with other vpon a bed." Nineteen months later, on October 2, 1650, the court, taking into account "diuers lasiuious speeches by her allso spoken," sentenced Mrs. Norman "for her vild behauior in the aforsaid particulars, to make a publick acknowledgment, so fare as conveniently may bee, of her vnchast behauior, and haue allso warned her to take heed of such cariages for the future, lest her former cariage come in remembrance against her to make her punishment the greater."[46]

The question of exactly what physical relations between women constituted punishable sodomy was raised by Luigi-Maria Sinistrari d'Ameno in his erudite and detailed treatise, *De Delictis et Poenis*, published in 1700. Sinistrari takes the radical position that penetration by an instrument should not be counted as legal sodomy. For Sinistrari, sodomy required fleshy union. If the insertion of a finger into the vagina was not a sodomitical act, why should it be a crime to insert an inanimate object? Yet Paul and Aquinas must have had some specific deed in mind when they equated female and male sodomy. Sinistrari thinks that the solution lies in the unusual features of some female anatomies. He cites the Danish anatomist, Kaspar Bartholin, to the effect that among Ethiopian women the clitoris protrudes and is cauterized in childhood to prevent its development, which would hinder male entry. He also notes a statement attributed to Galen that the ancient Egyptians circumcised their women to prevent lesbianism. He thinks some European women have similarly overdeveloped clitorises and gives a number of medical histories, including that of a noblewoman who was supposed to have penetrated a twelve-year-old boy. In cases of suspected lesbianism an enlarged clitoris should be a presumption of guilt and justify torture. Sinistrari implies that accusations of lesbian sodomy should be discountenanced unless such anatomical irregularities are found. But women who penetrate men or other women with such unusual organs should be burned.[47]

The researches of Claude Courouve into trials in France in the eighteenth century have identified a number of trials of males for sodomy but none for lesbianism, though, as we have seen, some took place earlier. French authorities, however, were still of the opinion that lesbian acts were as culpable as male sodomy and open to the same penalties. For example, Pierre-François Muyart de Vouglans in Chapter X ("Of Sodomy") of his *Institutes au droit criminel* of 1757 tells us that "This crime, which derives its name from that abominable city, which is mentioned in Holy Scripture, is committed by a man with a man, or by a woman with a woman." As to the penalty, he is similarly explicit. "The law *cum vir* 31. of the code *de adult.* ordains that those who fall into this crime should be punished by being burned alive. This penalty which our jurisprudence has adopted is equally applicable to women as to men."[48] This view was current until the very eve of the Revolution. Daniel Jousse, in his *Traité de la justice criminelle de France* (1777), expresses as lively a horror of sodomy as any Father of the Church, and devotes a special section in Chapter XLIX ("Of Sodomy, and other crimes against nature") to "Women who corrupt one another." "The crime of women who corrupt one another is regarded as a kind of sodomy, if they practice venereal acts after the fashion of a man and a woman, and is worthy of capital punishment *(la dernière supplice)* according to the law *foedissimam*, C. *ad L. Jul. de. adulter.*; and such is the common opinion of the authorities."[49]

The belief that lesbians should expiate their crimes on the scaffold or at the stake was also part of the legal tradition of Germany in the eighteenth century. In Halberstadt, a town in Saxony a few miles from the present East German border, two women were tried in 1721; as a result, one of them was executed. The trial records, preserved in the Royal Prussian Secret Archives, were discovered and published in 1891 by F. C. Müller as a case history in a German journal of forensic medicine. The English translation that Brigitte Eriksson has prepared for this issue of the *Journal of Homosexuality* brings to life the tragic history of Catherina Margaretha Linck and her lover, another Catherine Margaret, whose surname was Mühlhahn. Their story has something of the fascination of a play by Bertolt Brecht in its humanity, bawdiness, comedy, pathos, and horror. There must be few court records that give us so full, vivid, and intimate a picture of the lives of any lesbian couple.

These records also show how eighteenth-century courts applied the legal, theological, and physiological principles we have traced in this essay. The chief Renaissance authority on Saxon law was Benedict Carpzow, or Carpzovius, whose monumental *Practicae novae imperialis Saxonicae rerum criminalium* was first published in 1652. *Pars* II, *Quaestio*

LXXVI deals with penalties for sodomy. There Carpzov reprints section 116 of Charles V's Constitutions, which prescribed burning for men or women who had relations with their own sex. But Saxon law, he notes, is more specific. It differentiates three kinds of sodomy: first, masturbation, for which the penalty is "*relegatio*" (banishment); secondly, male and female homosexuality and sodomitical relations between men and women, which were punished by beheading; and, finally, bestiality, for which, as the most heinous crime, the penalty of burning is reserved.

It is interesting to see how lesbian cases were actually argued before the courts. Recognizing the legal importance of the Pauline tradition, Linck's defenders suggest (1) that Paul's words may have been limited in their reference to the one form of female sodomy for which the old testament did in fact provide the death penalty, that is, female bestiality; or, alternatively, (2) that what Paul may have had in mind was the kind of clitoral penetration African women were supposed to be capable of. (This second argument clearly echoes Sinistrari's treatise of 1700.) The court replied that according "to all the interpreters" Paul was indeed referring to lesbian relations in Romans I, 26, and that he may even have had in mind women who used instruments, since such devices were known to the Greeks, as Aristophanes' reference to *olisboi* shows. Though there is no emission of semen, mutual contact in an effort to achieve orgasm is enough to constitute the crime. Paul, by using general language, means to condemn all such relations. If he was writing against African practices, he did not intend to exclude others. Indeed, the African women at least used their natural members, while these depart farther still from nature. The guilt lies in the illicit sexual stimulus, and the emission of semen is irrelevant, though the court, in setting forth its reasoning in the case, notes a minority opinion that required emission. It is notable that though the court turns to Charles V's legislation and Saxon tradition when considering the punishment to be meted out, it is St. Paul's words that ultimately have the force of law in defining the nature of the offense.

Müller tells us that the recommended sentence of beheading was carried out. In Europe, later in the eighteenth century, homosexual men were also executed, though no further lesbian cases have come to light so far. Finally, however, the influence of the Enlightenment made itself felt. In 1791, the French National Assembly abolished sodomy as an offense between consenting adults, relegating it, in effect, to the same category as such archaic crimes as witchcraft, heresy, and blasphemy. This revolutionary reform was incorporated later into the Napoleonic Code. No executions of men or women are known to have taken place in continental Europe during the nineteenth century. In England hangings went on for another four decades, then ceased in 1835. A long nightmare had come to an end.

NOTES

1. In 1811, however, a useful twenty-page compendium, with many legal and literary references, chiefly in Latin and French, was prepared for a famous Scottish libel case under the title "Authorities with Regard to the Practice of Tribadism." This has been reprinted in Jonathan Katz, ed., *Miss Marianne Woods and Miss Jane Pirie against Dame Helen Cumming Gordon* (New York: Arno Press, 1975).

2. Derrick Sherwin Bailey, *Homosexuality and the Western Christian Tradition* (London: Longmans, Green, 1955), p. 161.

3. Yebamoth 76a, trans. Isaac Slotki; in *The Babylonian Talmud,* 18 vols. (London: Socino Press, 1961), 8: 513.

4. *Encyclopedia of Religion and Ethics,* 1908-27 ed., s.v. "Hierodouli (Semitic and Egyptian): Hebrew," by George A. Barton.

5. Bailey, p. 74.

6. Pierre Rapetti, ed., *Li Livres de jostice et de plet* (Paris: Didot Frères, 1850), pp. 279-80.

7. Sidney Lee, ed., *The Boke of Duke Huon of Bordeaux,* trans. Lord Berners. Early English Text Society, Series 2, vol. 40 (London: Trübner and Co., 1882), p. 727.

8. Bailey, p. 160.

9. St. John Chrysostom, *The Homilies of S. John Chrysostom, Archbishop of Constantinople, on the Epistle of St. Paul the Apostle to the Romans,* trans. J. B. Morris. Library of Fathers of the Holy Catholic Church, vol. 7 (Oxford: John Henry Parker, 1842), p. 47.

10. St. Ambrose, *Omnia opera,* 5 vols. in 3: *Commentarii in omnes Pauli epistolas* (Basel, 1567), 5: 178.

11. St. Anselm, *In omnes sanctissimi Pauli apostoli epistolas enarrationes* (Venice: ad signum spei, 1547), p. 8v.

12. Peter Abelard, *Commentarium super S. Pauli epistolam ad Romanos libri quinque,* in *Patrologia latina,* ed. J.-P. Migne, 221 vols. (Paris: J.-P. Migne, 1844-66), 178: 806.

13. The only commentator I am aware of before the twentieth century who interprets Paul's words as referring to heterosexual sodomy is David Pareus in his *Commentaria* of 1608. Pareus is cited on page 26 of "The Additional Petition of Miss Mary-Ann Woods and Miss Jane Pirie" in the 1811 libel case (see note 1). In the same case, the "Answers for Dame Helen Cumming Gordon," page 21, rebuts this reading in favor of the standard lesbian interpretation with references to Tertullian, Clement of Alexandria, Hugo Grotius, Mathew Poole and James MacKnight. In contrast to commentators, lawyers defending lesbians in the courts did challenge the received interpretation, as in the 1721 German trial discussed below.

14. Bailey, pp. 103, 105.

15. Emil Friedberg and Emil Richter, eds., *Corpus iuris canonici: Decretum magistri Gratiani,* 2 vols. (Graz: Akademische Druk-U. Verlaganstalt, 1959), 2: 1144.

16. St. Thomas Aquinas, *Summa theologica,* trans. Fathers of the English Dominican Province, 3 vols. (New York: Benziger Brothers, 1947-48), 2: 1825.

17. Vern Bullough, *Sexual Variance in Society and History* (New York: John Wiley & Sons, 1976), p. 353.

18. Paul Krueger and Theodor Nommsen, eds., *Corpus iuris civilis: Codex Justinianus,* 2 vols. (Frankfurt am Main: Verlag Weidmann, 1967), 2: 375.

19. Cino da Pistoia, *In Codicem commentaria,* 2 vols. (Frankfurt am Main: S. Feyerbrandt, 1578; reprint ed., Turin: Botega d'Erasmo, 1964), 2: 546A.

20. Bartholomaeus de Saliceto, *Lectura super IX libris Codicis,* 4 vols. (Lyons: Johannes Siber, 1496-1500), 4: no pagination. (Microfilm reprint, *French Books before 1601,* Lexington, Ky.: Erasmus Press, 1965, Roll 112.)

21. Hans Julius Wolff, *Roman Law: An Historical Introduction* (Norman, Okla.: University of Oklahoma Press, 1951).

22. Bullough, p. 391.

23. Henry Charles Lea, *A History of the Inquisition of Spain,* 4 vols. (New York: Macmillan, 1907), 4: 361-71.

24. G. Ruggiero, "Sexual Criminality in the Early Renaissance," *Journal of Social History* 8 (1975): 18-37.

25. Clark L. Taylor, Jr., "El Ambiente: Male Homosexual Social Life in Mexico City" (Ph.D. dissertation, University of California at Berkeley, 1978), pp. 17-20. See also Taylor, "Mexican Gaylife in Historical Perspective," *Gay Sunshine,* no. 26/27, 1975-76, pp. 1-3.

26. E. William Monter, "La Sodomie à l'époque moderne en Suisse romand," *Annales: E. S. C.* 29 (1974): 1023-33. (A revised and updated translation of this essay, entitled "Sodomy and Heresy in Early Modern Switzerland," is included in this issue of the *Journal of Homosexuality.*)

27. Louis Crompton, "Gay Genocide: From Leviticus to Hitler," in *The Gay Academic,* ed. Louie Crew (Palm Springs, Calif.: ETC Publications, 1978), pp. 69-91; and A. Harvey, "Prosecutions for Sodomy in England at the Beginning of the Nineteenth Century," *The Historical Journal* 21 (1978): 939-48.

28. Arthur Gilbert, "Buggery and the British Navy, 1700-1861," *Journal of Social History* 10 (1976): 72-98.

29. Claude Courouve, "Sodomy Trials in France," *Gay Books Bulletin* 1 (1978): 22-23, 26.

30. See Monter, in this issue, note 7.

31. Leopold August Warnkönig, *Flandrische Staats- und Rechtsgeschichte bis zum Jahr 1305,* 3 vols. (Tübingen: L. F. Fues, 1839), 3(2): 76.

32. Rudolf His, *Das Strafrecht des deutschen Mittelalters,* 2 vols. (Weimar: Hermann Bohlaus Nachf., 1935), 2: 168. Claude Courouve has drawn my attention to a fuller account of this case in Theodor Hartster, *Das Strafrecht der freien Reichsstadt Speier* (Breslau: Marcus, 1900), pp. 184-85.

33. Antonio Gomez, *Variae resolutiones, juris civilis, communis et regii* (Venice: Typographia Remondiniana, 1758), p. 328.

34. Jean Papon, *Recueil d'arrests notables des cours souveraines de France* (Paris: Jean de la Fontaine, 1608), pp. 1257-58.

35. Henri Estienne, *Apologie pour Hérodote,* ed. P. Ristelhuber, 2 vols. (Paris: Isidore Lisieux, 1879), 1: 178. I am indebted to Lillian Faderman for directing me to this source, and to Sinistrari, below.

36. Michel Montaigne, *The Diary of Montaigne's Journey to Italy in 1580 and 1581,* trans. E. J. Trechmann (New York: Harcourt, Brace, 1929), p. 6.

37. J. Kohler and Willy Scheel, eds., *Die peinliche Gerichtsordnung Kaiser Karls V: Constitutio criminalis Carolina* (Halle an der Saale: Verlag der Buchhandlung des Waisenhauses, 1900), p. 62.

38. *Statuta provisionesque ducales civitatis Tarvisii* (Venice, 1574), pp. 187v-188.

39. Joseph Berní y Catalá, ed., *Las siete partidas del rey D. Alfonso el Sabio, glossadas por el sr. D. Gregorio Lopez,* 4 vols. (Valencia: Benito Montfort, 1767), 3: 178.

40. Abulensis is presumably Alonso Tostado, Bishop of Avila, who died in 1455.

41. Antonio Gomez, p. 328.

42. Benjamin Uroff, "Grigorii Karpovich Kotoshikhin, *Russia in the Reign of Alexis Mikhailovich:* An Annotated Translation" (Ph.D. dissertation, Columbia University, 1970), p. 217; Kotoshikhin, *O Rosii v tsarstvovanie Alexseia Mikhailovicha,* 4th ed. (St. Petersburg: Tipografiia Glavnago Upravlenia Udelov, 1906; reprint ed., Slavistic Printings and Reprintings, vol. 126, The Hague: Mouton, 1969), p. 116. I am indebted to Dr. Ann Kleimola for these references.

43. Louis Crompton, "Homosexuals and the Death Penalty in Colonial America," *Journal of Homosexuality* 1 (1967): 279.

44. Ibid. Lillian Faderman has questioned whether we can be sure that the 1655 statute does indeed denote lesbian acts or whether it might refer instead to fellatio or to anal intercourse ("Lesbian Magazine Fiction in the Early Twentieth Century," *Journal of Popular Culture* 11 (1978): 814, note 4). It seems likely, however, that the framers did have lesbians in mind. First, as we have seen, ecclesiastical and legal authorities had customarily interpreted Paul's words as a reference to acts between women. As to oral relations, I am not aware of any law framed deliberately to include them before the late nineteenth century. And finally, in a later clause the statute makes it a crime to abuse "the contrary part of a grown woman," a provision that would not have been required if the earlier language had been intended to criminalize heterosexual anal relations.

45. Faderman, p. 814.

46. Nathaniel B. Shurtleff, ed., *Records of the Colony of New Plymouth in New England,* 12 vols. (Boston: William White, 1855-61), 2: 137, 163.

47. Ludovico Maria Sinistrari, *De Delictis, et Poenis* (Rome: Carlo Giannini, 1754), title 4, chapter 11 ("Sodomia"). This remarkable chapter, with 92 sections, is a major source of references for lesbianism and the law. A number of popular French and English translations have been published since 1883 under various titles (*De la sodomie, Peccatum mutum,* etc.), but with the legal references edited out of the text. These translations are listed in the *National Union Catalogue.*

48. Pierre-François Muyart de Vouglans, *Institutes au droit criminel* (Paris: Cellot, 1757), pp. 509-10.

49. Daniel Jousse, *Traité de la justice criminel de France,* 4 vols. (Paris: Chez Debure, 1771), 4: 122.

51. Ludovico Maria Sinistrari, *De Delectis, et Poenis* (Rome: Carlo Giannini, 1754), title 4, chapter 11 ("Sodomia"). This remarkable chapter, with 92 sections, is a major source of references for lesbianism and the law. A number of popular French and English translations have been published since 1883 under various titles (*De la sodomie, Pec-Peccatum mutum,* etc.), but with the legal references edited out of the text. These translations are listed in the *National Union Catalogue.*

52. Pierre-François Muyart de Vouglans, *Institutes au droit criminel* (Paris: Cellot, 1757), pp. 509-510.

53. Daniel Jousse, *Traité de la justice criminel de France,* 4 vols., (Paris: Chez Debure, 1771), vol. 4, p. 122.

A LESBIAN EXECUTION IN GERMANY, 1721
THE TRIAL RECORDS

Translated by
Brigitte Eriksson

ABSTRACT: In 1891, Dr. F. C. Müller of Alexandersbad published in Friedreich's Blätter für gerichtliche Medizin und Sanitätspolizei *a transcription from the Prussian State Archives of a trial of two lesbians that took place in Halberstadt in 1721. The records, translated here, describe in lively detail the religious life, wanderings, and lesbian relations of Catherina Margaretha Linck. Linck was tried for committing sodomy with her lover, Catherina Margaretha Mühlhahn. The trial documents also reveal with some particularity the legal questions raised by lesbian relations in the early eighteenth century with regard to moral theology, Saxon law, and psychological theories.*

INTRODUCTION

In 1891, Dr. F. C. Müller, head physician of Alexandersbad, near Bayreuth in Bavaria, published in Heft 4 of *Friedreich's Blätter für gerichtliche Medizin und Sanitätspolizei* an account of the trial, at Halberstadt in 1721, of Catharina Margaretha Linck and Catharina Margaretha Mühlhahn for lesbian relations. This document was transcribed from the royal Prussian Secret Archives, in which Müller claimed to have found records of over 100 sodomy trials. (In the eighteenth century, both Halberstadt in Saxony and Duisberg in the Rhineland, where the trial court and the review court had their respective seats, were under Prussian rule.) Müller, who titled his transcription "Ein weiterer Fall von conträrer Sexualempfindung," appended a brief and not very significant commentary, written from the point of view of late-nineteenth-century sexual psychopathology; that commentary is omitted here.

Requests for reprints should be sent to Brigitte Eriksson, 40876 Blossom Drive, Three Rivers, California 93271. *The translator wishes to acknowledge the assistance of John Poynter, Inge Worth, and Louis Crompton in preparing the text.*

The trial record is remarkable for its detailed account of the lives of the two women and for its discussion of the legal points raised by their relation. (The legal aspects of the trial are discussed in this issue of the *Journal of Homosexuality,* by Louis Crompton in his article, "The Myth of Lesbian Impunity: Capital Laws from 1270 to 1791.") As a result of their conviction, Müller tells us, Linck was sentenced to be beheaded and Mühlhahn to be imprisoned.

THE TRIAL OF CATHARINA MARGARETHA LINCK AND CATHARINA MARGARETHA MÜHLHAHN

The document is dated October 13, 1721, and contains the following text:

Concerning Catharina Margaretha Lincken,[1] *or the so-called Anastasius Lagrantinus Rosenstengel, and her alleged wife Catharina Margaretha Mühlhahn who were sent to us by the government of Halberstadt and who, according to the Halberstadt inquisition documents* (acta) *and the Duisberger verdict, were found guilty of various serious crimes, the government of Halberstadt most obediently asks your Royal Majesty to consider the matter and to give your gracious legal advice. Having examined and weighed the said documents, we find them legally correct.*

According to her mother's statement, the defendant, A. [*sic*] Marg. Lincken, approximately 27 years of age, was illegitimately born, after Mr. Lincken's death, to another man, at Gehowen. She was baptized there and then was sent to the orphanage in Halle. There she was instructed in the Christian religion until her fourteenth year. The mother still resides in Halle and freely admitted and confessed that the defendant, after leaving the orphanage, had remained for some time in Halle where she learned the trade of button-making and of printing cotton. Subsequently, she had stayed with her friends in Calbe. In order to lead a life of chastity, she had disguised herself in men's clothes. Dressed in this way she went to see her mother in Halle but took leave of her because she wanted to lead a holy life. She left for Sora with a troop of Inspirants she encountered in the Strohhof outside Halle and then went to Sechsstädten and Nuremberg. There she was baptized by the so-called prophetess Eva Lang in the river outside the town in the name of Jehova Almajo Almejo in the presence of a multitude of Inspirants from far and wide and took on the name of Anastasius Lagrantinus Rosenstengl. Immediately after the baptism the prophet is said to have made her swallow a rolled-up piece of paper, repeating once again the words Jehova Almajo Almejo. She also laid her hands crosswise on the defendant's head with the result that that same day the defendant went into ecstasy during a gathering which was being held in Nuremberg. The spirit appeared above her in the form of a veil, and, together with the other Inspirants who, in a frenzy, thumped the chairs with their behinds, rolled on the ground, hit their heads against the wall, and swallowed violently, the defendant finally regained both movement and speech. Afterwards, she became a prophet amongst the Inspirants for two whole years and preached and traveled with them throughout the country. They also kept the Eucharist amongst themselves. They confessed to God and no one else. For their sins they imposed penances on themselves, such as short or long fasts, wearing sackcloth, and so forth. They would not let themselves be absolved by any priest. The spirit pointed out one who was to deal out the Eucharist (after which he washed another's feet); whereupon the person whom the spirit had indicated took wine and a cake of unleavened bread such as the Jews have and spoke the words Christ himself had spoken. Then he broke a piece off one of the cakes, ate some, and gave the other piece to the next person, who broke a piece and ate and passed a piece on with the words: "Take and eat, this is the true body and blood of Jesus Christ." For when they ate the bread [they believed] it was the actual Last Supper and they received the true body and the true blood of Jesus Christ in this bread. The chalice, however, which was used after the supper, was only the covenant of the New Testament whereby they remembered Christ. A woman could bless and distribute the Eucharist just as well [as a man]. The defendant had seen for herself that the spirit often pointed out virgins and women to administer the Last Supper; however, it quite often happened that one spirit contradicted another one, which is what had happened to her in Cologne on the Rhine. She had prophesied to a maiden, Elizabeth, in the presence of her parents, that she must fast for 40 days and nights. Then another person with the name of Polt (who had come from Halle and, according to her opinion, was from Halberstadt, and had lived with the said Elizabeth as brother and sister) became inspired and pronounced that the maiden Elizabeth was too weak and would not be able to stand the fast. The same thing had happened to [the defendant] in Nuremberg, where the spirit had moved her to tell another young woman, [also] named Elizabeth, to fast for 40 days and nights. The male individual, however, who had been involved with the maiden and with whom Elizabeth had lived as brother and sister, also had been inspired and had contradicted the defendant and had said that this Elizabeth could not stand the fast. Furthermore, her prophecies had not come true. When she had prophesied to a rich merchant at Nuremberg that he would be able to walk on water, he had sunk just like the merchant at Cologne, who indeed would have drowned had he not been fished from the water just in time.

After these incidents, the defendant left the Inspirants since she no longer had the gift of prophecy. Rather, she had delusions which made bodies of water, no matter how small in size, appear so huge that nobody could cross them; or else it seemed to her that whole battalions of horsemen were after her. Later the spirit appeared to her sometimes as a white, sometimes as a black, male. The white spirit pleaded with her to unite herself with him again and to rejoin the sect of Inspirants. The black spirit, however, reappeared to her at various times: in Cologne, after she had left the Inspirants; in the Sauerland, where she was employed by a peasant, herding pigs; and in a big forest near Cologne, where she had kept herself for three days and nights without food or drink. He pleaded with her to unite herself with him for 20 years, after which time she would be his; in the meantime he would give her as much money as she wanted. The white spirit, however, always prevented this and always exhorted her to remain faithful to God. Later, no more spirits had appeared to her.

Following this she had gone back to Halle. After a few months, she joined the Hanoverian troops as a musketeer in Colonel Stallmeister's regiment, serving for 3 years under the name of Anastasius Lagrantinus Beuerlein or, according to page 89 of the affidavit from Hanover, as Caspar Beuerlein. In 1708, she deserted at Brabant; however, she was apprehended near Antwerp and condemned to death by hanging. But when she disclosed her sex and a letter in her behalf arrived from Professor Francken at Halle, she was reprieved.

After some time she joined the Volunteer Company of Royal Prussian troops in Soest, under General Horn, using the name of Augustus or Caspar Beuerlein. Her captain's name was Becker. When she had served approximately one year, Professor Francken wrote to the garrison priest and informed him that she was a female, whereupon she had been sent away with identification papers. Thereupon she returned to Halle, put on her woman's clothes, and stayed there one summer. Then she went to Wittenberg in men's clothing and joined the royal Polish troops as a musketeer with the name of Peter (or Lagrantinus) Wannich. When she participated in a campaign and was captured by the French on a march near Brussels, she ran away again. Having served for one year with the Hessian troops in Rheinfels in Major Briden's Volunteers, there was a fight for which she was to have run the gauntlet, but again she escaped. Serving amongst these troops she had called herself Cornelius Hubsch and had changed her name often so that, in case of desertion, interrogation would be more difficult. During her war service she had fluctuated between Catholicism and Lutheranism, taking both Catholic and Lutheran communion. After she had run away from the Hessian troops, she went back to Halle and made flannel for the university shoemaker; also she did spinning and printing and frequently kept 8, 9, and more spinning maids busy. She continued in this way of life for three or four years, sometimes wearing female, sometimes male clothing. Once she had been arrested by the soldiers in Halle, but, because of Professor Francken and his disclosure of her femaleness, she had been let go again. At this occasion she had been inspected at the Rathhaus to see whether she was a man or a woman.

After this inspection she once again changed her way of life, put on men's clothing, and, in 1717, went to work for a French stockingmaker, where she had become acquainted with the codefendant, Catharina Margaretha Mühlhahn. She became engaged to her and went to the former pastor of St. Paul's, Lic. Chauden, to inform him of her engagement to the Mühlhahn woman. On this occasion she had passed herself off as a dyer of fine colors and cloth maker and as a son of Cornelius Joseph Rosenstengl, former mine superintendent in Gültenberg near Prague. She asked for the usual reading of the banns and the wedding actually occurred shortly before Michaelmas in the year of 1717 in the church of St. Paul. At the first reading of the banns someone had called out that she had a wife and children in Halle; however, the defendant showed a letter from her mother, and also procured two witnesses to prove that such was not the case. After this, the reading of the banns and the wedding had continued.

After the wedding they lived together as an alleged married couple and kept the same table and the same bed. She had made a penis of stuffed leather with two stuffed testicles made from pig's bladder attached to it and had tied it to her pubes with a leather strap. When she went to bed with her alleged wife she put this leather object into the other's body and in this way had actually accomplished intercourse. When she had gone to bed with the bride for the first time she is said to have told her that she wanted to have intercourse 24 times, but she had done so only three or four times. Making love never lasted more than a quarter of an hour because the defendant was unable to perform any more. At these times, she petted and fondled somewhat longer. The defendant also added that during intercourse, whenever she was at the height of her passion, she felt tingling in her veins, arms, and legs.

She said that while she was a soldier she had hired many a woman whom she excited with the leather object. At times she ran for miles after a beautiful woman and spent all her earnings on her. Often when a woman touched her, even slightly, she became so full of passion that she did not know what to do.

Once she put the leather object, which she had first used down below, into the codefendant's mouth. Whether the latter had complained about this to her mother, the defendant did not know. The codefendant complained that her genitals had become very swollen and that her pelvic bones hurt so much that she had been unable to walk; but this was a lie, since the defendant had at first used a thin leather instrument, and only when the Mühlhahn woman's vagina had stretched had she acquired a thicker instrument. The Mühlhahn woman had frequently held the leather instrument in her hands and had stuck it into her vagina, which she would not have done if it had not felt pleasurable to her. The mother-in-law had taken her daughter away from the defendant and had insisted on a divorce; however, the defendant complained to the priests at St. Paul's so that the mother had to restore her daughter to the defendant.

The two women did not get along. Because the codefendant complained that she did not earn anything, the defendant beat her frequently. Also, she had taken from the codefendant linen, clothes, and sheets in the value of 77 Reichsthaler and sold these goods. If this was not stealing, then what was it?

After this she traveled cross country with her alleged wife and supported her mostly with begging. When they returned, neither had a shirt to her name. Then the codefendant had traveled to Hildesheim by herself; the defendant eventually followed. From there she moved to Münster, where she stayed for a year, since their hope to obtain money had persuaded them to become Catholic. She had herself publicly baptized in the Jesuit church and then married the codefendant for the second time. From Münster she went to Helmstadt where she called at M. Heinrich's and told him with dejected countenance and sad heart how she had been born of Inspirants or so-called Quakers in Nuremberg; that, however, she had not been baptized but that, on the day after her birth, in lieu of circumcision, she had merely been scratched with a pin and been given the name Lagrantinus; how, when she was twelve years old, she had been baptized at Cologne in the Quaker way by a prophetess named Eva and had received the name Jehova Almajo Almejo; and how when that particular sect had been expelled, the defendant had, after many mishaps, finally reached Münster, had been made doorkeeper by the local Jesuits, and been instructed by them in their religion and catechism. However, when she was forbidden to read the Bible, she had escaped from the monastery and had begged her way to Helmstedt. There, she pleaded for instruction in the Lutheran religion and for baptism so that she might not endanger her eternal salvation. After many complications, this finally took place. She received the name Julius Augustus, as well as 25 Reichsthaler as a christening gift. Of this she received 16 Reichsthaler; the rest had been kept by M. Heinrich. She had told him that she was willing to travel to Halberstadt to look up her spiritual sister, who had accompanied her during her Inspirant period, and to wed her in Helmstedt. She then embarked on the journey to Halberstadt, where she found her alleged wife sick. When she wanted to caress her and had actually spent 4 Rs for a jug of wine, wife and mother had shown the defendant the door. Furthermore, the mother had charged the defendant with being a woman and not a man, and when they got into a fight about it, the mother, together with a woman named Peterson, attacked her, took her sword, ripped open her pants, examined her, and discovered that she was indeed not a man but a woman. They also tore the leather instrument from her body, [as well as] the leather-covered horn through which she urinated and [which she had] kept fastened against her nude body. When the defendant had, nevertheless, insisted that she was a man, they had spread open her vulva and found not the slightest sign of anything masculine. They beat her up, and the mother-in-law submitted to the courts the leather instrument as well as the horn; the defendant was promptly interrogated.

The defendant had made the leather instrument herself while she was with the Hanoverian soldiers, and, using her ingenuity, she had used it with several girls when she was a soldier. Since she had to act like all the other soldiers, she caressed many a widow as well, who touched the leather penis and played with it and yet had not realized what it was; however, she had never inserted it into any of the widows' bodies.

The mother-in-law and the bride had known before the wedding that she was a woman, and she mentioned several incidents in this regard. Once in Münster, when the codefendant tore the leather object from the defendant's body and was therefore fully aware that she was no man, she nevertheless later let herself be tickled with it and they lived together even more intimately. Later, in Münster, they had been married a second time.

She had never been intimate with a man, neither had she ever used the leather instrument on herself or let someone else use it on her, and when she was finally asked how she could justify such misdeeds before God, she had replied:

a. As to her wearing men's clothes: She said other women had done this. Of course she knew that God had forbidden women to wear men's clothing, but this applied to married women only, not to maidens.
b. As to her going amongst the Inspirants: This was a holy life, and since she had wanted to receive the spirit of prophecy she had to be baptized once more; otherwise, the spirit would not appear and one received no inspiration.
c. As to her frequent desertions and perjuries: She had already received her punishment; in particular, she had spent weeks in chains and fetters and had stood under the gallows, ready to be hanged.

d. As to the public reading of the banns and her marriage to the codefendant: She thought she would be well able to answer this before God. Satan must have seen her because her mother had been possessed by the devil, for when the defendant was born on the first day of Pentecost, the devil had ordered the mother to hand over her child and he would set her free. In the end, to make her agree, he twisted the mother's hands behind her back, but since the mother still had not complied, the devil had stayed within her. However, he had singled out the defendant.
e. As to having acted as a man with her alleged wife and having tortured her so shamefully with the leather object: This she wished God to forgive her. Nevertheless, her wife had not suffered any pain because of it; the defendant now realized that she had committed an abominable sodomy, but up until this time she had been deluded by Satan.
f. As to having taken things from her alleged wife and having run through her money: That she could certainly justify, for she had supported the woman, and the codefendant had benefitted from whatever the defendant had sold.
g. As to having embraced the Catholic religion because of monetary gains, having let herself be baptized and married for the second time in Münster, also having repeated baptism in Helmstedt and in this way having committed a great offense: For all this she would ask God's pardon, and God was sure to grant it to her. In Helmstedt she had let herself be baptized not because of any monetary gains, but because she had entered a new covenant with God since she had felt that this was necessary. Whether she had committed an offense she did not know; she confessed and repented her sins; she deserved death tenfold; however, even if she were done away with, others like her would remain. She did not know what else to offer as an excuse; she had committed sins against God and was quite willing to die.

Concerning the codefendant Catharina Margaretha Mühlhahn, age 22, she confessed likewise and declared at the summary interrogation that she had had the banns read and entered marriage in the year 1717, 14 days before Michaelmas, with the so-called Rosenstengel in St. Paul's Church at Halberstadt. Also, at night she had shared the bridal bed with him. However, when the time came for actual intercourse, her supposed husband had been unable to insert his sexual organ into hers but had tortured and tormented her for about a week so that she endured great pains and her sexual organ had become very swollen. After a week it finally worked, but he had never been able to get in more than half a finger's length. Her bones and her vagina had always pained her a great deal since she had to suffer him in this manner morning, evening, and midnight, too. Often he had tormented her like this for a whole hour. Whenever night approached she had started shuddering. She had been a very naive maiden and had not realized that she had been deceived in this way. That is why the defendant had become so bold and made her handle his supposed male organ which had become quite warm in her body so that she had not noticed that it was made of leather. The defendant had always slept in pants and she had not been allowed to reach into them. It's true she had noticed that whenever he pissed he always wet his shoes and this made her suspicious so that she said to him: "Other men can piss quite a ways, but you always piss on your shoes." But he had called her a beast and scum and had threatened to beat her. In the year 1718, shortly before Gallen [St. Gall's Day], in Münster, she had been lying on the bed with her husband. Since she had been sick he had unwittingly taken off his pants. When she noticed that he had fallen asleep, she had inspected him closely since his shirt had slipped up, and she had found he had the leather sausage, which her mother had later handed over to the court, tied to his body, but that otherwise he was fashioned exactly like herself. This scared and amazed her terribly. Her supposed husband awakened, and, since she had torn off the leather male member with the bag, he looked for it in their bed under the pretext of having lost his cuff links. When she reproached him with his deception, he had begged her not to get him into trouble; what good would there be in her getting another's blood on her hands? Henceforth he would live with her as brother and sister and even offered to take her back home, but she had been afraid of him and had worried he might kill her on the way, and so she had stayed with him in Münster until Shrovetide. Neither was he to bother her any more with the object; she had thrown it into the river by their house.

In Halberstadt as well as in Münster the defendant had tried to talk her into believing that she was pregnant; and since this had not been true, he had told her to get herself with child by someone else. During Lent, he had left Münster and around Easter he came back. While he was away, he had supported himself with begging and had passed himself off as Catholic; he had claimed that he had been born of Anabaptists and that he had turned Catholic. Her husband had often begged the codefendant to become Catholic in order to help him out, and the priests had likewise tried very hard, but she had not wanted to do it.

Later, however, she confessed that she had become a Catholic at Münster. She had done so because of the defendant's desperation and coercion; she also confessed that she had been married once again by the Jesuits. But all this had happened before she had learned about the defendant's true nature; also, she steadfastly maintained that, once she had discovered that the defendant was not a man, she had not let him tickle her with the leather object; and she wanted to swear that earlier she had not known that the leather object had not been the defendant's own natural member. When her mother had wanted to inspect the defendant in Praetorius's Garden, he stood before her toward evening, took the thing out of his pants, and told her to look and see whether he was not a man after all. She had answered that the object was completely black, whereupon the defendant had answered that with little children it was different; when they grew up, it turned black; besides, he was black all over his body.

The court had wanted to let the codefendant free on bail, but the Minden judge and jury [that is, a lay assessor's court, a local tribunal consisting of a petty judge and 2 jurymen] decided that the inquest against the defendant had not been completed and that the special inquisition in regard to the imputed crime of sodomy should be continued. This was complied with and the codefendant was interrogated. Nothing much was discovered, except that the codefendant admitted that the defendant once stuck the leather thing into her mouth. At first, she had not wanted to do this, but when the defendant accused her of not loving him, she had suffered it in her mouth just once. She also told that once when the defendant had returned from Hildesheim and the codefendant's mother had not wanted to believe that he was a man, he was drunk, had pulled his thing from his pants, and had pissed on her mother and on the Catholic wife of the carpenter. He had been able to make this thing stiff or limp. She had followed her mother's order and after the wedding and during intercourse had tried to feel whether the defendant was a woman, but she had not been able to reach there; neither had she felt a strap or belt with which the leather thing was attached to his body, since it was kept between his legs.

When the defendant and the codefendant were confronted with each other, the defendant stated that once, when she put the leather thing into her mouth, she, Catherine Linck, had been stark naked and the codefendant, Margaretha Mühlhahn, had fondled her breasts and therefore should have known and felt that the object was made of leather or a fake. Here, however, the codefendant contradicted her and said that the Linck woman had not been naked but that she had been wrapped in a shirt; that although the codefendant had felt her breasts, the Linck woman had commented that many men had such breasts.

When questioned about her daughter's nature, the defendant's mother made a deposition that when her daughter was young she had not noticed anything masculine about her, but that she had not been perfectly female either, since in her youth the vagina had practically no opening and that because of this she might not have been capable of intercourse. Of course the witness had not examined the defendant since she had become an adult.

On the other hand, the testimony of the city physician, Dr. Bornemann, and the surgeon, Dr. Röper, instructs us that they inspected the defendant very carefully and that they found in her nothing hermaphroditic, much less masculine, but found her to be fashioned like a woman; and judging from the size of the breasts and the rather large womb and the largeness of the vulva, which was examined by a midwife, it could be concluded that her female member had not altogether been left alone, but that, during her extensive vagabonding, it undoubtedly had been disgracefully misused.

As for the defense, the defender asks for *poena extraordinaria* [that is, a penalty other than the ordinary (capital) punishment] for the defendant, that is, for life imprisonment. In regard to the codefendant, however, the defense asks her acquittal, particularly since she has had to lie in the squalor of prison all this time, citing also the extreme depression caused by her wanting to come to the aid of the accused. Consequently, the abovementioned city physician, Dr. Bornemann, has been instructed to examine her mood and condition. He attested that he did not find her suffering from depression. The documents were then completed and the case was sent to Duisberg, where the Judicial Faculty ordered that Marg. Cath. Linck, alias Anastasius Lagrantinus Rosenstengel, was to be delivered to the public executioner on account of her committed and confessed crimes. From there she was to be taken to the usual place of execution to receive her well-deserved punishment and to serve as an abominable example to others by being put to death by hanging. Afterward her body was to be burned.

Cath. Marg. Mühlhahn, however, was to be given a second-degree torture in order to arrive at the truth in her case.

The Halberstadt Municipal Government respectfully sent this decision with a report on reasons for compliance or modification. They would like to suggest respectfully that since the outrages perpetrated by the Linck woman were hideous and nasty, and it can furthermore not be denied that she engaged in repeated baptism for which she should be punished, the jurists are also of the opinion that a woman who commits sodomy with another woman with such an instrument could therefore be given poena ordinaria [that is capital punishment].

According to Carpzow and several others, the fact alone that she had practiced oral intercourse in the Mühlhahn woman's mouth with the leather instrument is enough to warrant capital punishment; however, since in this particular case and with these instruments semen cannot be sucked off or ejaculated, this reasoning may not be applicable. It further becomes evident from article 116 of the criminal code for capital offenses [the code of Charles V] that in cases of crimes of sodomy, when a woman is involved with another woman, the penalty is burning alive. It has been the practice to kill the evildoers before such burning in order to prevent despair; however, a few jurists have been of the opinion that according to Saxon law it is beyond doubt that, for people who commit sodomy, only the sword comes into consideration, in order that there may be a differentiation in penalties for sodomy between humans and sodomy between humans and animals. The court would like to leave it most respectfully to the discretion of your Royal Majesty whether to defer to the judgment of the Duisberg Judicial Faculty or whether to choose the latter, milder way and graciously prescribe the sword alone for the defendant; in any case they see no reason why the defendant should not first be killed with the halter rather than with the sword, and then burned, particularly since she is a female.

Concerning the codefendant Mühlhahn, she should expect a serious punishment since even after she discovered the deceit and the fact that the Linck woman, her alleged husband, was not a man, she nevertheless continued to commit these sexual acts.

And that the codefendant therefore not be entered for the *juramentum purgatorium,*[2] since she is rightfully suspect on many accounts and even her own mother denounces the actions. Yet, she regards second-degree torture as too severe a punishment. However, we wish to leave it to the discretion of your Royal Majesty whether to modify the torture somewhat or to let the sentence stand.

The question is whether, if the Duisberg judgment should stand, such grave crimes would escape [proper] punishment. For criminals of this sort forfeit their lives under the common law, that is article 116 of the criminal code, and are customarily sentenced to death by fire and, in addition, deserve punishment by divine law, since because of them God let fire and brimstone rain from the sky and whole cities be devoured.

On the other hand, it might appear that no genuine sodomy could be committed with a lifeless leather device, in which case capital punishment would not apply. Besides, nowhere in Holy Scripture does there appear an express discussion of women committing abominations with each other, as for example between men (Romans I, 26). About women it is written only that they perverted the natural custom into an unnatural one, and this happened when they were involved with an animal, which Leviticus 18 and 36 forbid and for which the death penalty is prescribed. Or, if it had to be admitted that a woman did indeed commit abominations with another woman, this probably would refer mostly to Eastern women, those with a so-called flaw of nature, a very large clitoris, with which they could perpetrate such abominations amongst themselves, which is not applicable to this case since only a leather instrument had been used.

Sodomy comprises various types of vice: firstly, the one so despicably perpetrated on oneself; secondly, more despicably yet, the one with the same sex, as man with man and woman with woman; and thirdly and most despicably, the one committed with nonreasoning animals. . . .

It is only fair to determine the penalty according to the seriousness of the crime. According to Carpzow, the first crime used to be punished with death by hanging, the second with the sword, and the third with fire. In addition, however, most people maintain that, as actually happened in this case, women actually do commit sodomy, which the heathens also detested and against which they wrote; likewise all the interpreters of Romans I, 26 expound on the unnatural sexual intercourse and libido of the female sex. No other interpretation is possible, for the famous St. Protius in the big Lexicon Septemvir. of Basilius explains the unnatural lewdness of the women mentioned by Paul in his first chapter, whom the well-known church father Tertullian calls *fricatrices,* that is, "rubbing women." The instrument which these women use in lieu of the male member is called an *Olisbo,* as the well-known Greek playwright Aristophanes observed when he said that *Olisbo* was the name of a male member made out of leather. Aristophanes himself explains it as a leather husk, which does not really add anything to our case. Even though the Holy Scriptures do not specifically mention that women committed lewd acts with each other, suffice it that the therein punished sin of women is of the same kind as that committed between men, that is, for those who commit unnatural acts. The effect is the same, for although the semen, which is normally sent into another part of the spouse, is not truly mixed, at least there is rubbing and a search for the extinction of the libido. This case also is stated unambiguously in the Bible when mention is made that a natural custom is changed into an unnatural one, which indicates just as much if not more as when it is said that the natural custom is left behind. Surely by this are meant not only the customs of African women, even if they are the main perpetrators, but that others are not excluded. Certainly, those who commit that certain act behave much more unnaturally than the African women, who, after all, use members with which nature endowed them merely in a wrong and improper way. These other women, however, imitate those members and therefore act against nature when nature refuses them her service. The result is the same, they do not achieve anything either way but use either method for the purpose of bestial rubbing and sexual stimulation of their lewd flesh. The vice is the same for all; just as it is between man and man, so it is between woman with woman. Consequently the penalty is the same for alike vices. This is why the capital code expressly prescribes the same penalty.

Because of those circumstances, the Duisberg sentence, as far as it prescribes the death penalty for Cath. Marg. Linck, alias Anast. Lagrantinus Rosenstengel, is to be confirmed. The manner of execution is to be performed according to the suggestions of the Halberstadt government, and the accused, because of her many committed and confessed serious crimes, is to be put to death by the sword, in accordance with the gravity of her crime.

Should your Royal Majesty be of the opinion that the Holy Scriptures nowhere expressly recommends the death penalty for women as well as for men who had committed lewd acts; and if, furthermore, in cases of different types of sodomy, when it was not committed for the purpose of emission of semen, which, for natural causes, could not be achieved in this case; then according to the opinion of many jurists, the death penalty should not be applied but only flogging.

Furthermore, several members of our department are of the opinion that in this case the death penalty is not applicable, since with these types of instruments actual fleshly union is not possible, much less can semen be released—both processes being required for the real offense in regard to the act of sodomy, consequently the same formal sin, if not our law, does not apply in this case. The other crimes, however, such as the abuse of holy baptism and the frequent apostatizing, do not in themselves require the death penalty, and the accused should be shown the mercy of the law which could be effected by way of flogging and subsequent incarceration for life in a penitentiary or a spinning room where she should be made to work.

Considering the codefendant, C. M. Mühlhahn, in order that the means by which the truth is obtained should not be harsher than the actual sentence, and since the death penalty is not applicable in the case of this simple-minded person who let herself be seduced into depravity, the Duisberg sentence should be changed so that instead of the second degree [torture] she should be punished *extraordinarie* and should be condemned to three years in the penitentiary or spinning room and afterwards should be banished from the country. Furthermore, both are responsible for paying all court costs incurred in this case, two-thirds of which are to be paid by the Linck woman.

NOTES

1. The forms of names and aliases vary throughout Müller's transcription. The most common spelling of the defendant's name, however, is Linck.

2. Literally, "purging oath." Presumably such an oath could, if accepted, lead to acquittal.

SODOMY AND HERESY IN EARLY MODERN SWITZERLAND

E. William Monter, PhD

ABSTRACT: The author compares records, from the early modern era, of sodomy trials in two parts of French Switzerland (Geneva, a Protestant city, and Fribourg, a Catholic pastoral area) and presents evidence that: (1) men charged with "sodomy" were prosecuted more often for homosexuality in cities and for bestiality in rural areas, (2) male homosexual subcultures were associated with the growth of large urban centers, (3) sodomy was punished with greater severity than any other crime than infanticide, (4) in both Geneva and Fribourg repression of sodomy increased during periods of religious zeal. With the advent of the Enlightenment, the number of sodomy trials fell as prosecutions for crimes of personal violence declined and prosecutions for crimes against property increased. This is the first English translation of Monter's article, originally written in French.

The history of sexual deviance in preindustrial Europe is gradually emerging from obscurity. Despite some significant recent contributions,[1] our knowledge of its general outlines between the age of the Crusades and the French Revolution could be summarized in two terse propositions: (1) Homosexuality was tacitly permitted at various times and places in the royal courts of Europe—Edward II of England was the first and last ruler to suffer personally for his deviant sexual preferences; and (2) among the rest of the population, male homosexuality was blanketed with bestiality under the rubric of "sodomy," and both were punishable by death throughout Christian civilization.

We have learned, moreover, that this intense hatred of sexual deviance in Western Christendom was closely associated with religious deviance. The association of sodomy with heresy, far more explicit and far more important in Latin than in Orthodox Christianity, became visible in the twelfth century, when the Latin church suggested that

---

This is a revised translation of the author's article, originally published as "La sodomie à l'époque moderne en Suisse romande," in Annales: Économies-Sociétés-Civilisations, *29 (1974): 1023-1033.*

Dr. Monter is with the Department of History, Northwestern University, Evanston, Illinois 60201.

neo-Manichean loathing for heterosexual relations implied a preference for male or female homosexuality. Such charges continued through the heyday of Catharism and became sufficiently commonplace to be transferred to such non-Manicheans as the Knights Templar, or even Pope Boniface VIII, by French lawyers soon after 1300.[2] By then, canon lawyers had decided that sodomy was a *delictum mixti fori,* that is, a crime within the jurisdiction of either secular or religious courts. Subsequently, only one inquisition (Aragon) claimed jurisdiction over all cases of sodomy, whether or not heresy was present.[3] Secular lawyers, who handled the vast majority of sodomy persecutions, argued that such deviants were akin to heretics and therefore punishable by a relatively new form of execution: burning. The martyrology of homosexual men and women (and other sexual deviates) burned for "heresy" by laymen begins in the fourteenth century and continues at least until the age of Voltaire.[4]

Both the geographical and chronological dimensions of the repression of sodomy between the fourteenth and the eighteenth centuries remain obscure, however. Much of our knowledge comes from prosecutions of ordinary homosexual men in such places as the cities of Renaissance Italy or from the British Navy in its glory days.[5] Nearly all our evidence is highly discontinuous, sparse, and unevenly distributed across European nations and occupational groups. Hazarding generalizations about the repression of sodomy in late medieval and early modern Europe is difficult, but a few working hypotheses do emerge from the available information. First, "sodomy" meant very different things in different places: Men were prosecuted for homosexuality in towns and for bestiality in the countryside, while women rarely were punished anywhere for it. Second, available evidence can be decoded to infer that continuous male homosexual subcultures existed in large Italian cities (with their high celibacy rates and late marriage ages for men) since the high Middle Ages; north of the Alps, such continuous and well-developed subcultures are difficult to find before the seventeenth century, when the great capital cities began to surpass 200,000 people for the first time.[6] Third, sodomites were punished in both town and country with relatively greater severity (although *not* greater frequency) than any other crime, with the possible exception of infanticide.[7] Fourth, in most parts of continental and transalpine Europe the repression of sodomy was probably most intense during the sixteenth and seventeenth centuries, during the peak of religious zeal generated by the Protestant and Catholic Reformations and during the peak of prosecutions for witchcraft, a form of nonsexual deviance that had similarly become confused with heresy.

This paper attempts to support all four propositions with evidence from French Switzerland, a region of relatively small political units containing relatively well-preserved criminal archives from the early modern period. The paper concentrates on the Republic of Geneva and the canton of Fribourg, each of which recorded several dozen trials for "sodomy" between the fifteenth and eighteenth centuries. These two states were different, insofar as one was urban and the other rural, but alike insofar as both were famous for religious zeal. The reputation of Calvinist Geneva spread rapidly throughout Europe, while Fribourg became (and still is) the capital of Swiss Catholicism (it was the first European city to demand an anti-Lutheran loyalty oath from its citizens). Of course, these are not the only Swiss archives that contain sodomy trials; isolated instances can be found almost anywhere, but they are extremely sparse.[8] The value of Fribourg and Geneva is that only those two places record enough sodomy trials to permit meaningful generalizations, especially when one considers the chronological distribution of the trials.

GENEVA

Geneva, though smaller in population than the canton of Fribourg, saw many more sodomy trials between 1400 and 1800. During the fifteenth century, Geneva was a commercially prosperous city ruled by a bishop, with Italian merchants attending its annual fairs. It is not too surprising that her archives contain traces of half a dozen trials and two certain deaths for sodomy before 1500, or that the two most scandalous cases involved an Italian and a Greek, or that there were serious jurisdictional clashes between episcopal and civic officials in sodomy trials.[9] (By contrast, fifteenth-century Fribourg had only one known case of sodomy.) The numbers of preserved trials and the severity of prosecution, however, increased dramatically in Geneva after the mid-sixteenth century. The first known death sentence for sodomy in over a century dates from 1555, when a French journeyman printer was burned after having been discovered sexually attacking the young son of his employer.[10] During the next century and a quarter, more than sixty people were tried for the crime in Geneva, and thirty were put to death for it. Sodomy was certainly not the most frequent capital crime in Calvinist Geneva—in absolute numbers it ranked well behind murder or witchcraft and about even with infanticide—but the laws against it were enforced with noteworthy strictness, especially considering how extremely private and how difficult to discover was the activity itself.

Geneva's sodomy trials were not distributed randomly but tended rather to cluster at a few points. For example, there were fifteen sodomy trials between 1561 and 1569, resulting in six deaths and eight banishments; but for the next twenty years there was only one recorded trial. In 1590 there were six trials and five deaths; in 1610 there were twelve trials and four deaths. From 1613 through 1623 there were five deaths and two banishments, but during the next forty years there were only five deaths and five banishments. Thus, sodomy trials appear to be concentrated in the 1560s and the decade following 1610. Furthermore, the clumps of trials and deaths in 1590 and 1610 can be explained easily. In 1590, during their war with the Duke of Savoy, the Genevans captured an enemy fort where Turkish prisoners were serving as galley slaves; of the thirty-odd Turks who fell into Genevan hands, three promptly confessed that they habitually engaged in homosexuality and were promptly burned for it, along with two French Catholic soldiers whom they implicated. (An older French galley slave also was accused but never confessed.)[11] In 1610, a prominent Genevan official, Pierre Canal, was arrested for high treason and attempted homicide; under torture he voluntarily confessed to several homosexual acts, implicating more than twenty men ranging from magistrates to gatekeepers. Canal was broken on the wheel (for treason) and then burned (for sodomy). Eleven of the men he accused were brought to trial that year. Four confessed (three were drowned and the other broke jail); six did not confess and were banished; the most prominent got off with a heavy fine and the loss of all political privileges.[12]

If the aftermath of the Canal scandal helps explain the small group of 1613-1623 trials, there still remains the series of trials between 1555 and 1569, when the accused were neither Turkish slaves nor prominent public officials but a group of unremarkable men (and one woman). Nearly all the homosexual defendants in Calvin's Geneva were recent religious refugees from France: a journeyman printer from Auvergne, a goldsmith from Normandy, wool-carders from Berry and Provence, weavers from Tours and Auvergne, a painter from Lyon, a carpenter from Perche, a student from Languedoc. Virtually none came from Geneva or its vicinity.[13] Why foreigners emerge as the homosexual element in the 1550s and 1560s is problematic, but it seems significant that Geneva's population more than doubled (to about 25,000) between 1550 and 1560 because of these refugees, most of whom returned home soon afterwards (Geneva's population fell to about 13,000 by 1590).[14] Unlike most European cities, which historically have contained a surplus of women, Geneva in 1560 was a remarkably crowded place with a large surplus of men, mainly young men. It was literally true that Calvinism made strange bedfellows, and it was difficult not to spy on one's neighbor under such conditions. All things considered, it is not surprising that among the thousands of religious refugees to Calvin's Geneva were a handful who practiced homosexuality and who were apprehended quickly by the omnipresent Consistory and handed over to secular justice.

Three other conclusions emerge from Geneva's sodomy trials. The first, not surprisingly, is that several incidents of homosexuality involved schoolboys; trials as far apart as 1555 and 1672 conform to this type.[15] Two students were put to death for homosexuality during the 1560s, including one denounced by a fifteen-year-old scholar who subsequently became a famous Huguenot author.[16] Younger boys accused of homosexuality usually were given a public whipping and sent home. Only those around age twenty risked their lives.

The second observation is that several accused men were Italians. This had been unusual at first—only two of the thirteen religious refugees accused before 1570 came from Italy, and Italians comprised perhaps one-tenth of all refugees then. It became more common after 1610, however: Pierre Canal explained to his interrogators that he had become homosexual while studying law at Italian universities. The final four men executed for homosexuality in Geneva were all visitors from Italy, men who traveled with valets whose services were apparently sexual.[17]

The final observation is that some Genevan sodomy trials were actually for bestiality rather than homosexuality. Like the Italian connection, this was relatively unimportant during the sixteenth century: There is only one known trial and no known death.[18] Bestiality, however, also became more significant after 1610: Three men (all non-Genevans) were burned for it between 1614 and 1617, and three of the final five seventeenth-century trials were for bestiality.[19] To some extent, this is simply the rural environment intruding into the history of a basically urban state. Peasants have fewer opportunities than town-dwellers for homosexual activities but many more opportunities for bestiality.

The most important conclusion that emerges from Geneva's sodomy trials, however, is the very strong chronological correlation between religious zeal and the punishment of sexual deviance. Geneva's first serious sodomy trials in over sixty years and her first death sentence for sodomy in over a century occur in the year Calvin's political allies finally took control of Geneva's magistracy. The relative frequency of sodomy trials in the period 1555-1570 exactly coincides with the greatest activity of Geneva's famous morals tribunal, the Consistory,[20] but the connection is even more direct than this. It can be seen in some of the first cases in the 1550s, which often include lawyers' opinions solicited by Geneva's courts. For example, the second post-Reformation death sentence involved a young Frenchman arrested at an inn. He confessed that he had tried to attack his roommate sexually, even threatening him with a knife to keep him quiet, but had been unable to carry out his plan because of the uproar made by the roommate.[21] Everyone else's evidence fully corroborated the Frenchman's story. Geneva's magistrates asked no fewer than three jurists (all French religious refugees) for opinions on this case. The first began by insisting that "this sin [N.B., not "crime"] ranks among the most execrable, prohibited by both divine and human laws, such that the Lord showed the rigor of his judgment on a part of the land by burning five cities for it. And in such grave and atrocious crimes, the attempt—even if no result follows—is gravely punishable." He concluded that the accused man deserved death but also pointed to mitigating circumstances: This was a first-time offense, it was never actually committed, and, above all, the defendant "has scarcely begun to live in the Reformed church." The second lawyer also began with Scripture, citing some of the same proof texts (I Cor. 10:6; Genesis 19; Exodus 20:1), and moved on to Roman law, again citing the same sources as the first jurist but concluding crisply and unequivocally that "punishment in this case is death by fire." The third and most famous jurist, Germain Colladon, didn't bother to cite Holy Writ but concentrated on the fact that the crime had certainly been attempted and that in Roman law such an attempt *(conatus perfectus)* is equivalent to the act itself. Colladon concluded, therefore, that the accused should be burned—but first should be tortured again, in order to discover whether he had attempted homosexuality before. Geneva's judges read all three opinions and decided to hang the defendant.

Perhaps the most interesting and revealing case of all involved a lesbian who was drowned in 1568.[22] Lesbianism is extremely rare in legal records—this is the only recorded trial in the rich Genevan series—and naturally it, too, required a legal opinion from Colladon. The suspect had originally been arrested for fornication but had irritated her judges by blasphemously insisting she was a virgin. A midwife reported otherwise, whereupon the defendant broke down and confessed both to ordinary fornication and to a lesbian episode four years previously with a woman now dead. Colladon argued that her blasphemy made it probable that she was guilty of homosexuality, and, to him, lesbianism equalled sodomy: "Such a detestable and unnatural case deserves the punishment of death by fire, according to Imperial law." (Colladon was referring to the revised code of 1532, the *Carolina,* which had in fact made both male and female homosexuality capital crimes.) He immediately added, concerning the public sentence which was read aloud at the time of the execution, that ". . . it is not necessary to describe minutely the circumstances of such a case, but only to say that it's for the detestable crime of unnatural fornication." Her official sentence, preserved in the same dossier, dwells on her blasphemy and fornication, adding that she also had committed "a detestable and unnatural crime, which is so ugly that, from horror, it is not named here." (By contrast, homosexual males had the circumstances of their crimes spelled out in detail at their execution.) Here, apparently, was the ultimate sexual taboo of Calvin's Geneva, ruthlessly condemned by a jurist who displayed consistent fairness and occasional leniency in his official opinions about the other great sixteenth-century perversion called witchcraft.[23] His particular horror of lesbianism fits oddly with the literary traditions of sixteenth-century France, which viewed this sexual deviation with tolerant amusement.[24]

FRIBOURG

Apart from one fifteenth-century case, all the recorded sodomy trials in early modern Fribourg date from the first half of the seventeenth century, and all were for bestiality rather than homosexuality. Of course, neither observation is surprising. The prevalence of bestiality resulted from the economy of the canton, which has been exporting Gruyère cheese since the Middle Ages and always has contained more cows than people: A pastoral economy with a capital city of about 4000 people produced a pastoral sexual deviation. The chronological clustering of Fribourg's trials, like Geneva's, also has a religious rather than an economic explanation: It corresponds to the apogee of the Catholic Reformation here. From the summer of 1599 to the spring of 1648, Fribourg's Council minutes contain references to thirty-two sodomy trials—then, nothing.[25] No more than two incidents occurred in any given year, but sodomy trials took place in twenty-three different years between 1614 and 1648. The time span coincides with the implantation of many post-Tridentine institutions at Fribourg, capped by the transferral of the Bishopric of Lausanne to Fribourg, where it was presided over by a famous local personage, the Grand-Vicar Schneeuwly.[26] Because there are no surviving legal opinions among the scattered sodomy cases preserved in Fribourg's prison registers *(Thurnrodellen)*, this cause-and-effect relationship must be inferred rather than documented; however, the analogy with Calvin's Geneva seems apparent.

The link between religious zeal and the detection of sexual deviance can, of course, be found elsewhere than at Fribourg or Geneva. In May 1595, in the Protestant village of Avenches (Vaud), a Catholic peasant from Savoy attended a sermon on different kinds of sin and was so moved that immediately afterward he made a voluntary confession to the Protestant pastor, who promised to pray for his soul. The affair came to the attention of the local *bailli,* who threw the peasant in jail. Without any torture, he promptly confessed to an act of buggery with the family cow thirty years before, and to adultery, perjury, and gambling more recently. Finally, he confessed to witchcraft; for the Devil had appeared to him after the peasant had moved to Fribourg, reminded him of his sodomitic act, and thereby convinced him that he was damned already and ought to do him homage. After making this long confession, the peasant shut up like a clam while undergoing three rounds of torture. He then was condemned to death for sodomy by a jury of Avenches men, and was burned at the stake together with his wife and twelve-year-old son, who had both confessed to witchcraft in the meantime.[27]

The links between sodomy and other crimes, particularly witchcraft, can be seen clearly in the Avenches case. This same dynamic was at work in Fribourg's first preserved witchcraft confession, made at a nearby Benedictine abbey in 1457. Its first sentence describes acts of bestiality with a cow, a goat, and a deer, and explains how the Devil appeared to the confessor afterwards, persuading him to do homage and thus become a witch.[28] This same sequence also recurs in a few other cases: a thirty-year-old Catholic vagabond, dying of the plague at a Genevan hospital in 1615; teenage boys arrested at Fribourg in 1620.[29] It even happened that a man being tortured about an accusation of witchcraft spontaneously confessed to bestiality while stubbornly denying the original charge; he was burned, of course, but for a crime truly committed.[30] Sodomy was occasionally linked with crimes other than witchcraft. At Fribourg, one man was arrested for sodomy and arson, another for sodomy and incest; at Geneva, a foreigner was arrested for sodomy and armed robbery.[31] The connections between sexual deviance and other capital crimes can also be seen in the case of the only known lesbian of early modern Fribourg, who was being questioned about witchcraft when she voluntarily confessed not only to homosexual activities before her marriage but also to attempted abortion after marriage—all the while firmly denying that she was a witch or had ever seen the Devil.[32]

The link between sodomy and witchcraft went even deeper than this. They nested together chronologically because both were frequently judged as forms of heresy. We have seen that the labeling of sodomy as heresy goes back to the Middle Ages; so does the assimilation of sorcery to heresy in the crime of witchcraft. By the time Charles V promulgated his famous law code, the *Carolina,* in 1532, sodomy was listed among other spiritual crimes whose special horror lay in their peculiar offense to God. Writing in 1629, a north German jurist explained that "In Tyrol, Switzerland, the Grisons, Valais, upper Alsace and thereabouts, such a monster *(unmensch)* is called a heretic, and generally punished as a heretic, by fire."[33] The same punishment, of course, was meted out to witches, for similar reasons. If the very name of sodomy came directly from Genesis 19, and if (as Antoine de Lautrec reminded Genevan officials in 1556) Jehovah had burned five cities because of it, then it went against divine laws even more than human law. This aspect, in turn, explains why the repression of sodomy in Switzerland tended to cluster at points of extreme religious zeal, at the very zenith of either the Protestant or the Catholic Reformation.

CONCLUSIONS

Labeling sexual deviations as heresy can also help explain why recorded sodomy trials declined after 1650 at both Fribourg and Geneva. In general, sodomy trials ended at approximately the same time as witchcraft trials. At Fribourg, the last preserved sodomy trial dates from 1661 and the last typical witchcraft confession dates from 1683;[34] at Geneva, the last death sentence for sodomy occurred in 1662 and the final death for witchcraft in 1652.[35] We know that other forms of heresy were also viewed more tolerantly by public officials in the later seventeenth century, although the reasons for this shift remain obscure. Justice generally became far milder by the early eighteenth century, as crimes of personal violence shrank in importance relative to crimes against property. At Geneva, even infanticide, the only crime to be punished more severely than sodomy, saw no executions after 1712.[36] Although bestiality cases still cropped up from the vicinity of Geneva as late as 1721, and a death for this crime occurred in a nearby Lutheran state as late as 1724, the overtones of religious horror so prominent during the first half of the seventeenth century had diminished.[37] Perhaps some discreet homosexuality was still practiced occasionally in the Geneva of Voltaire and Rousseau (the latter seems to have had his lone homosexual encounter in Italy), but it no longer attracted public notice—partly because the great watchdog of Genevan public morality, the Consistory, had had most of its teeth pulled by the mid-eighteenth century.

What can these two examples from Protestant and Catholic Switzerland tell us about the history of sodomy elsewhere in early modern Europe? Perhaps only that the relatively large numbers of recorded trials in these two states, compared with their scarcity in neighboring districts, resulted from the unusually high degree of religious motivation behind these two governments during the sixteenth and seventeenth centuries. In most other parts of Western Europe the connections, verbal and otherwise, between sodomy and heresy were not so close as in Switzerland and in neighboring states, as the North German jurist noted. Legal systems that punished homosexual sailors or schoolboys were less interested in uprooting heresy than in maintaining discipline on shipboard or at school.

Enlightenment Europe, a civilization that stopped executing witches and proclaimed religious toleration, desacralized the crime of sodomy. Religious zeal came to be confined to the lower classes, who ordinarily did not control the machinery of justice; consequently, sexual deviance became a morals offense and a matter of public order. At the same time, highly visible male homosexual subcultures flourished in the major cities of Western Europe: We possess vivid pictures of the homosexual worlds of Regency Paris and of London in the 1720s.[38] The results were interesting. As Michel Foucault has observed, the Parisian police investigated about 4000 suspected homosexual persons during the eighteenth century but almost never executed them, preferring to banish them or put them in prisons or asylums: ". . . one has the impression that sodomy, formerly condemned under the same rubric as magic and heresy and in the same context of religious profanation, is now condemned only for moral reasons."[39] By the 1780s even the provincial Genevans were following the example of Paris. Homosexuality reappears in legal records for the first time in over a century, but an Enlightened judiciary ensured that no one was menaced with death because of it; the soldiers on guard duty, rather than the zealots of the Consistory, now turned in the culprits.[40] Geneva entered the modern world, at least in this respect, slightly before the French Revolution.

NOTES

1. As recently as 1964, a prominent historian complained in a major synthesis that "the history of medieval sodomy has not been written, either for theory or practice": Jacques Le Goff, *La civilisation de l'Occident médieval* (Paris: Arthaud, 1964), p. 392. A dozen years later, another Frenchman finally attempted an overview in a lesser work of popularization: Jacques Solé, *L'amour en Occident à l'époque moderne* (Paris: Albin Michel, 1976). Comparable recent improvements in English-language scholarship—much of it covering either the Middle Ages or the Enlightenment—are visible in these notes.

2. See the overview by Michael Goodich, "Sodomy in Ecclesiastical Law and Theory" *Journal of Homosexuality* 1 (1976): 427-34; and his recent book, *The Unmentionable Vice: Homosexuality in the Later Medieval Period* (Santa Barbara, Calif.: A.B.C. Clio, 1979). There are also valuable pieces of information in the works of Vern Bullough, especially *Sex, Society and History* (New York: Science History Publishers, 1976), pp. 74-92; and in Jeffrey B. Russell, *Witchcraft in the Middle Ages* (Ithaca: Cornell University Press, 1972), pp. 95n., 162, 341.

3. See Goodich, *Ecclesiastical Law* and *Unmentionable Vice*; and Henry Kamen, *The Spanish Inquisition* (London: Weidenfeld & Nicolson, 1965), pp. 200f.

4. See Goodich, "Sodomy in Medieval Secular Law," *Journal of Homosexuality* 1 (1976): 295-302. For France, a census of homosexual individuals burned by decree of the Parlement of Paris during the reigns of virtually every French king from Philip V (1317-22) to Louis XVI (1776-92) is available from the Centre International d'Information et de Documentation sur l'Homosexualité, run by M. Claude Courouve (ALEPH,

71 rue de Bagnolet, 75020 Paris). It is certainly incomplete (see Soman's work cited below, n. 7) but does offer some long-range perspectives.

5. See Goodich, *Ecclesiastical, Unmentionable Vice,* and *Secular.* For instance, Venice had seven cases in twenty years (1338-58), all punished by death: G. Ruggiero, "Sexual Criminality in Early Renaissance Venice," *Journal of Social History* 8 (1975): 22f.; Florence set up a special anti-sodomy magistracy in 1432: Gene Brucker, ed., *The Society of Renaissance Florence* (New York: Harper & Row, 1971), pp. 201-6; and the smaller city of Ferrara saw eight executions for sodomy from 1440-1500 (4% of all capital punishments): Werner Gundesheimer, "Crime and Punishment in Ferrara," in L. Martines, ed., *Violence and Civil Disorder in Italian Cities 1200-1500* (Berkeley: University of California Press, 1972), pp. 114f. For the English sailors, see A. N. Gilbert, "Buggery and the British Navy 1700-1861," *Journal of Social History* 10 (1976): 72-98.

6. The assumption that there was a "relatively continuous" (*sic*) homosexual subculture in the great cities and royal courts of Europe since the twelfth century vitiates a highly erudite and valuable study of Randolph Trumbach, "London's Sodomites: Homosexual Behavior and Western Culture in the Eighteenth Century" *Journal of Social History* 11 (1977): 9-11; this assumption led him to implausible criticisms of my 1974 article, on p. 10. At Geneva, a city of 12,000-20,000 people, no "relatively continuous subculture" could possibly have escaped the notice of the Consistory, especially during the sixteenth and seventeenth centuries. Below a certain population line (probably 100,000 for northern Europe and 60,000 for Italy) it was impossible to sustain a true homosexual subculture.

7. Recent statistics from the largest court system in Europe confirm this assertion. From 1565 until 1640, the Parlement of Paris, an appellate court serving at least ten million people, judged 176 sodomy cases, including 121 (69%) appealing death sentences; overall, 77 men were executed (44% of all accused). These were far higher averages than for persons appealing convictions for murder or witchcraft, but lower averages than for women appealing convictions for infanticide (90% appealed death sentences, 70% were finally executed)—who were eight tımes as numerous as sodomites in the records of this court. See Alfred Soman, "The Parlement of Paris and the Great Witch-Hunt," *The Sixteenth Century Journal* 9 (1978): 36 and n. 7. At Geneva, rates of conviction were about equal for sodomy and infanticide, and the number of trials in each category was close: I counted 26 deaths in 43 infanticide cases from 1573-1735 and 30 deaths in 62 sodomy cases, 1555-1678.

8. For example, at Neuchâtel two homosexual men were burned in 1597: Archives de l'Etat, Neuchâtel, # 60 (Criminal Trials, 1535-1667), pp. 191-95. In the Bishopric of Basel, a man who attempted a pilgrimage to Rome because of his many deeds of sodomy and bestiality was burned in 1615: Archives de l'Ancien Evêché de Bâle, Porrentruy, B 168, liasse 18 (Francois des Boeufs). At Lausanne, a man was quartered alive and burned face downwards for bestiality in 1627: Archives Cantonales Vaudoises, Bh 20, pt. 2 (Michel Uldry). Across the frontier in Franche-Comté, a man was killed for sodomy in 1604: Francis Bavoux, *Hantises et diableries dans la terre abbatiale de Luxeuil* (Monaco: Editions le Rocher, 1956), p. 187. In Lutheran Montbéliard, a teenage swineherd was let off with a whipping in 1660, but the sow he had sodomized was burned: Alexandre Tuetey, *La sorcellerie dans le pays de Montbéliard au XVIIe siècle* (Dole: Vernier-Arcelin, 1888), p. 21. The relative rarity of sodomy cases in rural zones is suggested by Henry Heigel, *Le bailliage d'Allemagne de 1600 à 1632* (Saarguemines: Imprimerie municipale, 1961), pp. 183f: the large German-speaking part of the Duchy of Lorraine, which saw 638 witchcraft trials in 790 hamlets between 1580 and 1632, held only a dozen sodomy trials during the same period.

9. See Appendix I, cases 1-5; apparently # 4 remained in the episcopal prison for a

dozen years and then confessed (see *R.C.* 5/48). See also Louis Binz, *Vie religieuse et réforme écclesiastique dans le docèse de Genève 1378-1450* (Geneva: Société d'Histoire et d'Archéologie, 1973), pp. 193, 279, 291. After city officials tried the first two homosexual suspects in 1444, episcopal officials jealously guarded further suspects from lay courts, and defendants went through elaborate procedures to gain benefit of clergy, even when accused of raping minors (cases # 3, 4).

10. See Appendix I, case # 8.

11. See Appendix I, cases # 28-33. For the other evidence about these galley slaves, see my "Calvinists in Turbans," *Bibliothèque d'Humanisme et Renaissance* 29 (1967): 443-45.

12. See Appendix I, cases # 39-50.

13. See Appendix I, cases # 8, 11-17, 19, 22, 23.

14. For a full discussion of these problems, see William Monter, "Historical Demography and Religious History in Sixteenth-Century Geneva," *The Journal of Interdisciplinary History* 9 (1979): 399-427. Geneva remained under 15,000 until about 1680, then rose slowly to ca. 25,000 by 1780.

15. See Appendix I, cases # 9, 69.

16. See Appendix I, cases # 17, 21; the chief plaintiff in the latter case was Agrippa d'Aubigné.

17. See Appendix I, cases # 21, 25, for the Italian refugees of the 1560s; and cases # 60, 63, 64, 66, for the mid-seventeenth-century visitors.

18. See Appendix I, case # 20. For an overview of early modern opinions on bestiality, see J. Solé, pp. 139-50; and for a list of preserved Parisian trials, see Fernand Fleuret and Louis Perceau [Dr. Lodovica Hernandez], *Les procès de bestialité aux XVIe et XVIIe siècles* (Paris: Bibliothèque des curieux, 1920).

19. See Appendix I, cases # 53, 55, 52, 65, 62, 68, 70, 71.

20. See William Monter, "The Consistory of Geneva, 1559-1569," in *Bibliothèque d'Humanisme et Renaissance* 38 (1976): 475-84.

21. See Appendix I, case # 10.

22. See Appendix I, case # 24. The only other Protestant lesbian known to me from early modern Swiss evidence was the widow Isabel Galandre, who was burned as a witch at Neuchâtel in 1623: Archives de l'Etat, Neuchâtel, # 60 (Criminal Trials, 1535-1667), pp. 765-70.

23. For Colladon's role in witch trials, see William Monter, "Witchcraft in Geneva, 1537-1662," *Journal of Modern History* 43 (1971): 189-91, 204.

24. See Solé, pp. 209-10. Other literary evidence from Renaissance sources (e.g., Erasmus) suggests considerable de facto tolerance of artistocratic or convent lesbianism.

25. In Fribourg's Archives d'Etat (hereafter AEF), entries for "sodomy" appear in contemporary indices to the *Ratsmanualen.*

26. See Gaston Castella, *Histoire du Canton de Fribourg* (Fribourg: Fragnière frères, 1922), for a clear and succinct account of the Catholic reformation.

27. Archives Cantonales Vaudoises, Lausanne, Bh 20, Pt. I (Pierre Guedon, 6-5-1595).

28. AEF, Papiers de l'Abbaye de Hauterive, Tiroir 2, # 9. With one exception fifteenth-century theorists never associated sodomy directly with witchcraft (see Russell, p. 239); but this may be just one more indication that "theorists lagged behind the witch trials in the formation of the phenomenon" (ibid., pp. 243, 250).

29. See Appendix I, case # 53; and AEF, Thurnrodell # 11, procès H. Peller (26-8-1620) or A. Feudy (20-3-1623).

30. AEF, Thurnrodell # 14, procès Claude Pillet (14-6-1644).

31. See Appendix I, case # 55; and AEF, *Ratsmanualen,* indices for December 1615 and March 1641.

32. AEF, Thurnrodell # 13, procès J. Cuasset (10-9-1635).

33. Melchior Goldast, *Rechtliches Bedencken von Confiscation der Zauberer- und Hexen-Güther* (Bremen, 1661), p. 54, quoted by Siegfried Leutenbauer, *Hexerei- und Zauberdelikt in der Literatur von 1450 bis 1550* (Berlin: J. Schweitzer Verlag, 1972), p. 100.

34. AEF, Thurnrodell # 16, procès P. Chappalay (12-8-1661): the accused was a deaf-mute and thus could not be tortured with the strappado (which required one's hands to be tied) and had to be liberated almost at once; for the last witch-trial, see Thurnrodell # 17, procès Marie Ribotel (4-2-1683).

35. See Appendix I, case # 66; and AEG, P.C. I/3465 (1652) for the final witchcraft death.

36. See AEG, P.C. I/6169, for the final recorded death for infanticide. Unlike sodomy, infanticide continued to figure in Genevan trial records throughout the eighteenth century, but no one was convicted for it after 1712. In France, the Parlement of Paris amended its old, ferocious law on infanticide in 1731, and death sentences fell off rapidly thereafter: see Léon Abensour, *La femme et le féminisme en France avant la Revolution* (Paris: Ernest Leron, 1923), p. 26.

37. See Appendix I, case # 71 (he seems to have been allowed to escape before his formal arrest); and Bibliothèque Municipale, Besancon, ms. Duvernoy # 61, fol. 61, for the Montbéliard case of 1724.

38. For Paris, the remarkable trial of Etienne Benjamin Deschauffours (1723) is in Fernand Fleuret and Louis Perceau [Dr. Lodovico Hernandez], (Bibliothèque des curieux, 1920), pp. 88-190; for London, see Trumbach, pp. 11-22.

39. M. Foucault, *Histoire de la folie à l'âge classique* (Paris: Librairie Plon, 1961), pp. 108-10 (quote, p. 109): he mentions only two known deaths after 1725. See also Jeffry Kaplow, *The Names of Kings* (New York: Basic Books, 1972), pp. 141f, 204.

40. See Appendix I, cases # 72-75.

APPENDIX I:

GENEVAN SODOMY TRIALS, 1400-1800

#	Date	Reference*	Judgment	Remarks about Suspects
1	1444	P.C. I/81	Hanged	Greek, episcopal cook
2	1444	P.C. I/105	Hanged	Genevan, partner of #1
3	1460	R.C. I/414-25	Unknown	Milanese, jurisdiction quarrel
4	1480	R.C. 3/128-35	Unknown	Physician, jurisdiction quarrel
5	1485	R.C. 3/427	Unknown	Genevan, tried by bishop
6	1513	R.C. 7/347-50	Unknown	Genevan, tried by bishop
7	1542	P.C. II/529	Banished	Genevan, also adultery
8	1555	P.C. I/517	Beheaded	Frenchman, journeyman printer
9	1555	P.C. II/1073	Whipped	Genevan schoolboy
10	1556	P.C. I/561	Hanged	Frenchman
11	1561	P.C. I/957	Banished	Frenchman
12	1561	P.C. I/957	Banished	Frenchman, partner of #11
13	1561	P.C. I/971	Banished	Frenchman
14	1561	P.C. I/971	Banished	Frenchman, partner of #13
15	1562	P.C. I/1078	Drowned	Frenchman
16	1562	P.C. I/1078	Drowned	Frenchman, partner of #15
17	1563	P.C. I/1167	Drowned	French student, age 20
18	1563	P.C. I/1168	Whipped	Three Genevan schoolboys
19	1565	P.C. I/1324	Banished	Frenchman
20	1565	P.C. II/1284	Unknown	Local peasant, bestiality
21	1566	P.C. I/1359	Drowned	Italian student, age 22
22	1567	P.C. I/1405	Banished	Frenchman
23	1568	P.C. I/1452	Drowned	Frenchman
24	1568	P.C. I/1465	Drowned	Genevan, lesbian
25	1569	P.C. I/1560	Banished	Italian
26	1569	P.C. I/1560	Banished	Frenchman, accuser of #25
27	1576	P.C. II/1433	Banished	Swiss, servant
28	1590	P.C. II/1634	Unknown	French galley slave, age 50
29	1590	P.C. II/1634	Burned	Turkish galley slave
30	1590	P.C. II/1634	Burned	Turkish galley slave
31	1590	P.C. II/1634	Burned	Turkish galley slave
32	1590	P.C. II/1634	Burned	French soldier, age 25
33	1590	P.C. II/1634	Burned	French valet of #32, age 18
34	1593	P.C. II/1751	Unknown	Genevan citizen
35	1593	P.C. II/1751	Unknown	German artisan, partner of #34
36	1595	P.C. II/1813	Unknown	French boy, age 12
37	1600	P.C. I/1818	Drowned	Genevan citizen
38	1600	P.C. I/1818	Drowned	Local peasant, partner of #37
39	1610	P.C. I/2013	Burned	Genevan official (P. Canal)
40	1610	P.C. I/2016	Fined	Genevan official, partner of #39
41	1610	P.C. I/2017	Drowned	Genevan gatekeeper, partner of #39
42	1610	P.C. I/2017	Drowned	Genevan, partner of #39
43	1610	P.C. I/2017	Drowned	Genevan, partner of #39
44	1610	P.C. I/2018	Banished	Genevan, accused by #39
45	1610	P.C. I/2018	Banished	Genevan, accused by #39
46	1610	P.C. I/2018	Banished	Genevan, accused by #39
47	1610	P.C. I/2018	Banished	Genevan, accused by #39
48	1610	P.C. I/2019	Banished	Genevan, accused by #39

APPENDIX I (CONTINUED)

#	Date	Reference*	Judgment	Remarks about Suspects
49	1610	P.C. I/2019	Banished	Genevan, accused by #39
50	1610	P.C. I/2212	Banished	Genevan, accused by #39 (escaped)
51	1613	P.C. I/2212	Banished	Genevan, began as plaintiff
52	1614	P.C. I/2238	Drowned	Catholic stableboy, bestiality
53	1615	P.C. I/2297	Burned	French Catholic, bestiality and witchcraft
54	1617	P.C. I/2350	Burned	Swiss visitor, age 80
55	1617	P.C. I/2378	Burned	Catholic, age 46, bestiality
56	1621	P.C. I/2505	Burned	Catholic, age 50, Savoyard
57	1623	P.C. I/2579	Banished	Genevan citizen, age 83
58	1633	P.C. I/2948	Burned	Genevan citizen
59	1633	P.C. I/2948	Banished	Genevan boy, age 15, partner #58
60	1634	P.C. I/2981	Burned	Neapolitan
61	1634	P.C. I/2982	Banished	French valet, partner of #60
62	1636	P.C. II/2393	Banished	Frenchman, bestiality
63	1647	P.C. I/3330	Hanged	Italian
64	1647	P.C. I/3331	Burned	Italian, partner of #63
65	1660	P.C. I/3696	Released	Stableboy, age 17, bestiality
66	1662	P.C. I/3768	Burned	Italian officer, age 42
67	1662	P.C. I/3777	Banished	French valet, partner of #66
68	1663	P.C. I/3777	Banished	Genevan carpenter, bestiality
69	1672	P.C. I/4215	Unknown	Two Genevan schoolboys
70	1678	P.C. I/4405	Unknown	Local peasant age 18, bestiality
71	1721	P.C. I/6896	Unknown	Catholic stableboy, bestiality
72	1785	P.C. I/14478	Unknown	Genevan citizen, watchmaker
73	1786	P.C. I/14930	Banished	German, age 23, accused by guard
74	1787	P.C. I/15178	Banished	Genevan, accused by guard
75	1789	P.C. I/15711	Unknown	Genevan, billiard-parlor owner

Abbreviations

P.C. = Series of Procès Criminels at Archives d'Etat, Geneva
R.C. = *Registres du Conseil de Genève*, ed. Rivoire and van Berchem, 13 vols. (Geneva, 1900-1940). Series stops in 1536.

CONCEPTIONS OF HOMOSEXUALITY AND SODOMY IN WESTERN HISTORY

Arthur N. Gilbert, PhD

ABSTRACT: This essay explores recent attempts to write the history of homosexuality and identifies two distinct approaches: the biographical approach, which reports on the private lives of individuals and charts the formation of homosexual subcultures; and the approach that studies the labeling and treatment of homosexual men and women by the heterosexual majority and examines the reasons why hatred of homosexuality increases and decreases over time. The author warns against applying modern definitions to words that have had different connotations. As an example of the possible confusion, the author discusses the two meanings of the word sodomy*: unspecified sexual relations between males; and the act of anal intercourse, whether heterosexual or homosexual. Western civilization's association of the anus with evil, the devil, and bestiality is examined.*

Recently and tentatively historians have begun uncovering the roles of homosexuality and homosexual men and women in history. It is not an easy task. Proscriptions against homosexuality have always been enormously powerful, and prudent individuals rarely left any record of this aspect of their lives. Documents that might have shed some light on the subject were more often than not destroyed by friends, relatives, or heirs anxious to avoid scandal and preserve the family name. Court records can tell us something about the treatment of offenders in a number of countries, and newspaper accounts occasionally record a homosexual scandal, especially if it involved someone of prominence. Here and there one finds a pamphlet or observation by a chronicler of the day writing about covert or overt homosexual behavior. Beyond this, however, there is silence, for what was called in English law "the crime not fit to be named" was not likely to leave many traces.

Still, the history of homosexuality is being written, and it has taken a number of predictable forms. As one might expect, there have been books and articles about individuals as well as studies of homosexual life during particular historical periods. Representative of the biographical approach are a number of works by Roger Casement, the Irish patriot who was condemned, tried, and executed for treason in 1916.[1] Casement's life is of great interest to historians of homosexuality

Dr. Gilbert is Associate Professor, Graduate School of International Studies, University of Denver, Denver, Colorado 80210.

Journal of Homosexuality, Vol. 6 (1/2), Fall/Winter 1980/81

because after he had been condemned to death the discovery of his diary, the notorious black books, effectively destroyed any likelihood that friends and acquaintances in positions of power would draw attention to themselves by intervening to have his sentence commuted. As such, the example of Roger Casement shows how the violation of one of Western culture's most powerful sexual taboos could mean the difference between life and death.

Raising consciousness by demonstrating historical continuity has always been an important function of the historian's trade. Both the women's movement and the black movement have been given considerable legitimacy by the publication of numerous books and articles on historically important, but generally ignored, women and black people. In this same vein there are books that attempt to rediscover a homosexual past by telling the stories of a number of historically important homosexual men and women. A. L. Rowse's *Homosexuals in History*[2] is an example—an unfortunate one in my judgment—of the effort to identify "great gays" and thus, presumably, to dignify the lives of homosexual individuals of the present day.

Alongside these popular accounts, there are many scholarly articles that stress the environment that spawned and shaped homosexual subcultures at various periods. An example is the fine article by Randolph Trumbach, "London Sodomites: Homosexual Behavior and Western Culture in the Eighteenth Century."[3] Trumbach's thesis is that, in the large cities of Europe, underground homosexual communities lived a sometimes furtive but nonetheless flourishing existence, with a full panoply of modes of recognition and behavioral patterns, and a distinct argot. In other words, underground homosexual communities shared many of the characteristics often exhibited by other secret and forbidden societies. Trumbach's study is an interesting blend of history and that branch of sociology that deals with subcultures and deviance.

Another attempt to deal with homosexual subcultures is Peter Allison's "The Secret Sharer."[4] Unlike Trumbach, Allison is less concerned with organized homosexual activity in time and place but focuses rather on the various conditions that gave rise to homoerotic sensibilities in late nineteenth- and early twentieth-century England. According to Allison, upper-class and upper-middle-class males of this period were virtually isolated from contact with females. The public school, the military, the university, and professional training all helped to create, as Allison writes, "values, allegiances, and shared experiences to which women were almost inconsequential."[5] He does not discuss actual sexual practices, as does Trumbach, for Allison is more interested in the symbolic meaning of the institutional encouragement of all-male environments.

As biographers probe more deeply into the homosexual proclivities of their subjects, we all may come to a deeper understanding of the public and private behavior of well-known men and women. More importantly, we may learn how homosexual people survived and functioned as subgroups in Europe and America and about the kinds of sociocultural traditions that explain the cause, incidence, and awareness of homosexuality at various times in history. Research in the first two areas mentioned would be an important adjunct to modern studies of homosexual subcultures and the psychosocial dimensions of homosexual individuals and their communities. The work of psychologists and sociologists in this field usually suffers from a lack of historical referents.

A second and larger field of study concentrates not on the history of homosexual persons but the history of their treatment by society. In many ways this is a more interesting subject, for it ranges beyond the problem of subculture formation and survival to the roots of Western fears of certain modes of sexual behavior. The focus is not so much on individuals but on the reasons why they were mistreated, persecuted, and even killed for their sexual activities. Implicitly or explicitly, those who work in this area are interested in the sociology of deviance. The central dictum of deviance theory, with its emphasis on interaction and labeling, is significant here. As Albert Cohen noted, "[T]hat which we deplore and that which we cherish are not only part of the same seamless web: they are actually woven of the same fibers."[6] For Kai Erikson,

> [*D*]*eviance is not a property* inherent *in certain forms of behavior: it is the property conferred upon these forms by the audience which directly or indirectly witnesses them. Sociologically, then, the critical variable in the study of deviance is social audience rather than individual person, since it is the audience which eventually decides whether or not any given action will become a viable case of deviation.*[7]

The sociologist of deviance sees normality and deviance, acceptable and unacceptable behaviors, as mirror images, with the audience playing a major role in defining deviant behavior. This audience can be defined historically in broad or narrow terms. We have respectable contributions on the treatment of homosexual people from Arno Karlen, who deals mainly with Western culture, and from Vern Bullough, who adds not only to our understanding of Western culture but measures it against the attitudes and practices of the non-Western world, in particular, Hindu, Buddhist, Islamic, and Taoist approaches to sexual behavior.[8] These general studies have many obvious virtues and provide a framework for better understanding of an entire heritage. The defects, however, are equally apparent. Sometimes lost in an overview of thousands of years of history is the sensitivity to nuances, to the change of attitudes, provided by narrower but more intensive studies.

Bullough's work is a good example of this latter point. Attitudes toward homosexuality in the West were shaped early by Platonic philosophy in ancient Greece and Rome and later by Christian horror of unnatural and non-procreative sex. Differences in attitude and practice over the next couple of millenia seem less important to Bullough than the overwhelming fact of repression of homosexuality. A number of questions come to mind. If Christianity was indeed perenially hostile to homosexuality, why was this the case? Other early Christian beliefs were modified when confronted with changing world-wide realities. The history of Christian attitudes toward war is a good example of how ideas have been modified by new situations. An essentially pacifist religion turned into a crusading one in the eleventh and twelfth centuries. Why were Christian attitudes toward things sexual, as opposed to matters of external violence, reinforced? This process cannot be explained simply by reference to "the power of ideas" without careful attention to the economic, political, and social conditions that allowed for the unchanging transmission of these ideas. In addition, although Bullough notes the perceptible changes in attitudes that *do* occur, he does not account for them. Bullough merely states that there were times of tolerance and times of harsh repression, that there were royal courts dominated by homosexual courtiers but also fierce persecutions of homosexual men and women, persecution that led to the stake and the gallows.

More modest studies, like William Monter's on the interconnection between witchcraft and sodomy in the Swiss Romande in early modern times, help to remedy the shortcomings of general surveys.[9] Monter probes beneath cultural generalities to pick up spatial and temporal differences. He notes that in the Swiss Romande accusations of sodomy and other sexual offenses often were paired with witchcraft accusations, implying that the fear of witches and the fear of sexual deviance were similar. Monter suggests that the great age of witch persecution, in the sixteenth and seventeenth centuries, had a sexual parallel. Whether Monter is correct is problematic, but at least his study undertakes the kind of correlations that must be made if we are to understand fear of deviance in history.[10] Other studies, such as some articles by Bullough and Karlen, link charges of sodomy to fear or heresy, once again joining sexual and religious deviance.[11]

Yet connections between heresy, witchcraft, and sexual deviance explain only partially the fear of sexual deviance. We need more information on the social and economic conditions that exacerbate fear of deviance, and we must uncover the social explanations for why society's fears change from time to time. My own studies of sexual deviance in the eighteenth and nineteenth centuries, both in the British Navy and in Great Britain in general, are useful in this connection. With respect to the British Navy we have an institutional explanation for fear of deviance.[12] British naval society—highly structured and disciplined—could not tolerate an activity that might interfere with the smooth running of the ship. Further, it was an all-male and therefore a "marginally" puritanical society.[13] In British society generally, we find an intensification of fear of deviance that parallels involvement in the long and threatening Napoleonic Wars. Pressure on homosexual men was particularly intense in 1810, when war weariness and fear of anti-religious and revolutionary French ways were combined with economic strife.[14] This analysis suggests a link between persecution of homosexuality and perceived or imagined social disaster.

The narrower studies, such as Monter's and mine, raise some important cautionary banners to which historians in this field must pay heed. In attempting to understand fear of homosexuality contextually, one becomes acutely aware that there are difficulties in defining terms and a great danger that one will apply current definitions to a past that saw sexual deviance quite differently. As an example of this pitfall consider a short article by Louis Crompton, entitled "Gay Genocide: From Leviticus to Hitler."[15] The term genocide is used inappropriately in his discussion of homosexual offenders. Genocide, the systematic execution of large numbers of people because of their beliefs, race, or origins, does not fit the occasional and sporadic violence against sodomites. A graver error is Crompton's contention that there were about 2000 years of repression and violence directed toward a definable group called gays, homosexuals, or whatever. In his recent book, *The History of Sexuality,* Michel Foucault makes some distinctions that are important for historians of homosexuality.[16] Foucault correctly notes that terms such as "homosexuality" and "homosexual" are modern, originating in the late nineteenth and early twentieth centuries. This linguistic development stemmed not from some arbitrary desire to find a new word to replace the earlier ones, but rather from the recent creation by society of a new class of deviants. Suddenly there were "homosexuals"—a group of males who because of heredity or childhood training chose to seek sexual partners from members of their own sex. The sodomite had been someone who *sinned* by performing a deviant social *act.* The homosexual was not a sinner in the old religious sense but someone with an identifiable lifestyle revolving around the choice of sexual partners of the same sex. The distinction is important, for it marks the beginning of the treatment of a segment of the population as a race apart. For Crompton, apparently, the persecution of a sodomite in the fourteenth century is pretty much the same as harassment of homosexual communities in the twentieth. He may be correct, but it is wrong simply to assert this sameness without taking a more intense look at similarities and differences among historical views of deviance.

Because of the historical silence surrounding the subject of homosexuality, it is not all that easy to determine what was being punished in the past. One thing is clear, however: The words "sodomy" and "sodomite" had dual meanings. On the one hand sodomy referred to unspecified sexual relations *between males,* and on the other it meant a particular mode of sexuality, usually anal sex. Understanding the dual nature of sodomy is an important antidote to the false assumption made by so many scholars that there was only one meaning, a relational one.

This distinction can best be understood by a quick review of the writings of clergy and the surviving penitentials. Thomas Aquinas is representative of the first category. Aquinas attempted to define and rate those sins that fell under the general heading of "unnatural vice."[17] One unnatural vice, according to Aquinas, was the act of "procuring pollution without any copulation, for the sake of venereal pleasure." Aquinas called this the sin of uncleanliness, and it seems likely that he was referring to masturbation. Another unnatural vice was bestiality, and a third was the "vice of sodomy," which Aquinas defined as "male with male and female with female." Finally, Aquinas included "unnatural manner of copulation," which appears to cover unacceptable positions, for example, oral and anal heterosexual sex. Aquinas regarded all these unnatural vices as grave sins, more serious than incest and rape, but he also rank-ordered the four categories. The worst sin was bestiality "because use of the right species is not observed," followed by sodomy "because use of the right sex is not observed." These two most grievous sins were followed by "not observing the right manner of copulation" and by "pollution without any copulation."

It should be stressed that Aquinas was concerned with sin in the traditional Christian sense: sexual acts forbidden by God. As Foucault warns us, we must not assume Aquinas viewed homosexuality as a lifestyle. Nonetheless, in placing all homosexual behavior in the forbidden category, he seemed to support writers like Crompton who define sodomy in modern-day relational terms.

We should also examine surviving handbooks of penance, which give a somewhat different view of the nature of sexual deviance. The penitentials are much closer to law as it might be applied in a modern court than to the expository writings of clergy on sexuality. The definition of penances required precision because confessor and sinner needed to know precisely what was sinful. A sinner was a lawbreaker and the punishment had to fit the crime. As a result, penitentials were *act specific;* there were no penances for illicit *relationships* such as homosexuality.

In a study of penitentials, John Noonan remarks that "anal and oral intercourse is treated as a serious sin by everyone who mentions such behavior" and, he continues, "many writers prescribe a more serious penance for it than for homicide committed by a layman . . . "[18] Noonan also notes that the penitentials were designed essentially to control lust and not simply as an adjunct to the church's stance against birth control. Further, so far as we can tell, there were no distinctions made between oral and anal sex as performed by heterosexual couples and by homosexual couples. If the length of penance is an indicator, then among those acts, anal intercourse was clearly the more heinous crime.

The dual definition of sodomy led to endless confusion in the public mind, as well as in law courts throughout Europe when civil law later replaced church control of sexual misconduct cases. In England the law was unclear on this matter for years. In the seventeenth century Edward Coke had defined sodomy as sex between males (there was no mention of lesbianism), presumably eliminating the possibility that heterosexual deviance would be punishable by law.[19] In practice, however, sodomy was defined quite differently. In the seventeenth century the Earl of Castlehaven was convicted of sodomy on his wife. In the early eighteenth century, in his important decision of a case involving anal sex committed on a twelve-year-old girl, Judge Fortescue ruled that prosecution under the sodomy statute was perfectly appropriate here because it was inconsistent for the law to claim that only males could be sodomized.[20] There can be no question that Fortescue favored a behavioral rather than a relational interpretation of what constituted sodomitic offenses.

Fortescue's decision set the tone for English legal interpretation of the sodomy statute during the eighteenth and early nineteenth centuries. While the vast majority of cases tried under the sodomy statute involved two or more males, there were exceptions. Every now and then a man would be tried for sodomizing his wife or another female, and the courts never ruled that the indictments were illegal because sodomy referred solely to homosexuality.[21] Following Aquinas, homosexual males were still tried under the sodomy statute, but, in accordance with the penitential tradition, heterosexual anal sex was forbidden too. As the eighteenth century progressed, it became increasingly necessary to prove penetration (and sometimes emission) into the anal passage in order for the judge and jury to convict. This suggests sodomy had come to be defined as a specific act under English law. Clear proof of this can be found in the surviving courts-martial records, which, unlike civilian records, have lengthy trial minutes. While military law had many unique features, in crimes for which there were civilian counterparts (murder, rape, robbery, sodomy), it followed the precedence and practices of English law. Sodomy was sodomy whether the offender was in or out of uniform. The army and navy trial records show intense preoccupation with whether or not anal penetration was achieved. Where penetration could be proved, the verdict was guilty and a death sentence usually followed. If there was no penetration, the accused would not be executed, although he might be punished for attempted sodomy or uncleanliness.[22] Neither the military nor civilian society executed men for fondling, kissing, or oral sex, or for the myriad other activities homosexual males might perform.

Let us be clear on this, that narrowly defining sodomy as an act did not mean that English society or even the courts ignored homosexual behavior as unimportant and of no threat to the community. Many individuals were tried and convicted of *attempted* sodomy, even though there was very little evidence that anal sex had been intended. When the existence of homosexual clubs was discovered, both courts and populace could punish with incredible ferocity. A man convicted of attempted homosexual advances had every reason to fear for his life if he were pilloried in London, for the mob would turn out to hurl missiles at offenders. Nonetheless, the dual definition of sodomy and sodomite seriously qualifies the assertion that homosexual repression was equivalent to the repression of sodomy in past times.

In a short essay, it is not possible to explore these themes in great depth. But in light of the present-day misconception that sodomy and homosexuality were one and the same, it is crucial to examine the link between sodomy and anal sex. This is particularly important because the facts substantially qualify the gay-genocide or gay-repression hypothesis. Fear of anal sex in Western culture is part of a complex of values that developed out of the Judeo-Christian tradition. Hostility to all nonprocreative sexual acts is significant but is only a partial explanation for the proscription of sodomy. Many modes of sex interfere with procreation, but, as the penitentials reveal and as the later application of civil law indicates, none was punished as harshly as anal sex. While Christianity frowned on self-abuse, oral sex, and the like, penances were shorter for those offenses and men were not normally executed for them. Furthermore, many if not all societies have taboos against the waste of semen. Such taboos are part of Taoist thought, Tantrist Buddhism, and other traditions that do not show any particular horror of anal sex per se. Disapproval of wasting semen is not a sufficient explanation for Western fear of sodomy.

To understand the anal sex taboo, as opposed to the homosexual relationship taboo, we must return to the origins of Christianity. From its beginning, the new religion was characterized by a dichotomy between body and spirit. Paul, for example, states in the Epistle to the Romans: "Those who live on the level of our lower nature have their outlook formed by it, and that spells death; but those who live on the level of the spirit have the spiritual outlook, and that is life and peace." Soon after this passage, Paul writes:

It follows, my friends, that our lower nature has no claim upon us: we are not obliged to live on that level. If you do so, you must die. But if by the Spirit you put to death all the base pursuits of the body, then you will live.[23]

The words lower, base, and death contrast explicitly with higher, spirit, and life; however, at the same time, Paul and other Christian writers referred to the human body as a temple, a holy vessel. Paul writes in Corinthians, "Do you not know that your bodies are limbs and organs of Christ? Shall I take then from Christ his bodily parts and make them over to a harlot? Never!"[24] He adds, "Do you know that your body is a shrine of the indwelling Holy Spirit and the Spirit is God's gift to you?"[25] The spiritual strivings in Christian thought clashed with the unassailable fact that life ends in death, that human flesh, like that of all other animals, rots and decays. Even more disturbing to the Christian mind was the admission that the living body constantly enacts the drama of death in its physical functions. Excrement was always the clearest and most persistent reminder of the fate of man. Humans usually defecate in secret, and in the Western imagination the anal function became a symbol of evil, darkness, death, and rebellion against the moral order. It is not accidental that Zoroastrianism, with its Manichean emphasis on the opposition of good and evil, body and soul, also treated the sodomite with the same hatred we associate with the Christian West. Early Christian asceticism and its attitude toward the body is most significant, for as Derek Bailey writes:

The rigorist tendency . . . in the New Testament came to its full development during the patristic age in an asceticism which sought, like its Hellenistic counterparts, to attain perfection through renunciation of the world and subjugation of the body. To this end every means was employed—fasting, solitude, prayer, mortification (not to mention a deliberate neglect of elementary hygiene), but always the decisive test, the critical discipline, was that of sexual continence![26]

Still, after punishing the body and denying the delights of the flesh in order to come closer to God, there was always, for even the holiest, a reminder of animality and mortality: that stinking bit of fecal matter that proved one was, after all, brother to the sheep, the dog, and the goat. For someone aspiring to overcome earthbound mortality, defecation was a sign of the ugliest fact of all: man is a dung-producing animal.

It was for these reasons that sodomy was inextricably linked in Western thought with bestiality. Just as sodomy was a reminder of "lower" physical impulses, so bestiality evoked man's link with the animal kingdom. Both were acts in defiance of the spiritual nature of man. Rather than striving upward toward God and the angelic, copulation with animals was a deliberate turning of one's back (or backside) to the deity and plunging, like Lucifer, to a level below man's assigned role. It was to break the links with animality that Christianity had condemned heterosexual intercourse from the rear. For a man to mount a woman as the stallion does the mare was unclean—too close to the sodomitic and the bestial for comfort. In sodomy trials the imagery of animals and bestiality was always in evidence.

Sodomy, then, elicited the combined fears of sexuality, animality, and anality. This triumvirate came to personify evil to the Western sexual imagination. More particularly, the anal-evil link was established firmly. As one modern scholar has noted, "Dante's hell is one vast excremental dungeon."[27] The very structure of hell, with its tortuous downward spiralling in the belly of the earth, is suggestive of the excremental organ, as are its features of darkness, wind, and stench. Since sin is the most hateful thing, only the language of the privy is adequate to express the disgust it generates. In the fifteenth century, Jan Van Eyck painted a remarkable rendition of the Last Judgment, which parallels Dante's anal-evil theme.[28] Christ is shown welcoming the saved into heaven in the usual fashion, but of much greater interest is Van Eyck's views of the punishment of the damned. The earth is pockmarked with gaping holes into which sink the struggling, naked sinners. Astride the earth is a gigantic skeleton—death personified—with arms and legs akimbo, defecating the damned into a hell inhabited by monsters and wild beasts of the most terrifying sort, who tear, dismember, and devour those who did not lead the holy life. Hell is a giant privy and death turns human beings into waste. Men and women are metamorphosed into the products of their own bowels.

The anal-evil link is, if anything, even more dramatically presented in Martin Luther's writing, as both Norman O. Brown and Erik Erikson have indicated.[29] Also in eighteenth-century England, when sodomites were punished with death, the symbolic link between anality and evil was unmistakable. One sees it in the writings of Jonathan Swift, in the etchings and engravings of Hogarth, and most pointedly in the political and social satires of James Gillray.[30] More research is required to discover why anality as evil was reinforced from generation to generation and why this theme dominates in some periods and not others. Already it is certain, however, that sexual acts involving the anal passage were regarded as the ultimate form of evil, a pact with the devil, a violation of the upwardly striving Christian attempt to find salvation. Fear of anal sex was certainly as powerful a force in the Western imagination as fear of homosexual relations.

The error of reading the present into the past is well known and yet common in the historical enterprise, as evidenced in examples cited here. Advice to respect the integrity of the past is hardly earthshaking, but it seems particularly important to remind historians who are studying sexual deviance to exercise some caution in their admirable attempts to write the history of homosexuality. While empathy for other times is difficult to achieve in the best of circumstances, it is particularly difficult in this case because of the secrecy and ambiguity surrounding the subject of deviant sexuality and because of the consequent paucity of data. Yet scrupulous historical accuracy is essential; indeed, it is the only way in which we will begin to understand not only homosexuality as a forbidden relationship but sodomy as a forbidding mode of sexual activity.

NOTES

1. Brian Inglis, *Roger Casement* (London: Hodder and Stoughton, 1973); B. L. Reid, *The Lives of Roger Casement* (New Haven: Yale University Press, 1976).
2. A. L. Rowse, *Homosexuals in History: Ambivalence in Society, Literature and the Arts* (New York: Macmillan Publishing Co., 1977).
3. Randolph Trumbach, "London's Sodomites: Homosexual Behavior and Western Culture in the Eighteenth Century," *Journal of Social History* (Fall 1977): 1034.
4. Peter Allison, "The Secret Sharer: The Symbolic Significance of Homosexuality in Late Victorian and Edwardian England" (unpublished paper).
5. Ibid., p. 16.
6. Albert Cohen, "The Study of Social Disorganization and Deviant Behavior," in Robert Merton, Leonard Brown, and Leonard Cothell, *Sociology Today* (New York: Basic Books, 1959), pp. 473-74.
7. Kai Erikson, "Notes on the Sociology of Deviance," in Howard Becker, *The Other Side: Perspectives on Deviance* (New York: Free Press, 1964), pp. 10-11.
8. Arno Karlen, *Sexuality and Homosexuality: A New View* (New York: W. W. Norton, 1971); Vern Bullough, *Sexual Variance in Society and History* (New York: John Wiley & Sons, 1976).
9. E. William Monter, *Witchcraft in France and Switzerland: The Borderlands during the Reformation* (Ithaca, N.Y.: Cornell University Press, 1976), p. 197. See also Monter, "La Sodomie à L'Époque Moderne en Suisse Romande," *Annales* 29 (1974): 1023-33, reprinted in a revised translation in this issue of the *Journal of Homosexuality.*
10. See also, Guido Ruggiero, "Sexual Criminality in the Early Renaissance: Venice, 1338-1358," *Journal of Social History* (Summer 1975): 18-31.
11. Vern L. Bullough, "Heresy, Witchcraft, and Sexuality," *Journal of Homosexuality* 1 (1974); Arno Karlen, "The Homosexual Heresy," *The Chaucer Review* 6 (Summer 1971): 44-63.
12. Arthur N. Gilbert, "Buggery and the British Navy, 1700-1861," *Journal of Social History* (Fall 1976): 72-98.
13. On marginality see Martin S. Weinberg, "The Nudist Management of Respectability" in Jack Douglas, ed., *Deviance and Respectability: The Social Construction of Moral Meanings* (New York: Basic Books, 1970).
14. Arthur N. Gilbert, "Sexual Deviance and Disaster during the Napoleonic Wars," *Albion* 9 (Spring 1977): 98-113.
15. Louis Crompton, "Gay Genocide: From Leviticus to Hitler" in Louie Crew, ed., *The Gay Academic* (Palm Springs, Calif.: ETC Publications, 1978), pp. 67-91.
16. Michel Foucault, *The History of Sexuality,* Vol. 1, *An Introduction* (New York: Pantheon Books, 1978), pp. 42-43.

17. *Summma Theologia* (New York: Benziger Brothers, 1947) II-11 Q 154 art. 11 & 12.

18. John Noonan, *Contraception* (Cambridge: Harvard University Press, 1966), p. 166.

19. Alex Gigeroff, *Sexual Deviation in the Criminal Law: Homosexual, Exhibitionistic, and Pedophilic Offenses in Canada* (Toronto: Toronto University Press, 1968), pp. 8-9.

20. Rex V. Wiseman, *English Law Reports,* XCII (London, 1909), 774-76.

21. For example, see the case of Edward Bishop, who was convicted of attempted buggery on his wife Mary, Middlesex Session Books, MJ/SPB/15, June 1746.

22. See my article, "Sodomy and the Law in Eighteenth and early Nineteenth Century England," *Societas* (forthcoming).

23. Romans 8:5, 6, 7, 12, and 13.

24. Corinthians 6:15.

25. Ibid.

26. Derek Bailey, *Sexual Relations in Christian Thought* (New York: Harper & Brothers, 1959), p. 19.

27. Jae Num Lee, *Swift and Scatalogical Satire* (Albuquerque: University of New Mexico Press, 1971), p. 18.

28. The painting is in the New York Metropolitan Museum of Art.

29. Erik Erikson, *Young Man Luther* (New York: W. W. Norton, 1962); Norman O. Brown, *Life Against Death: The Psychoanalytic Meaning of History* (New York: Vintage Books, 1959).

30. For example, see Hogarth's *Four Stages of Cruelty,* Plate I.

HO HUM, ANOTHER WORK OF THE DEVIL
BUGGERY AND SODOMY IN EARLY STUART ENGLAND

B. R. Burg, PhD

ABSTRACT: A study of contemporary handbooks for justices of the peace, sworn depositions, and other judicial records shows that in early Stuart England people were relatively tolerant of homosexuality. Sodomy was a minor felony, but more than homosexual activity was required to prosecute an offender. Persons accused of religious heresy, political offenses, or violating social-class distinctions also might be charged with sodomy, as illustrated by the cases of Lord Audley, Earl of Castlehaven and John Atherton, Bishop of Waterford and Lismore. Although the Puritans expanded the list of sexual acts proscribed as vices, even they did not react to it with the extreme horror characteristic of the Victorian era and the present day.

The England of the early Stuart monarchs was a land far different from modern Britain or America. Aside from the obvious changes created by three centuries of technological evolution, the lives of the seventeenth-century English followed patterns widely divergent from those familiar to people now living. Ideals, values, moral codes, conceptions of humankind, and the very nature of social reality were so substantially distinct from those of the twentieth century that one modern historian of the period was moved to entitle his book on the structure of society 300 years ago *The World We Have Lost.*[1] Among the many features that distinguished Stuart England from modern times were the attitudes of its citizens toward homosexual activity. Unlike the present day, when sexual contact between members of the same sex is anathema to large segments of the population in both England and America, homosexuality was greeted with little hostility or opprobrium in the early seventeenth century.

Although one authority on the period, Caroline Bingham, contends that homosexual acts were considered abominations in the first decade of the seventeenth century, other sources indicate it is unlikely that this was the case. Bestiality, homosexual child molestation, and homosexual acts were all lumped together under the heading of "buggery,"

Dr. Burg is with the Department of History, Arizona State University, Tempe, Arizona 85281.

Journal of Homosexuality, Vol. 6(1/2), Fall/Winter 1980/81

which in Elizabethan times often was used interchangeably with sodomy. Despite the potential for confusion inherent in this overlapping nomenclature, the operation of the law made sharp distinctions among the different offenses. The first two (bestiality and homosexual child molestation) were exceedingly serious crimes. Details of their commission were described clearly in the records, and conviction drew severe penalties, often including the death sentence. Consenting adults convicted of having engaged in homosexual acts also were subject to the death penalty, but in practice it was rarely or never imposed.

This toleration is hardly surprising. It was only since the reign of Henry VIII that buggery had been a civil crime. Previously, it had been subject to ecclestiastical censure, but religious authorities rarely prosecuted unless the homosexual acts were compounded with heresy, sorcery, witchcraft, or other sacrilegious practices. The first statute prohibiting buggery was enacted in 1533 and, like a later Elizabethan law of 1562 prohibiting sodomy, was the result of a struggle for power between the church and expanding secular authority, rather than a sympton of a definite policy to restrict the varieties of sexual activity practiced by the English. The only celebrated sodomy case during the Tudor period was that of Nicholas Udall (1505-1556), the noted churchman, playwright and Eton headmaster. Udall's taste for paddling and sodomizing his adolescent charges, however, did no lasting harm to his career. He was not prosecuted and, although dismissed from his post at Eton, was given severance pay equal to a year's salary. Later he became headmaster at Westminster and in due time received ecclesiastical preferment under both Edward VI and Mary. Evidently, the ecumenical nature of his sexual preferences made him acceptable to both a Protestant king and a Catholic queen. There were no other prosecutions for homosexual acts under the buggery or sodomy statutes until well into the next century. Indeed, at the end of the Elizabethan age, Richard Barnfield was composing graceful pastorals on obviously homosexual themes. At one point he softly denied the existence of homoerotic motifs in his work, but went ahead writing more of the same. There were no serious objections to Barnfield's advocacy of love between shepherds and their boys.[2]

The lack of alarm is nowhere more apparent than in the treatment accorded homosexual practices in various manuals written to aid justices of the peace in the conduct of their official tasks. In a compendium of instructions for justices, the early Tudor author Anthony Fitzherbert devoted only a single sentence to buggery, explaining that it was a felony without benefit of clergy. The same lack of concern was evidenced in William Lambarde's manual for instruction of justices, published in 1582. His *Eirenarcha* was the best of the sixteenth-century handbooks and had enormous influence, going through numerous editions despite competition from similar works by John Goldwell of Gray's Inn and Richard Crompton. Although in his diagram of felonies Lambarde distinguished buggery with man from buggery with beast, the treatment in the text indicated an obvious lack of horror. His fifteen-word explanation was inserted narrowly between putting out "the eies of any of the King's subjects" and "the taking of any maid, widdow, or wife, unlawfully, against her will, that hath lands, or tenements, goods or chattels." Sir Edward Coke, one of England's foremost judicial scholars during the reign of James I, was another who dealt with the legal aspects of buggery. In his comprehensive examination of the nation's laws, he explained that the crime originated in pride, excess of diet, idleness, and contempt of the poor. Nowhere did he seek to connect its beginnings with heresy or any other satanic machinations; it was an ordinary felony of human origins. Coke noted that even the adjectives describing buggery as "detestable" and "abominable" dated only from the prohibition enacted under Henry VIII. Coke also attempted to extend the definition to cover at least one heterosexual situation—being an accessory to rape—and tried to restrict the grounds on which convictions for homosexual acts could be obtained: Penetration had to be established to prove guilt; emission alone was insufficient. When Coke sought to buttress his arguments, he found sodomy cases were exceedingly rare. The best precedent he could locate did not involve two adult males. It was instead a 1608 case of homosexual child molestation; as mentioned, this act was legally distinct from those involving consenting adults.[3]

Sir Edward Coke and the justices of the peace all were drawn from the upper strata of English society, and their attitudes were not necessarily identical with those of people from lower levels of the social scale. On the matter of buggery, however, ordinary Britons appear to have agreed with influential justices in their lack of animosity toward homosexuality. This is evidenced in one of the rare quarter sessions proceedings against an individual accused of sodomy. The only surviving documents of the 1622 Somersetshire case are depositions sworn by men who had been sexually involved with the accused, a George Dowdeny, or who had rejected his advances at one time or another. The precise reasons for bringing Dowdeny to public account are not clear, but according to testimony his penchant for buggery was of long standing, one deponent recalling that he had been raped by the defendant fourteen years earlier. Two of the three depositions mention excessively enthusiastic importuning by the accused during the months previous to the trial, an indication that Dowdeny's homosexual solicitations may have become too frequent and conspicuous to ignore. There is also a possibility that one of his objects of seduction was a boy. Throughout the testimony, however, there was little expression of anger or revulsion at any of Dowdeny's homosexual acts or attempts. The only moment of stark terror recoverable from the written record is in the statement of Walter Wiseman. Recalling an incident from the preceding year, Wiseman told how, at Christmas time, Dowdeny made preparations to engage in bestiality with the mare belonging to one William Checkenton. When he realized Dowdeny's intention, Wiseman was seized with fear that even discussion of the topic was sufficient to send them both to the gallows and immediately fled from the stable. The final disposition of the case has not survived, but the extant testimony makes it clear that more than homosexual acts was required to provoke the law. Dowdeny was probably a nuisance with his attempted seductions; he may have been a pederast, and allegedly he had an eye for a well-turned equine ankle. The sworn depositions indicate, however, that for all his offenses bestiality was considered far more serious than his homosexual acts, masturbations, and occasional exhibitionism.[4]

The Dowdeny case was a rarity in early seventeenth-century England. During the reign of James I a wave of prosecutions for homosexuality was unlikely, since the king himself was notoriously involved with a series of male lovers. Even after James was succeeded in 1625 by his son, Charles I, there was no rush to root out sodomites at any level of English society. Among the gentry, it required more than a homosexual act to bring a person to justice. John Hockenhull of Prenton was brought before the Chester Sessions on April 21, 1628 and charged with buggery, but there was more to his proscribed behavior than the sex charge. He was accused additionally of the more ominous crime of sorcery.[5] The record of the verdict has been lost but for such a case to be tried was anomalous in itself.

The earliest successful prosecution for homosexual acts involving adults did not come until 1631, half a dozen years into the reign of Charles I. In this instance the accused was a nobleman, Mervin Touchet, Lord Audley, Earl of Castlehaven. It is apparent that more was involved than a simple matter of anal penetration. Audley was a Roman Catholic, an unpopular set of beliefs in virulently Protestant Stuart England, but, of greater importance, the Earl was charged with far more than simple buggery. He was accused of committing a series of sex crimes including "Abetting a Rape on his Countess, . . . Sodomy with his Servants, and Commanding and Countenancing the Debauching [of] his Daughter."[6] He also was accused of voyeurism, child molestation, and buggering the servants who had raped the Countess on his orders. Not only was this style of conduct far more extreme than sodomy alone, but the Earl had made his crimes more despicable by violating class taboos. He was, in addition, charged with dispensing lands and large sums of money to his companions in debauchery. The indictment against Castlehaven contained the standard legal phraseology describing sodomy as contrary to nature and a crime not to be named among Christians, but in the judicial proceedings against him no attempt was made to label sodomy as more brutish or less natural than heterosexual rape.[7] The Lord High Steward presiding over the Westminster Hall trial condemned both crimes as "Great and Heinous" but also cautioned the lords who sat in judgment to make certain that "Reasons and Consciences sway your Judgments, and your Heads direct your Hearts."[8] During the course of the proceedings, rape and sodomy were both described as abominable and felonious, but it was explained emphatically that these were crimes not because of their repellant nature but because they were violations of English law. The only unflattering adjective applied exclusively to sodomy by the Lord High Steward was a moderate "vile." On the single occasion when the prosecution described the Earl's actions as not fit to be named among Christians, it was in a quotation from the legal phraseology of the indictment.[9]

The Earl of Castlehaven was convicted of both rape and sodomy, yet the noble lords who decided his guilt did not condemn him equally on each of the two counts. The evidence presented to the tribunal substantiated the facts of the accusations, and in his defense the Earl did not dispute the truth of the testimony. He argued instead that while he had forced his unwilling wife to submit to a series of sex acts, because she was a promiscuous woman, this did not legally constitute rape. In like manner he denied being guilty of sodomy since the testimony of witnesses proved only emission but not penetration. The Lord Chief Justice explained to the court that under English law the unwholesome character of a woman was no defense against rape and that, despite Coke's arguments to the contrary, the emission of semen, whether or not penetration took place, constituted buggery. With all legal questions settled, the twenty-six peers who sat in judgment then were asked to render their verdict. Each of them pronounced Castlehaven guilty of rape. On the second charge, however, some jurors felt less need to convict. The majority necessary to condemn the Earl was available, but it is apparent that if the lords had thought sodomy to be as ghastly a crime in 1631 as it was to be considered in the nineteenth and twentieth centuries, even eleven of them would not have attested to their belief in the defendant's innocence by voting for acquittal.[10]

No proceedings for similar but unrelated crimes followed the trial of the Earl of Castlehaven, and sodomy continued to be regarded as a rare occurrence. The extreme events of this particular case enabled zealous English Puritans to bring a Catholic nobleman to trial under circumstances where the Romish Charles I and his Catholic queen could not possibly exert influence. Only under such a constellation of events could charges be preferred against Lord Audley. Social circumstances also were vital in bringing indictments against Castlehaven's companions in debauchery. Two of the servants who had provided testimony against him in exchange for immunity from prosecution were tried, convicted, and executed. As was the case with their Catholic master, it was the aggregate of their social behavior rather than a specific crime that earned them a death sentence. Their trespass over sacred class boundaries only amplified their sexual transgressions. These ordinary men, common household servants, had engaged in repeated sexual acts with a noble lady and her child daughter while insinuating themselves into the nobleman's favor to the pecuniary detriment of his rightful heirs. In an era when rigid social stratification was a pillar of all national institutions, such men could not be tolerated.[11]

A decade after Castlehaven's execution another public figure was condemned for sodomy, and again more was involved than a sex act between consenting males. John Atherton, Anglican Bishop of Waterford and Lismore, was hanged at Dublin on December 5, 1640. An account of his penitence and preparations for death was later written by Dr. Nicholas Bernard, a cleric who attended Atherton in his final days. Bernard's pamphlet is concerned with Atherton's humility and his longings for Heaven rather than with the specifics of his crime, but it reveals that the disgraced bishop was well aware that political offenses were the actual cause of his death. Atherton was being made to answer, Bernard explained, for "too much zeale and forwardnesse, both in introducing and pressing some Church-observations, and in dividing himself from the house of Convocation Anno 1634 in opposition to the Articles of Ireland then voted to be received."[12] Atherton created some of his own difficulties by serving as local champion for conforming Anglicanism at a time when Puritans were gaining the upper hand in England, but in fact his errors went beyond those recorded in the pamphlet. During his years of service in Ireland he had made the compound mistake of creating powerful enemies while at the same time becoming the protégé of the Earl of Strafford, a man who was soon to lose the power to protect himself and his retainers. The most dangerous of those in opposition to Atherton was the influential Earl of Cork. He and other leading landowners had some time before been forced by Strafford to surrender portions of their holdings, and later Cork was sued by Atherton in an attempt to make him return lands once owned by the See of Waterford. Under the circumstances, Atherton needed all the support he could muster, but Strafford could not have protected him even if he had desired to do so. At the very time the convicted bishop mounted the scaffold in Dublin, the Earl was in serious difficulty with the Puritan-dominated parliament. Within months after Atherton's death, Strafford was charged with treason through a bill of attainder, condemned to death, and executed on May 12, 1641.[13]

English history from 1630 to 1650 was characterized by disruptions so severe that any attempt to apply the lessons learned in Castlehaven or Atherton's prosecutions and to bring accusations of homosexuality against a major figure for political or ecclesiastical purposes would have been doomed. At this time the nation was deeply divided on truly substantive issues. The English were vitally concerned with the form of the national church, the collection of taxes, and the apportionment of governmental authority. Charles I had antagonized large numbers of his subjects, including many Puritans whose hopes for religious reform he had dashed prior to 1630 with royal edicts demanding conformity to the doctrines and ceremonies of the Church of England. Many of the Puritan reformers, who included in their ranks those responsible for condemning Castlehaven, Atherton, and Strafford, were rich, powerful, and determined not to accept "Romish corruptions" as integral parts of the national religion. Their hostility was carried into Parliament, where a large bloc supported the cause of ecclesiastical reform, and their anger over religious problems spilled into the debates on other issues. Under the direction of John Hampden, John Pym, and Oliver Cromwell, Parliament decreed that it could not be dissolved without the members' own consent, it abolished the king's courts of Star Chamber and High Commission, and it ordered that no taxes could be collected without the permission of Parliament. Charles attempted to halt the flow of events by arresting the legislative leadership, but this failed. Full-scale civil war erupted in the 1640s and raged for seven years before the Puritans and their supporters were able to gain complete victory.

During the war years, when the Puritans were gaining domination of religious life in England, they tried to restrict what they regarded as the moral lapses of the people. In addition to alterations in ecclesiastical doctrine and polity, the Puritans expended great efforts to make patterns of living accord with those prescribed by God. Attempts were made to eliminate dicing, cardplaying, bearbaiting, cockfighting, drunkenness, whoring, homosexual acts, and a whole host of objectionable activities. One of the best contemporary catalogs of these various sins was John White's *The First Century of Scandalous, Malignant Priests*. The book was a veritable roster of sins committed by members of the Anglican clergy. The most frequent charge lodged by White against clerics of the established religion was heresy, as might be expected, but among behavioral lapses the most offensive acts were drunkenness and whoremongering. Homosexual conduct was proscribed and a number of ministers were denounced for it, but these were relatively minor matters according to White, who was much more agitated over heterosexual rape, lusting after neighbors' wives, and adultery. Nicholas Bloxam, a Suffolk clergyman denounced in the volume, was accused of being a common drunkard, a swearer, a man who neglected his ecclesiastical duties, and of having a lascivious carriage toward several women. He was, in addition, accused of being an enticer of others to "that beastly vice," but the exact nature of this final accusation is uncertain and may or may not have been buggery. John Peckham, like his colleague Bloxam, stood accused of numerous crimes ranging from drunkenness to adultery, opposing Parliament, and a failure to observe the Lord's supper. Another charge, that he engaged in heterosexual sodomy, was a minor matter compared with his serious violations of divine command. Even in the case of a third minister, who had engaged in buggery eighteen times according to testimony, the penchant for sodomizing males was mitigated in White's opinion by the minister's expression of horror at fathering bastard children. His other offenses could not be so easily excused. Among the genuinely serious sins were attempted bestiality, drunkenness, baptizing an illegitimate child, defending imagery in churches, asserting that sins committed after baptism were imitations rather than corruption, and calling Christ a bastard.[14]

One of the most precise of the Puritan moralists was William Prynne, whose monumental work denouncing the theater had considerable effect on religious dissenters seeking to extirpate sin in England. The corrupting influence of drama on all classes of people had long been an article of faith among the Puritan clerics and the artisans, merchants, and laborers who followed their teachings. Prynne pointed out, as had other writers of the same ilk, that the examples of easy morality provided by the stage had substantial effect on people too young and too unsophisticated to distinguish between theatrical fancy and reality. He charged that theatrical performances instigated and abetted "Love-passions, Lusts, Adulteries, Incests, Rapes, Impostures, Cheates, Conspiracies, Treacheries, Murthers, Thefts, Debates, and other abominable villanies."[15] Among the many vices he cataloged was the acting of female parts by men and boys. Women were not permitted on the stage in the early decades of the seventeenth century, and this resulted in the encouragement of transvestism among players, both during and after performances. Prynne denounced the practice of males donning female garb for any purpose, calling it disgusting, revolting, repugnant, counter to the judgments of both pagan and Christian scholars from earliest recorded history, and contrary to the revealed will of God. Transvestism was a wickedness, Prynne explained, of "which my Inke is not blacke enough to discypher."[16] In addition, men donning the raiment of women encouraged the practice of sodomy. Not only did "Players and Playhaunters in their secret conclaves play the Sodomites,'' but their effeminate manner and their example encouraged homosexuality among the general population.[17] In proper Puritan fashion, Prynne did not ignore the opportunity to denounce buggery in his excoriation of transvestism among players, and he left no doubt that he considered it lewd, unnatural, abominable, and worse than adultery; however, in his condemnation he did not venture very far beyond that point. He was willing to admit that the lives of players were characterized by ''more than Sodomiticall uncleanness,'' and in his denunciation of the theater, a tirade running over 1000 pages, the few paragraphs labeling sodomy as one of the evil results of men dressing as women indicated Prynne was not overly concerned with it, or at any rate was less concerned with buggery than with the host of other pernicious practices allegedly encouraged by actors and the stage.[18]

The surviving documentary materials relating to homosexuality in England during the reigns of the early Stuarts are few, and generalizations based on these documents are by nature tentative. The small amount of evidence indicates, however, that there was no abiding concern with restricting homosexual acts in the age of James I and Charles I. Although bestiality was as severely punished as was homosexual child molestation, there was little alarm over sexual relations between adults of the same sex. Accusations of sexual irregularity were employed occasionally against political foes, but severe penalties were imposed only when public figures were involved and political motives were present. This is not to imply that homosexual behavior was an acceptable style of conduct, even though common at the royal court. It was a felony but a minor one. It aroused none of the horror later to be characteristic of Victoria's reign and the present day. To people of early Stuart England, homosexuality was simply another work of Satan, and most Britons, whether wealthy or poor, foolish rustic or sophisticated jurist, Puritan or conforming Anglican, did not see in it sufficient evil to evoke a passionate negative response.

NOTES

1. Peter Laslett, *The World We Have Lost* (New York: Scribners, 1965).

2. Caroline Bingham, ''Seventeenth-Century Attitudes Toward Deviant Sex,'' *Journal of Interdisciplinary History* 1 (Spring 1971): 447-68; Frederick Pollock and Fredric W. Maitland, *The History of English Law Before the Time of Edward I,* 2 vols. (Cambridge: Cambridge University Press, 1895), 2: 554-55; A. L. Rowse, *Homosexuals in History: A Study of Ambivalence in Society, Literature and the Arts* (New York: Macmillan, 1977), pp. 24-25; for an excellent survey of assorted sexual practices during the seventeenth and eighteenth centuries, see Vern L. Bullough's compendious *Sexual Variance in Society and History* (New York: John Wiley & Sons, 1976), Chapter XVI; Hyder Rollins and

Herschel Baker, "Richard Barnfield," in *The Renaissance in England* (Boston: D. C. Heath, 1954), pp. 396-97.

3. Anthony Fitzherbert, *Loffice et Auctority de Iustices de Peace* (London, 1606), folio 50; William Lambarde, *Eirenarcha, or Of The Office of the Justices of Peace in Foure Books* (London, 1610), pp. 224-25; Retha M. Warnicke, *William Lambarde, Elizabethan Antiquary* (London: Phillimore, 1973), pp. 61, 70-72; Lambarde's absence of concern was again evident in Michael Dalton's *Countrey Justice* published over half a century later, in 1655: Dalton barely touched on the crime, although he did extend it to include sex acts involving only women and several unspecified heterosexual practices (pp. 340-41); Sir Edward Coke, *The Third Part of the Institutes of the Laws of England* (London, 1644), pp. 58-59; Coke, *The Twelfth Part of the Reports of Sir Edward Coke* (London, 1658), pp. 36-37.

4. Quarter Session Rolls, SR/49, Taunton, 1622, Somerset Record Office, Taunton, Somersetshire.

5. Chester Quarter Sessions 21/3/174a, 24/119/3-6164.

6. *The Tryal and Condemnation of Mervin, Lord Audley Earl of Castle-Haven* (London, 1699), t.p.

7. Ibid., p. 9.

8. Ibid., p. 4.

9. Ibid., pp. 10-12.

10. Ibid., pp. 22-31.

11. Ibid., p. 9. There is no evidence in accounts of the trial to substantiate Caroline Bingham's contention that the execution of the two servants proves the members of the court were revolted by sodomy. See Bingham, pp. 463-65.

12. Nicholas Bernard, *The Penitent Death of John Atherton* (Dublin, 1641), p. 15.

13. Ibid., pp. 15, 26, et passim; Atherton's accuser was hanged some days or weeks before Atherton (ibid., p. 26); *DNB,* I, pp. 689-90.

14. John White, *The First Century of Scandalous, Malignant Priests* (London, 1643), preface, pp. A2 (recto, verso), A3, 1-2, 11, 23-24, 28.

15. William Prynne, *Histrio-Mastix: The Players Scourge* (London, 1633), pp. 75-76.

16. Ibid., p. 211.

17. Ibid., pp. 208-14.

18. Ibid., p. 135.

DEFINING SODOMY IN SEVENTEENTH-CENTURY MASSACHUSETTS

Robert F. Oaks, PhD

ABSTRACT: Legal and theological definitions of sodomy in the Massachusetts Bay Colony, and various recommendations for its punishment, are discussed. A notorious case of heterosexual child molestation illustrates the differing views as to definitions of the crime and the requirements for imposing the death penalty. The author suggests that the strict legal procedures later established in order to avoid the confusion attendant upon this case actually reduced the number of arrests and convictions for homosexual activity.

In the 1630s, when Puritan settlers in Massachusetts began to codify the colony's laws, they drew heavily upon the Old Testament, especially for their list of capital crimes. By 1641, the colony had accepted a compilation of crimes drawn up by Nathaniel Ward. The list of capital crimes, published first in Massachusetts and later in London, included "sodomy": "If a man lyeth with mankinde, as he lyeth with a woman, both of them have committed abomination, they both shall surely be put to death. *Lev.* 20:13." The phrasing, as with nearly all other definitions of capital offenses, was lifted verbatim from the Old Testament. The only exceptions to this rule were the laws concerning rape and child molestation. These were amended after a sensational case, which, among other things, indirectly clarified the definition of sodomy and the legal requirements for conviction.[1]

In 1641, authorities were horrified to discover that three men regularly had been molesting two young girls over the previous two years. One Daniel Fairfield "abused the tender body" of Dorcas Humfrey and her younger sister, Sara, beginning when Dorcas was only seven years old. The girls' father, John Humfrey, had been a prominent leader of the Puritan settlers even before they left England. In Massachusetts, Humfrey had served as magistrate, but after a few years, possibly because he did not get along with Governor John Winthrop, he returned to England, leaving the girls in the care of "a company of rude servants." This arrangement was unusual. Parents often sent their children to live away from home, but not until the children were older than the Humfrey girls. Humfrey's action appears to have

Requests for reprints should be addressed to Dr. Oaks at 575 Pierce Street, #105, San Francisco, California 94117.

Journal of Homosexuality, Vol. 6(1/2), Fall/Winter 1980/81

been child abandonment. With little supervision, the girls were easy prey for Fairfield: "This wickedness was committed very often. . . usually. . . on the Lords dayes & lecture dayes."[2]

Jenkin Davis, a servant formerly employed by Humfrey, and John Hudson, another servant, also abused the little girls. Davis's pregnant wife was "scrupulous" about not having "fellowship" with him in her condition, and "he was hurried by the strength of his lust to abuse the elder of these girls." Hudson, "having no woman to lodge with. . . did abuse [Dorcas] many times, so that she was grown capable of a man's fellowship and took pleasure in it."[3]

The story finally came to light when Dorcas told an older married sister what had happened. Dorcas claimed that two of her brothers had also "used such dalliance with her," but they were so young that they were simply admonished. Not so the three men, however. The colony was outraged and demanded death sentences, particularly for Fairfield. Several legal problems were involved, however, as no one knew exactly how to define the crime. The girls had apparently consented to the treatment; could it, then, be considered rape? Even if it were rape, there was as yet no specific law against that crime in Massachusetts, and Winthrop noted, "there was no express law in the word of God" that rape be punished by death. So the authorities tried to apply the recently adopted sodomy statute to the case. This created even more difficult legal problems, for although the men confessed to molestation, they "denied entrance of her body." English precedent for sodomy convictions generally required proof of actual penetration. The English Chief Justice Edward Coke had made this clear only a few years earlier, when he published the Third Part of his influential *Institutes of the Laws of England.* The magistrates had only the girls' testimony to go on, but the law provided that no one could be compelled to testify against himself and that two witnesses were needed to any crime which resulted in a sentence of death.[4] Even if the sodomy statute could have been construed to fit this situation, it would have been extremely difficult to obtain a conviction under these conditions.

Stymied by legal restrictions, the magistrates wrote for advice to other New England colonies, soliciting written opinions from prominent ministers, the nearest equivalent to legal experts. The magistrates' first question was phrased in Latin, and while it was common to use that language in legal discourse, the fact that their other questions were in English suggests that this one may have been too sensitive a subject to render in English. The question concerned the necessity of proof of penetration for a capital sodomy conviction: *"an contactus et fricatio usque ad seminis effusionem sine penetratione corporis sit sodomia morte plectenda?"*[5] From the outset it was clear that many of the responding ministers clearly and understandably equated "sodomy" with male-male sexual activity and found it difficult to apply the term to the case of Fairfield and the Humfrey girls.

There was no general consensus among the ministers' replies. The Rev. John Rayner, for instance, drew examples from the Bible to show that it was not necessary to have *"penetratio corporis"* for sodomy to be capital: "his sin is not mitigated where there is no penetration, nor augmented where it is." The Rev. Ralph Partridge, on the other hand, though he thought it "probable that a voluntary effusion of seed. . . of man with man, as of a man with woman," without penetration might allow a death sentence, was not entirely confident of his opinion. The Rev. Charles Chauncy, who later became President of Harvard, wrote that all "evident attempts" to commit capital crimes were themselves capital. Chauncy then tried to apply sodomy specifically to the case in question: ". . . if. . . unnatural lusts of men with men, or women with women, or either with beasts [are to] be punished with death, then *a pari* natural lusts of men towards children under age are so to be punished."[6]

The majority of the respondents concluded that evidence of actual penetration was necessary to prove sodomy. The ministers disagreed as to whether accused individuals could be forced to testify against themselves, though nearly everyone ruled out torture as a means of exacting a confession. As to the number of witnesses required, the ministers generally insisted on two, except where there was a confession by the accused or "concurrent and concluding circumstances."[7]

Because of the confusion, when the General Court met in May 1642 the members were divided as to the sentence for the three defendants. Several magistrates wanted the death penalty, especially for Fairfield. After much dispute, they ruled that the case did not fit within the definition of sodomy and agreed on a lighter sentence, because the "sin was not capital by any express law of God." Instead of a death sentence, Fairfield was sentenced to be "severely whiped at Boston. . . & have one of his nostrills slit so high as may well be, & then to be seared, & kept in prison, till he bee fit to bee sent to Salem, & then to be whiped againe, & have the other nostrill slit & seared." After that, he would be confined to Boston Neck, under penalty of death if he ever left. Also, he had to "weare an hempen roape about his neck, the end of it hanging out two foote at least." And, finally, he was to pay forty pounds to the girls' father. Davis was whipped at Boston, then again at Lynn, and confined to that town under penalty of death. He, too, had to wear a rope around his neck and pay forty pounds to Humfrey. Hudson was whipped at Boston and Salem, and ordered to pay Humfrey twenty pounds. Dorcas Humfrey "was ordered to be privately severely corrected."[8] How ironic that the girls' father, whose neglect of his daughters helped create the problem in the first place, was rewarded by the court, probably because his daughters now would be more difficult to marry off.

One result of applying scrupulous legal standards to sodomy, as in this case, was to make it extremely difficult to convict people for homosexual activity. The requirement that penetration be proved not only restricted the definition of sodomy to anal copulation but also made it nearly impossible to obtain the necessary evidence. Prosecution was made even more difficult by the rulings that accused individuals could not be forced to testify against themselves and that two witnesses were necessary for conviction. These very rigorous standards may explain why there were so few arrests and only one execution for sodomy (for a rather extreme case) in seventeenth-century New England.[9]

The authorities attempted to tighten up the laws dealing with rape and child molestation, so that similar confusion would not recur. On the same day that the men involved in the Humfrey case were sentenced, the General Court adopted several laws to eliminate some of these problems. Drawing on English laws dating from the reign of Elizabeth I, the Court accepted the concept of statutory rape and decreed that any man having "carnal copulation" with any "woman child under ten yeares ould" would be put to death, regardless of whether or not the girl consented. Rape of a married or engaged woman also carried the death penalty. Rape of an unmarried woman over ten years old could carry a death penalty, but judges were given the discretion of applying lesser penalties. Finally, a man who committed "fornication with any single woman" with her consent could be punished by being forced to marry her, by a fine, by corporal punishment, or by any combination of these penalties at the judge's discretion.[10]

The attempt to link homosexuality with child molestation failed in seventeenth-century Massachusetts. By the time the Humfrey case was concluded, the colony had established legal procedures for enforcing laws against homosexuality and had instituted other harsh laws to punish rape and child molestation. While it is difficult to use the word "liberal" in reference to Puritan New England, in some respect homosexual males received more stringent legal safeguards in the seventeenth century than did their counterparts in later and presumably more "enlightened" times.

NOTES

1. Charles M. Andrews, *The Colonial Period of American History* (New Haven: Yale University Press, 1934-38), I: 454-59; George L. Haskins, "The Capitall Lawes of New-England," *Harvard Law School Bulletin*, February 1956, pp. 10-11; Louis Cromp-

ton, "Homosexuals and the Death Penalty in Colonial America," *Journal of Homosexuality* 1 (1976): 277-93.

2. *Records of the Governor and Company of the Massachusetts Bay in New England,* ed. Nathaniel B. Shurtleff (Boston: Commonwealth of Massachusetts, 1853-54), II: 12-13; John Winthrop, *The History of New England from 1630 to 1649,* ed. James Savage (Boston: Little, Brown & Co., 1853), II: 54-58; Samuel Eliot Morison, *Builders of the Bay Colony,* rev. ed. (Boston: Houghton Mifflin Co., 1958), pp. 32-33, 65, 98-99; Edmund S. Morgan, *The Puritan Family: Religion and Domestic Relations in Seventeenth-Century New England* (New York: Harper & Row, 1966), pp. 75-78.

3. Winthrop, II: 54-58. Mrs. Davis' refusal to have sex during pregnancy hints at what may have been one of the Puritans' beliefs about sex. Since Protestants generally (and Puritans more specifically) did not accept the Catholic view that sex should be used for procreation only and should, therefore, be avoided at times (such as during pregnancy) when procreation was impossible, Mrs. Davis probably acted out of medical considerations. Sex during the latter stages of pregnancy was often discouraged in the belief that the fetus might be crushed or aborted. See Lawrence Stone, *The Family, Sex and Marriage in England, 1500-1800* (New York: Harper & Row, 1977), pp. 263, 496.

4. *Records of Massachusetts Bay,* II: 12-13; Winthrop, II: 54-58; Vern L. Bullough, *Sexual Variance in Society and History* (New York: John Wiley & Sons, 1976), p. 437; Edward Coke, *The Third Part of the Institutes of the Laws of England,* 4th ed. (London, 1669), p. 59.

5. Winthrop, II: 54-58. The question asked "whether contact and friction leading to the flow of semen without penetration of the body is sodomy punishable by death."

6. William Bradford, *Of Plymouth Plantation 1620-1647,* ed. Samuel Eliot Morison (New York: Alfred A. Knopf, 1970), Appendix X, pp. 404-13.

7. Winthrop, II: 54-58.

8. Ibid., *Records of Massachusetts Bay,* II: 12-13.

9. See Robert F. Oaks, " 'Things Fearful to Name': Sodomy and Buggery in Seventeenth-Century New England," *Journal of Social History* 12 (1978): 268-81.

10. *Records of Massachusetts Bay,* II: 21-22. Consensual sex with a married or engaged woman constituted the crime of "adultery," one of the original capital offenses drawn up from the Old Testament.

"WRITHING BEDFELLOWS": 1826
TWO YOUNG MEN FROM ANTEBELLUM SOUTH CAROLINA'S RULING ELITE SHARE "EXTRAVAGANT DELIGHT"

Martin Bauml Duberman, PhD

ABSTRACT: In 1826, twenty-two-year-old Jeffrey Withers, later a judge in the South Carolina Court of Appeals and a delegate to the conferences that established a provisional government for the Confederacy, wrote two letters to his young friend, Jim Hammond, who would attain prominence as governor, member of congress, senator, and major apologist for slavery. The letters discussed homosexuality in a guilt-free manner. The author suggests that this nonchalance may have been typical of this class and race in the antebellum South. The author's account of the difficulties surrounding his efforts to publish the Withers/Hammond letters provides historians with useful advice on how to deal with archivists when printing sensitive material.

BACKGROUND

The two manuscript letters that form this article's centerpiece have been concealed from public view for 150 years. No portion of them has ever previously appeared in print, not even in the form of disguised paraphrase or oblique reference. No single hint at their *existence* is anywhere to be found in the scholarly literature of the period. Yet, as

Dr. Duberman is Distinguished Professor of History at Lehman College, the City University of New York. The author of nine books, Duberman has won the Bancroft Prize, the Vernon Rice/Drama Desk Award (for his play, "In White America"), a nomination as Finalist for the National Book Award, and a special prize from the National Academy of Arts and Letters for his "contribution to literature." Active in the gay movement since 1972, Duberman was one of the founders of the Gay Academic Union and has served on the board of a variety of gay organizations (Lambda Legal Defense Fund, The National Gay Task Force, The Glines Theater, etc.). He currently is completing for publication a selection of his essays and diaries from the Seventies.

Journal of Homosexuality, Vol. 6(1/2), Fall/Winter 1980/81

will be seen at a glance, the letters' startling content opens up immensely suggestive new avenues for historical interpretation. It is therefore important that they be "introduced" on several levels.

To start with the simplest, we need to identify the letters' author (Jeff) and the recipient (Jim). When the letters were written in 1826, both Jeff and Jim were still inconsequential young men—yet both on the brink of distinguished careers. Of the two, Jim (James H. Hammond) eventually achieved by far the greater eminence. But Jeff (Thomas Jefferson Withers) was himself to cut a considerable swath—as a journalist, lawyer, "nullifier," and Judge of the South Carolina Court of Appeals.

In 1826, the twenty-two-year-old Jeff Withers was studying law at South Carolina College—discontentedly. "An useful man," he wrote Jim Hammond, "must, at last, be *self-educated.*" In Withers' opinion, time spent in college was time "murdered;" in concentrating as they did on the "dead languages" of Greek and Latin, the colleges of the day were hopelessly "behind the state of society" and ill prepared their students for "the duties of life." In spite of his education, by 1826 Withers had reached certain basic decisions about his future. Henceforth, he wrote Jim, he would "sacrifice" his "Northern mania" and devote himself to what he now realized was his "appropriate sphere of action"—the Southern states. Though in general "not strenuous in opinions upon political matters," Withers did feel strongly about the mounting argument between "strict" and "broad" constructionists over the kind and amount of power the Constitution had granted the federal government. Withers sided with the strict constructionists. His hero was South Carolina Senator William Smith, in the early 1820s probably the country's fiercest defender of the sovereign and "inviolate" rights of the individual states against the threatening encroachments of national power.[1]

Activating his beliefs, in 1828 Jeff Withers became editor of the Columbia *Telescope*, one of several organs of the powerful nullification movement that had recently arisen in South Carolina to protest and defy the federal tariff of 1828. For several years thereafter he gave his full energies to the struggle, delaying the completion of his law studies until 1833 (the same year he married Elizabeth Boykin, whose niece, Mary Boykin Chestnut, later won enduring fame for her extraordinary Civil War journals, *Diary from Dixie*). Elected a common-law judge soon after, Withers moved up to the state Court of Appeals, where he served until his death in 1866. His moment of greatest public prominence came in 1861, when he was chosen as one of fifty delegates sent by the seven seceded states of the lower South to Montgomery, Alabama to draw up a provisional government for the pending new "Confederacy."[2] Beyond a few additional details, little more is known about Withers' public career.

Still less is known about his private life. He apparently was considered an "irritable" man, quick-tempered and sarcastic, although one friend insisted Withers was withal "a very kind-hearted gentleman and most indulgent and affectionate in all relations of life."[3] It's tempting—given the contents of his two letters printed below—to read innuendos into that friend's description; but since such phraseology was perfunctory for its day, the temptation is better resisted.

We know a great deal more about the later life of Withers' friend, Jim: James H. Hammond. One of the antebellum South's "great men," his career ranged from politics to agricultural reform to pro-slavery polemics. At various times Hammond was Governor, Congressman and Senator from South Carolina, a leading exponent of Southern economic diversification, and a highly influential "moralist" whose varied theories in defense of slavery became cornerstones in the South's "Pro-Slavery Argument." If Hammond's name is scarcely known today, in the antebellum period he was sometimes bracketed in importance with John C. Calhoun—and considered by many his likely heir.[4]

For our limited purpose of elucidating two 1826 letters, any detailed description of Hammond's later public career would be gratuitous, especially since it has been recounted ably many times.[5] Yet a few aspects of that career, as well as what little is known of his later private life, do need to detain us, for they bear directly on our interpretation of the "meaning" of young Jim's erotic activities and on whether we can establish any continuities in the behavior of James H. Hammond, the adult.

First, however, we need to get acquainted with young Jim himself—with the lusty roisterer revealed for the first time in these hitherto unpublished letters from 1826.

THE DOCUMENTS

The following letter was from Withers to Hammond, May 15, 1826, Columbia, South Carolina.[6]

Dear Jim:

I got your Letter this morning about 8 o'clock, from the hands of the Bearer . . . I was sick as the Devil, when the Gentleman entered the Room, and have been so during most of the day. About 1 o'clock I swallowed a huge mass of Epsom Salts—and it will not be hard to imagine that I have been at dirty work since. I feel partially relieved—enough to write a hasty dull letter.

I feel some inclination to learn whether you yet sleep in your Shirt-tail, and whether you yet have the extravagant delight of poking and punching a writhing Bedfellow with your long fleshen pole—the exquisite touches of which I have often had the honor of feeling? Let me say unto thee that unless thou changest former habits in this particular, thou wilt be represented by every future Chum as a nuisance. And, I pronounce it, with good reason too. Sir, you roughen the downy Slumbers of your Bedfellow—by such hostile—furious lunges as you are in the habit of making at him—when he is least prepared for defence against the crushing force of a Battering Ram. Without reformation my imagination depicts some awful results for which you will be held accountable—and therefore it is, that I earnestly recommend it. Indeed it is encourageing an assault and battery propensity, which needs correction—& uncorrected threatens devastation, horror & bloodshed, etc. . . .

The remaining two pages of the letter deal with unrelated matters of no particular interest. The way in which the letter signs off, however, is of decided interest:

With great respect I am the old
Stud,
Jeff.

The second letter was from Withers to Hammond, Sept. 24, 1826:

My dear Friend,

. . . Your excellent Letter of 13 June arrived . . . a few weeks since . . .[7] Here, *where anything like a systematic course of thought, or of reading, is quite out of the question—such system as leaves no vacant, idle moments of painful vacuity, which invites a whole Kennel of treacherous passions to prey upon one's vitals . . . the renovation of spirit which follows the appearance of a* friend's Letter—*the diagram of his soul—is like a grateful shower from the cooling fountains of Heaven to reanimate drooping Nature. Whilst your letters are Transcripts of real—existing feeling, and are on that account peculiarly welcome—they at the same time betray too much* honesty of purpose *not to strike an harmonious chord in my mind. I have only to regret that, honesty of intention and even assiduity in excition* [?] *are far from being the uniform agents of our destiny here—However it must, at best, be only an a priori argument for us to settle the condemnation of the world, before we come in actual contact with it. This task is peculiarly appropriate to the acrimony of old age—and perhaps we had as well defer it, under the hope that we may reach a point, when 'twill be all that we can do—*

I fancy, Jim, that your elongated protruberance—*your* fleshen pole—*your* [*two Latin words; indecipherable*]—*has captured complete mastery over you—and I really believe, that you are charging over the pine barrens of your locality, braying, like an ass, at every she-male you can discover. I am afraid that you are thus prostituting the "image of God" and suggest that if you thus blasphemously essay to put on the form of a Jack—in this stead of that noble image—you will share the fate of Nebuchadnazzer of old. I should lament to hear of you feeding upon the dross of the pasture and alarming the country with your vociferations. The day of miracles may not be past, and the flaming excess of your lustful appetite may drag down the vengeance of supernal power.—And you'll "be dam-d if you don't marry"?—and felt a disposition to set down and gravely detail me the reasons of early marriage. But two favourable ones strike me now—the first is, that* Time *may grasp love so furiously as totally* [?] *to disfigure his Phiz. The second is, that, like George McDuffie,*[8] *he may have the hap-hazzard of a broken backbone befal him, which will relieve him from the performance of affectual family-duty—& throw over the brow of his wife, should he chance to get one, a most foreboding glooming—As to the first, you will find many a modest good girl subject to the same inconvenience—and as to the second, it will only superinduce such domestic whirlwinds, as will call into frequent exercise rhetorical displays of impassioned Eloquence, accompanied by appropriate and perfect specimens of those gestures which Nature and feeling suggest. To get children, it is true, fulfills a department of social & natural duty—but to let them starve, or subject them to the alarming hazard of it, violates another of a most important character. This is the dilemma to which I reduce you—choose you this day which you will do . . .*

COMMENTARY

The portrait of young Hammond that emerges from these letters is at startling variance with the adult Hammond of the history books. Nineteen-year-old Jim, with his "flaming excess" and "lustful appetite," seems to bear no resemblance to James H. Hammond, conservative moralist, staid pillar of the traditional Old South. To try to reconcile this disparity, some additional biographical details become necessary at this point.

Hammond, by birth, was a "commoner"—his father a native New Englander who had gone south to teach school, his mother a native South Carolinian of undistinguished ancestry. It was only through his own talent and diligence (he graduated near the top of his class at college), and then through what is called a "fortunate" marriage, that Hammond entered the ranks of the planter aristocracy. His marriage to the Charleston heiress, Catherine Fitzsimmons, was of critical importance. Through his wife, Hammond became owner of Silver Bluff, a 10,000-acre plantation on the Savannah River worked by 220 slaves, and gained instant membership in the ruling elite.[9]

Hammond used his opportunities well. Always an apt pupil, he quickly acquired the cultivated externals—the manners, rituals, and social preoccupations—of the master class. No less quickly, he internalized its values. By the mid-1830s, Hammond was already highly regarded as a "brilliant" advocate of "states' rights," a zealous defender of slavery, and a "superb" manager of his landed estates. (He had also acquired a reputation for willingness to use the lash and to send his slaves to cut fodder in malaria-infested swamps.)[10] Contemporaries found Hammond's temperament more enigmatic than his views, often describing him as mercurial and impetuous. They also found him aloof, vain, willful and proud—not, for that region and class, necessarily pejorative terms, uncongenial qualities.

That the adult Hammond was sometimes thought "impetuous" suggests that the tumultuous young Jim of 1826 never got wholly swallowed up in the later overlays of Statesman and Seer. None of the few details of that impetuousness suggest it ever took the form, as it had in his youth, of "furious lunges" at male bed partners or ever expressed itself in "charges over the pine barrens" to bray at "she-males." Perhaps those youthful penchants and impulses did continue to exert some hold over his adult fantasy life (and given how pronounced they had been in his youth, it's difficult to believe they had lost all force). But if homoeroticism did maintain a subterranean life in Hammond's fantasies, there is no scintilla of evidence that as an adult he acted on them.

But if no direct evidence exists from Hammond's later years of the homoerotic zest he had shown as a young man, there is a good deal to suggest that his lusty appetite in general—however much its loci may have shifted—continued to be strong, his public image to the contrary. As an adult, Hammond gained a reputation as a man of stern rectitude, and he was at pains periodically to reinforce it. For example, he haughtily rebutted abolitionist "propaganda" that racial mixing was common on Southern plantations, denouncing the charge as "grossly and atrociously exaggerated"; the actual incidence of miscegenation, he insisted, was "infinitely small" in contrast to the "illicit sexual intercourse" known to be widespread among the factory populations of England and the North. Hammond's own reputation as a planter who sternly enforced traditional sexual mores among his slaves further reinforced his puritanical public image. He did advocate allowing slaves to marry, but not to divorce. He would grant a divorce decree only if a slave couple could convince him that "sufficient cause" existed; even then, both members of the couple were given one hundred lashes and both denied the right to remarry for three years.[11]

Hammond's reputation as guardian and exemplar of traditional morality got a sudden, nasty jolt in 1846. In that year, George McDuffie resigned his seat in the U.S. Senate, and the state legislature seemed on the verge of choosing Hammond as his successor. But then Hammond's brother-in-law, Wade Hampton, warned him that he would publicly reveal an incident that had taken place three years earlier if Hammond allowed his name to remain in contention for the Senate seat. It was only fifteen years ago—when the historian, Clement Eaton, discovered a secret diary of Hammond's and published part of its contents—that we learned the nature of the "incident": Hammond had seduced Hampton's teenage daughters.[12]

Hardly a peccadillo, one might think. Yet Hammond himself, remarkably, seems to have viewed it in precisely that light. He did agree to withdraw his candidacy for the Senate (rumors of the sexual scandal had already circulated and Hammond could scarcely afford to let Hampton confirm them). He also gave up his mansion in Columbia and retired to the management of his estates—a retirement which, in the upshot, lasted fourteen years. Hammond did none of this, however, in a spirit notable for contrition or chagrin. To the contrary, the dominant tone he adopted (in diary entries and in letters to friends) was one of aggrieved petulance—*he* was the wounded party! Merely for "a little dalliance with the other sex," for an incident marked by "impulse, not design," he wrote, he had been forced into political retirement, though numerous other public figures, past and present, had indulged "amorous & conjugal infidelity" without incurring censure or retribution of any kind.[13]

Hammond's tone, astonishing in itself, reveals a great deal about his actual (as opposed to rhetorical) attitudes on sexual morality. His casual view of "dalliance" suggests far more personal experience with it than we are able to document (indeed, aside from the 1846 episode, we have no documentation). But his attitude toward "dalliance" is the least of it. If Hammond could treat the seduction of teenage girls—relatives through marriage, no less—as an event of no great import, nor cause for particular remorse, it is hard to imagine what if any erotic experience he might have considered untoward, beyond the pale.

It would seem the young sexual adventurer of 1826 and the staid eminence of 1846 are not the alien, unrelated beings we thought them. As an older man, Hammond's range of sexual tastes may have narrowed (*may*; that impression could be due to the paucity of extant evidence), but his sex drive itself seems to have remained not only strong, but impulsive, determined, and—judged by the conventional mores of the day—"indiscriminate." If Hammond's external circumstances changed radically from youth to middle age, his inner life apparently underwent less of a sea change.

Both as a young and a middle-aged man, his lust—whether aroused by male college friends or by teenage female relatives—could be ungovernable. Not that Hammond seems ever to have struggled very hard to contain it. Certainly not as a young man. We get no sense from the 1826 letters that Jim Hammond expended much energy, nor saw much reason, to control his impulses or curtail his pleasures. As an older man he may have, if only to maintain his image and protect his privileges. Yet even that is conjecture; and conjecture based, moreover, on *our* assumptions about what would constitute "logical" behavior for a man of Hammond's position. Judging from his actual behavior in the mid-1840s and his indignant reaction to discovery and threatened exposure, our logic and Hammond's may not coincide.

This deepens the puzzle further. How *are* we to understand this uncategorizable, curious man? Looked at from the angle of 1826, Hammond seems (by my mores) rather admirable: exploratory and free-wheeling, uninhibited and attractively unapologetic. Looked at from the angle of 1846, he seems merely repulsive: a grossly insensitive and irresponsible man, willful and arrogant, perhaps pathologically so. Yet it may be the only real change is in *our* angle of vision (and the moral assumptions underlying it), not in the man himself, the shift in context between the 1826 and 1846 episodes encouraging us to radically different judgments of what were in fact consistent, enduring traits of personality.

In truth, the discomforting fact is that we "understand" very little—not only about Hammond the man, but even about the lesser enigma of the two letters Jeff Withers sent him in 1826. Having exhausted what little historical information exists for trying to construct a plausible context in which to read the erotic content of those letters, conjecture, not confident conclusions, is the best we can offer.

The consistent tone of Withers' letters—ironic and playful—does suggest strongly that his sexual encounters with Hammond carried no emotional overtones of a "romantic" involvement between the two men. Not that we can be sure. Irony, as we know, is a common device for concealing emotions. Besides, an occasional phrase in the letter—such as Withers' reference to the "exquisite touch" of Hammond's "long fleshen pole"—can be read as more than "playful." Unfortunately, no other correspondence from the period exists of remotely comparable content, nothing that might allow us to draw parallels, to clarify, consolidate, or amplify tentative "conclusions" now derived wholly from the skimpy internal evidence of the two letters themselves.

Given the impoverished results of our efforts to pin down the *meaning* of the two letters, it probably is foolish to move beyond the Withers/Hammond relationship and pose still broader questions; "foolish" because to do so invites additional futility and frustration. Yet broader questions are implicit in the material—they seem to suggest themselves—and posing them may alone be of value, though answers prove elusive.

The critical question, historically, is whether their erotic experiences should be regarded as "anomalous" or "representative." Was their behavior unique, or does it reveal and illustrate a wider pattern of male-male relationships—one hitherto unsuspected and undocumented but nonetheless in some manner "typical" of their time, region, race, and class? The question, on its face, is an enigma wrapped in a mystery. At best, we can approach, not resolve it. But the reader should be forewarned: What follows is hypothesis nearly pure, to be taken with generous grains of salt.

The best clue by far provided by the internal evidence of the letters themselves is their *tone*. It has a consistent ring: off-handed, flip. Jeff's bantering appeal for repentence is transparently mocking, his "warnings of retribution" are uniformly irreverent—"campy," in the modern vernacular. The letters are *so* devoid of any serious moral entreaty or fervor, of any genuine attempt to inspire shame or reformation, as to take on negative significance. To be sure, the values and vocabulary of evangelical piety had not yet, in the 1820s, come to permeate consciousness and discourse. It is also true that even when those values were at the height of their influence—roughly 1830-1870—they seem not to have held sway in the South to the same extent they did elsewhere in the country.

In other words, the geographical locale and time period in which Jeff and Jim grew up may well be important factors in explaining their free-wheeling attitudes. The South of the latter part of the eighteenth and early part of the nineteenth centuries was (for privileged, young, white males, that is) one of those rare "liberal interregnums" in our history when the body could be treated as a natural source of pleasure and "wanton" sexuality viewed as the natural prerogative—the exemplification even—of Manliness.

In at least this sense, therefore, Jeff and Jim's relaxed attitude toward sex in general, far from being anomalous, may have been close to mainstream mores. Whether the same could be said for their high-spirited, unselfconscious attitude toward *same*-gender sexuality is far more problematic. Jeff's comedic descriptions of male bedfellows "poking and punching" each other with their "fleshen poles" are so light-hearted, so devoid of furtiveness and shame, that it becomes difficult to believe male-male sexual contact was deeply stigmatized in the culture at large. Withers and Hammond, after all, saw themselves as *insiders,* as ambitious aspirants to positions of leadership and power. Would Hammond have indulged so freely (and Withers described so casually) behavior widely deemed disgraceful and abhorrent, outside the range of "permissible" experience? Had homoeroticism been utterly taboo, one would expect Withers' tone to betray *some* evidence of guilt and fear. Since instead it is markedly breezy and nonchalant, it seems fair, at a minimum, to raise the possibility that sexual contact between males (of a certain class, region, time, and place) was, if not commonplace, not wholly unacceptable or anomalous either. If that surmise is even marginally correct, then our standard view of the history of male homosexuality in this country as an unrelieved tale of concealment, opprobrium, and woe stands in need of major revision.

One might challenge that surmise by pointing to the lack of any confirming evidence—the absence of additional documentation from the period recounting attitudes and experiences comparable to Jeff's and Jim's. That we lack such supporting data is undeniable. But this in itself is not sufficient proof that same-gender sexuality never (or rarely) happened, nor is it even proof that records of it may not still survive (though not yet retrieved). After all, to date we have accumulated only a tiny stockpile of historical materials that document the existence of *heterosexuality* in the past. Yet no one claims the miniscule amount of evidence is an accurate gauge of the actual amount of heterosexual activity that took place.

Just so with Jeff and Jim. What now appears unique and anomalous behavior may one day be seen to have been unexceptional—casually tolerated, if not actively encouraged or institutionalized. This will happen only if the new generation of scholars continues to press for access to previously suppressed materials and if the new generation of archivists continues to grow in sympathy toward such scholarship, declassifying "sensitive" data at an accelerated pace. I myself believe that additional source material, possibly a great deal of it, relating to the history of homosexuality has survived and awaits recovery from well-guarded vaults. I base this belief on my own research experiences over the past half-dozen years. The two Withers/Hammond letters are a case in point. Until they turned up, few if any scholars (including myself) would have credited the notion that "carefree" male-male sex took place in this country in the 1820s—or that off-handed, unemphatic descriptions of it could ever be found.

For this reason, it may be worth providing additional details about the discovery of the Withers/Hammond letters: to encourage other scholars to persevere in their search for long-suppressed materials, to suggest certain tactics for extracting them, to alert them to some of the obstacles and ploys custodial guardians will use to deflect their search, and to suggest how these might be neutralized and counteracted.

RECOVERING THE WITHERS/HAMMOND LETTERS

Let me state at the outset of this cautionary tale that its chief purpose is *not* to extablish the villainy of archivists. As a group, they are no more the enemy of innovative scholarship nor the defenders of traditional mores than are historians as a group, most of whom scornfully dismiss the study of sexual ideology and behavior as not being a proper discipline. During my research travels, individual archivists at manuscript libraries have been enormously supportive. People like Stephen T. Riley of the Massachusetts Historical Society, Sandra Taylor of the Lilly Library in Indiana, and Richard J. Wolfe of the Countway Library of Medicine in Boston not only helped me gain access to "sensitive" material but pointed me to other pertinent sources of whose existence I had been unaware. Such people (and I could name others) acted from their conviction that research into the "history of intimacy" was long overdue and of great potential importance to a better understanding of our national experience and character.

That attitude is still a minority one in the archival profession (and in the historical profession, too). Many who stand guard over the nation's major manuscript collections see their function as protective and preservative—of traditional moral values in general and of a family's "good name" in particular. They tend to equate—as is true everywhere in academia (and perhaps to a greater degree than in the population at large)—the libidinous with the salacious and to be profoundly distrustful of both. Given this discomfort, some archivists will invent obstacles to put in the researcher's path or will claim to be hamstrung (and, in truth, even sympathetic curators sometimes *are*) by certain restrictions to access which the donor of a given manuscript collection appended to the original deed of gift.

My six-month tangle over the Withers/Hammond letters illustrates the prevailing climate. The tale begins (and I will confine myself to its main outlines) with Catherine Clinton, a doctoral student in history at Princeton. It was she who first brought the letters to my attention, and though she has modestly asked that her efforts not be detailed, I did at least want to acknowledge her pivotal role.[14] Once having seen the letters and realized their importance, I started in motion the standard procedures for acquiring permission to publish them, sending out on March 6, 1979, a formal request to that effect to the South Caroliniana Library (henceforth, SCL), where the original manuscripts of the two letters are housed as part of the Hammond Papers.

That, according to one of the several experts I was later to consult, was my first, and worst, mistake. In applying for formal permission, I was (to quote the expert) being "super-dutiful" and, in the process, making life infinitely more difficult for *all* parties concerned. Technically, I had done the "correct" thing—I had gone through proper channels, abided by the terms of the agreement (one that most manuscript libraries require of scholars) to request formal permission before publishing any material. But in real life, my chiding expert added, what is technically correct is often functionally awkward. In practice, it seems (and after twenty years of research, this came as news to me), many scholars proceed to publish manuscript material without ever formally requesting permission to do so.

And many libraries, it seems, prefer it that way. A formal request, after all, requires a formal reply. The library must make a clear-cut decision, one that could place it (sometimes unwillingly and unfairly) in a no-win situation: Should the library grant permission, it risks the wrath of a donor or a family descendant, the charge of dereliction, the possible loss of future acquisitions; should the library deny permission, it risks an outraged scholar's accusations of censorship. Let others take profit: though archivists will not or cannot say so openly, they may well prefer to be handed a *fait accompli;* they may be silently grateful to researchers who adopt what might be called the Macbeth ploy: "do what ye need to do, but tell me not of it till after 'tis done" (rough paraphrase).

Lacking this wisdom at the time, I instead sent off my formal letter of request. It left SCL with two choices: to act on the request (which, given the letters' contents, almost certainly meant a negative response), or to do nothing. They chose the latter course: My letter went unanswered. If SCL had thereby meant to signal me to go ahead, and not to demand their formal acquiescence, I misread the signal. Instead of quietly retreating, I noisily persisted. On April 15 I sent a second letter, near duplicate of the first. When that, too, was ignored, I got angry (blame it on the zodiac: Leos cannot stand being ignored). In early June, thirteen weeks having gone by without a response of any kind, I sent—no, shot off by certified mail—a third letter, this one longer and decidedly more testy than its predecessors. SCL's obdurate muteness, I wrote, could be interpreted in one of two ways: as "silence giving consent" or as a calculated attempt at censorship. Should I decide to opt for the first interpretation, my letter continued, I would simply proceed to publication without further ado (and on the assumption that I had their tacit blessing). Should I opt instead for the second interpretation, I'd feel an obligation to other scholars to report the incident to the prestigious Joint Committee of Historians and Archivists, a group empowered to deal with matters of censorship. While making up my mind between the two courses of action, my letter concluded, "I would be glad to receive any information which might have a bearing on my decision." (Leos get snotty when pushed.)

Within the week, I had a reply—proving yet again, I suppose, that if threats do not bring out the best in man, they do bring out *something*. The reply came from SCL's Director (Dr. Archer, I'll call him). He expressed regret, at the top, that I had "found it necessary to write such a sharp letter"—though he acknowledged that the delay in responding to my letters might have been contributory. Still, he continued, I surely could understand that he had had to put my letters aside while "awaiting a convenient opportunity" to seek advice "on the status of the restrictions" attached to the Hammond Papers. Such an opportunity had finally presented itself; he now was able to report that the original donor of the Hammond Papers had "asked" (the choice of word, as subsequently pointed out by several of my consultants, is significant, implying as it does a request from the donor, not a binding stipulation) that none of the manuscripts be used in a way that might "result in embarrassment to descendants." Although the donor was dead, Dr. Archer viewed the "restriction" as "still in force." Since he also viewed the two Withers letters as unquestionably "embarrassing," he had decided to deny my request to publish them.

In a curious concluding paragraph, Dr. Archer suggested that my request might be reconsidered if I could provide "full assurances" the letters would be published in such a way that no one could identify them with the Hammond Papers or with Hammond or Withers themselves. In short, that I agree to strip the letters of all historical context—a context integral to their meaning and importance—and treat them as floating objects unanchored in time or space. To me, that seemed comparable to requiring that a Vivaldi string quartet be performed solely with tambourines and vibraharp. I declined to pursue the suggestion.

Instead, I embarked on a double course of action: I started to draft a reply to Dr. Archer and at the same time began a round of consultations with various scholars, friends, and legal experts about what to say in that reply. My advisors diverged in their advice on this or that minor point, but concurred that I was justified, legally and morally, in proceeding straightaway to publication. In support of that conclusion they cited various arguments but put special stress on the legal doctrine of "fair usage": an author's right to quote (without permission) an appropriate amount of copyrighted material. Legal decisions relating to fair usage have varied widely in regard to what constitutes an appropriate amount of unauthorized quotation, but in recent years (most significantly in *Nizer v. Rosenberg*) the courts have leaned consistently toward a liberal definition.

One of the experts in copyright law whom I consulted felt "absolutely confident" I was entitled to publish the two Withers letters *in full,* if I so wished. (Ultimately I decided that only the erotic portions were relevant to my purposes.) In his opinion, SCL "had long since weakened its copyright claim to the Hammond Papers, however unintentionally." By which he meant that the library's long-standing practice of allowing scholars access to the papers (instead of sealing them off) amounted to a tacit admission that the original deed of gift had been unencumbered by substantive, detailed restrictions—that aside from some vague admonitory advice, the donor had left final discretionary power to the library itself. The fact that SCL, in addition, had catalogued the two Withers letters and had also provided photocopies of them on request compounded their "errors" and, in the view of the copyright lawyer, made my legal position on publication rights "airtight."

All this I dutifully incorporated in the ongoing draft of my letter to Dr. Archer. That letter, in the upshot, was never sent, my Council of Experts persuading me that I had nothing to gain thereby and might needlessly stir quiet waters. As one consultant put it, "If you formally notify SCL of your intention to publish, the library might feel obligated to bring suit, though they'd much prefer not to, given their shaky legal case and the additional publicity any litigation would give to the contents of the letters. Do yourself *and* them a favor: Say and write nothing further; simply proceed to publication."

Which is what I've done. Though not, I should add, without misgivings. A direct challenge to SCL, though likely to involve time-consuming, expensive litigation, might have yielded an important precedent of use to future scholars. I also regret that Dr. Archer never got to read my letter, especially the part in which I asked him to spell out his specific grounds for deciding the letters were an "embarrassment." As I had written (hot tongue in hard cheek), "For two men like Hammond and Withers who have gone down in history as among the country's staunchest defenders of human slavery, I should think their reputations could only be enhanced by the playful, raucous—the *humanizing*—revelations contained in the two letters." Yes, I was being patently ingenuous; and yes, I was unlikely to force from Dr. Archer an explicit avowal of homophobia. Still, it would have done my soul good to try (it's doing it some good just to quote the unsent letter here).

But what I remain most uncomfortable about in my decision to print portions of the Withers letters without specific authorization are certain implicit ethical implications: that familiar array of moral conundrums (in however diminutive a form) long associated with any act of "civil disobedience." To explain why I proceeded nonetheless, I must step back a bit and approach the issue indirectly, through some general observations.

The long-sanctioned notion of a "community of scholars"—in the ideal sense of a disinterested collectivity of truth seekers— is an exalted but illusory conceit. In practice, the notion has served as a useful justification for codifying professional behavior and for denying credentials to those—women, gays, ethnic minorities—who might challenge those established codes. The conceit of a community of scholars, in short, has characteristically been a blind for parochialism and discrimination.

Yet the *ideal* of a community of scholars remains attractive—just as the role that a genuinely unharnessed scholarship might play in providing data for challenging the status quo and nurturing alternate visions of the good society remains potentially vital. It seems obvious that a scholar's prime allegiance and responsibility should be to the ideal itself, not to those academic guilds claiming to represent it (even as they enforce standards for membership and employ definitions of "legitimate" inquiry that straightjacket and subvert it). Most of the scholarship emanating from the universities functions primarily, if "unintentionally," to rationalize existing arrangements of power; and the academic guilds, in excluding or ostracizing mavericks, play their role in perpetuating those arrangements.

What seems obvious on an abstract level becomes less so on a personal one; the question of "responsibility" becomes stickier. As one who chose to join the academic community and to remain in it (with attendant profit, such as a professorial salary), it could be argued that I, and others like me, are obligated either to abide by academe's conventions or—if certain we cannot—to resign from it. In response, I would argue that a scholar owes *primary* allegiance to what academe might be, to its promise, not its practice. Besides, the standards of what constitutes acceptable professorial behavior and proper scholarly inquiry have themselves been muddled and slippery. To give one example, no agreement exists among university-affiliated historians as to correct (or even preferred) research procedures, modes of analysis, or styles of presentation: Cliometricians battle impressionists, generalists disparage specialists, literary stylists war with statistical analysts.

Adding to the confusion is academe's contradictory record in its treatment of dissenters. The record is not one of monolithic repression. While it is indisputably true that many innovative academicians have suffered grievously—by being fired or not hired or not promoted—for political, personal, and professional nonconformity (as well as for their sex, class, and race), it is also true that academe sometimes honors its insurgents, if often belatedly. (The political radical, William Appleman Williams, is current President-elect of the American Historical Association.) The academy is assuredly not the free-swinging arena of open inquiry its champions would claim, but neither is it as tightly sealed against novelty and innovation, as unvaryingly hostile to fractious upstarts, as its detractors insist.

Academe's ambiguous tradition helps to persuade many scholars who by temperament, conviction, or lifestyle are "deviant"—outside mainstream orthodoxy—to maintain their university affiliations. Some of these scholars would claim ("lull themselves into believing," skeptics would say) that academe is one of the few remaining arenas in which innovative inquiry is possible, and that the "long march through the institutions" is the only promising tactic for social change now available. More academic deviants would admit, however, that in retaining their ties to academic disciplines and institutions that function essentially as "conservators" (preservers and transmitters of conventional knowledge and norms) they open themselves to considerable peril. The danger of cooptation is omnipresent; unorthodoxy and personal integrity can be gradually (sometimes undiscernibly) sapped. To guard against such risks, one can try to stay vigilant—in touch with the different drummer within, resistant to any effort to muffle its sound. But vows of vigilance, as we know, are more easily made than kept.

All of which is about as close as I can come to describing (perhaps idealizing) the kind of general relationship I myself have tried to maintain with the academic world, and also to describing something of the inner debate I went through over the specific matter of the Withers/Hammond letters. In making the decision to publish them against the wishes of their official custodian, my personal discomfort played a considerable role: discomfort at the prospect of yielding to the prevailing, and to my mind dangerously narrow, view of what is acceptable historical inquiry and, by implication, "permissible" norms of behavior. I also felt, to speak more generally, that the public *does* have the "right to know"—and that moreover, in regard to the Withers letters, the gay public has a desperate *need* to know.

That last consideration, to the extent I can judge, was decisive. It seemed essential to challenge the tradition and break the cycle of suppressing information that could help gay people better understand the historical dimensions of our experience, the shifting strategies we have adopted over time to cope with oppression, and the varied styles we have developed to express our special sensibility. If the "lawless" tactics I've chosen seem extreme to some, well, so is our need; and more orthodox tactics (like polite letters of inquiry) have done little to meet it. The heterosexist world has long used legal niceties and ethical proprieties as devices for denying us access to knowledge of our own antecedents. Let heterosexism take the blame then if, having finally despaired of gaining that knowledge by humble petition through proper channels, we now turn, by default and in anger at the continuing impasse, to "improper" tactics. It is better to stand accused of impropriety or illegality than to continue to accept someone else's right to control access to *our* heritage.

Power has created that "right" in the past. But we no longer need to concede that it should in the future. Nor need we fail to press other claims to "right"—the right of a people to knowledge of its own history (to *memory*)—an indispensable prerequisite for establishing a collective identity and for enjoying the solace of knowing that we too have "come through" and are bearers of a diverse, rich, enduring heritage. In pressing these claims, it may be necessary to defy entrenched conventions and to risk the consequences, professional and legal, of doing so. Not prospects one welcomes. But the alternatives are less palatable still: to continue to abide by anachronistic definitions of what constitutes "sensitive material" and "acceptable" areas of historical inquiry. To do that is to collaborate in sustaining those definitions, to be complicit in our own oppression.

NOTES

1. Thomas J. Withers to James H. Hammond, 24 September 1826, Hammond Papers, South Caroliniana Library, Columbia, S.C. (The preceding quotations and paraphrases are from portions of his letters *not* printed in Part II of this article.)

2. Most of what is known about Withers can be found in two studies: William H. Freehling, *Prelude to Civil War: The Nullification Controversy in South Carolina, 1816-1836* (New York: Harper & Row, 1965); and Charles Robert Lee, Jr., *The Confederate Constitutions* (Chapel Hill: The University of North Carolina Press, 1963).

3. Lee, pp. 28, 71, 75, 135.

4. See, for example, Clement Eaton, *The Mind of the Old South* (Baton Rouge: Louisiana State University Press, 1964), p. 21.

5. For those interested, the following studies (along with those by Freehling and Eaton, already cited) are the most authoritative. For Hammond's political career: Charles

S. Sydnor, *The Development of Southern Sectionalism* (Baton Rouge: Louisiana State University Press, 1948); Allan Nevins, *The Ordeal of the Union* and *The Emergence of Lincoln* (New York: Scribners, 1947; 1950); Avery Craven, *The Growth of Southern Nationalism* (Baton Rouge: Louisiana State University Press, 1953); Holman Hamilton, *Prologue to Conflict* (Lexington: University Press of Kentucky, 1964); and Steven A. Channing, *Crisis of Fear* (New York: Simon & Schuster, 1970). For Hammond's economic views: David Bertelson, *The Lazy South* (Oxford: 1967); Robert S. Starobin, *Industrial Slavery in the Old South* (Oxford: 1970); Richard C. Wade, *Slavery in the Cities* (Oxford: 1964); R. R. Russel, *Economic Aspects of Southern Sectionalism* (Urbana: University of Illinois Press, 1924); and Eugene Genovese, *The Political Economy of Slavery* (New York: Pantheon, 1965). For Hammond's theories on slavery (and his treatment of his own slaves): William S. Jenkins, *Pro-Slavery Thought in the Old South* (Chapel Hill: University of North Carolina Press, 1935); William Stanton, *The Leopard's Spots* (Chicago: University of Chicago Press, 1960); Eugene Genovese, *The World the Slaveowners Made* and *Roll, Jordan, Roll* (New York: Pantheon, 1969; 1974); Kenneth Stampp, *The Peculiar Institution* (New York: Knopf, 1956); William Taylor, *Cavalier and Yankee* (New York: Braziller, 1957); John Hope Franklin, *The Militant South* (Boston: Beacon, 1956); and Herbert G. Gutman, *The Black Family in Slavery and Freedom* (New York: Pantheon, 1976).

6. For reasons explained in Part IV of this article, I've excerpted and published here only the erotic portions of the two letters. The remaining material is at any rate of little historical interest, dealing as it does with various mundane matters—news of friends, complaints about the Boredom of Life, youthful pontifications on public events and personalities.

7. If Hammond's letter is extant, its whereabouts is unknown.

8. A leading figure in politics in the antebellum period.

9. Freehling contains the best description of South Carolina in this period and of the life-style of its ruling elite (see especially pp. 11-24). Eaton is most helpful for biographical detail on Hammond himself. I've relied heavily on both books for the factual material in this section.

10. For additional details on Hammond's severity as a slaveowner, see Gutman, pp. 221-2; Freehling, pp. 68-71; and Genovese, *Roll,* p. 455, 561. For more on Hammond's skills as a planter, see Nevins, *Ordeal,* pp. 482-3.

11. Wade, p. 122; Gutman, pp. 62, 572.

12. Eaton's account (pp. 30 ff.), or perhaps the secret diary itself, is blurred on the central question of whether (and in what sense) Hammond's seduction "succeeded"—though the weight of the blurred evidence suggests it did.

13. Eaton, pp. 31-32.

14. This seems the appropriate point to thank several other people whose advice or expertise proved of critical importance: Jesse Lemisch, Joan Warnow, Jonathan Weiss, Eric Foner, Martin Garbus, and Ann Morgan Campbell. To prevent any one of them being held accountable for actions and decisions for which I alone am ultimately responsible, I deliberately refrain from specifying which individual gave what advice or recommended which line of strategy.

THE "THIRD SEX" THEORY OF KARL HEINRICH ULRICHS

Hubert C. Kennedy, PhD

ABSTRACT: In the 1860s, with an innovative theory of the origin of homosexuality that saw it as neither a sin nor a sickness, the German lawyer Karl Heinrich Ulrichs became an outspoken defender of its practice. This paper describes the theory, placing it historically in the context of Ulrichs' life, and shows why, although progressive for its time, the theory eventually was abandoned.

Noting that "in most corners of Western civilization, homosexuality came to be labeled both sinful and criminal, an outrage to God and man, indicative of social decay," Bell and Weinberg add: "This view persisted for more than nineteen centuries until it was replaced, at least in some quarters, by medical authorities' equation of homosexuality with disease."[1] Although the foundations for the change were laid in the eighteenth century, the transition from the religious model to the medical model of homosexuality occurred mainly during the nineteenth and took firm hold during the first half of the twentieth century. It has been argued that "one of the causal factors for the change was the attempt of certain elements in the medical community to bolster traditional Western attitudes toward sex—attitudes that were being challenged by the new rationalism of the period."[2] One of these challenges to traditional attitudes was the theory of Karl Heinrich Ulrichs that the homosexual male has a "feminine soul confined by a masculine body."[3] Ulrichs' popularization of his theory in the 1860s brought comfort to many, but the rise of the medical (disease) model of homosexuality, in combination with the internal weakness of the idea of a "third sex," brought about the downfall of Ulrichs' theory. The theory may be considered progressive for its time, however, since it not only allowed Ulrichs to accept his own homosexuality but also led him

Dr. Kennedy is Professor of Mathematics, Providence College, Providence, Rhode Island 02918.

Journal of Homosexuality, Vo. 6(1/2), Fall/Winter 1980/81

to speak out for the rights of homosexual men and women. He was perhaps the first person in modern times to do so publicly.

Karl Heinrich Ulrichs was born on August 28, 1825, the son of an architect in the civil service in the town of Aurich in northwestern Germany.[4] Karl Heinrich had an elder and a younger sister; another sister and a brother did not survive infancy. Among his relatives were jurists, civil servants, and several Protestant ministers, including his mother's brother and her father, who was supervisor of a church district. After attending primary school in Aurich and secondary schools *(Gymnasia)* in Detmold and Celle, Ulrichs studied law at the universities of Göttingen and Berlin and won an award at each university for a Latin dissertation.

His studies completed, Ulrichs entered the civil service of the Kingdom of Hanover as a junior attorney, but, following the death of his mother in 1857 (his father had died in 1835) and the marriage of his sisters, he gave up his position in order to travel. In the following years he visited Cologne, Mainz, Stuttgart, Munich, Vienna, Graz, Prague, and Leipzig. The year 1861 found him in Frankfurt am Main, where he met Justin T. B. von Linde, representative of Lichtenstein, Reuss, and Homburg to the diet of the German Confederation, and became Linde's personal secretary.[5] In this diplomatic circle, Ulrichs formed a lasting friendship with Ludwig Windthorst, who began his second term as Minister of Justice to the Kingdom of Hanover in late 1862.

The summer of 1862 was a busy time for Ulrichs. Besides the work for Linde, he was correcting the manuscript of a law book for Heinrich August Tewes (later, Professor of Roman Law at the University of Graz and a lifelong friend of Ulrichs) and reporting to several newspapers on the All German Shooting Contest, at which it is probable he met Johann Baptist von Schweitzer, corresponding secretary of the central committee of the Contest and the publisher of its official newspaper. Schweitzer, whose speech at a workers' rally on May 25, 1862 may be taken as the beginning of Social Democracy in the Frankfurt area,[6] became notorious two weeks after the Contest when he was arrested for an act of "public indecency" with a young boy in a city park in Mannheim. Ulrichs wrote a defense and sent it to Schweitzer, but part of it was intercepted and confiscated by the authorities.[7]

The Schweitzer incident may have helped determine Ulrichs to publish his views on "the riddle of love between men." This had occupied his thoughts and studies since his early teens, when he first recognized that he was sexually attracted to other men, and he now felt that he had solved the "riddle." In a letter of November 28, 1862, circulated to eight of his relatives, Ulrichs announced his plan to publish a monograph on the subject, provisionally entitled: "The Race of Uranian Hermaphrodites, i.e., the Man-Loving Half-Men."[8] Despite his relatives' opposition to the project, he continued with his plan and completed the first volume in 1863, although its publication was delayed until 1864 because of legal difficulties. In deference to his family, at first Ulrichs used the pseudonym "Numa Numantius." He did not reveal his true identity until 1868.

In the years from 1864 to 1879, Ulrichs published twelve volumes on the subject, collectively entitled: *Forschungen über das Rätsel der mannmännlichen Liebe* [Researches on the Riddle of Love Between Men]. The first five appeared in 1864-1865, the next five in 1868-1869, and one each in 1870 and 1879. At the outset, Ulrichs seems to have based much of his theory on an analysis of his own sexual preference, supposing that all other homosexual men were like himself. After his first writings brought him into contact with a wider range of homosexual types, through his publisher, the theory had to become more complex, but by 1868 it had achieved a fixed form.[9]

Ulrichs found the basis for his theory in contemporary studies of embryology. He was particularly impressed with the fact that the future sexual organs are not differentiated in the early developmental stages of the human embryo. (It may be recalled that the first evidence suggesting a chromosomal basis for gender determination was published in 1905, by Nettie M. Stevens of Bryn Mawr College and Edmund B. Wilson of Columbia University.[10] This fact suggested to Ulrichs the possibility that an embryo could develop in either direction, both with regard to the differentiation of the sexual organs and to the sex drive. The first of these would be accomplished by the suppression of one direction (female or male) of development. At the same time, the direction of the future sex drive, to be awakened at puberty, would be determined by a mechanism more difficult to construe. Ulrichs was convinced that the existence of the sex drive is dependent on the sexual organs but emphasized that the "masculine or feminine direction" of the sex drive is independent of the "masculine or feminine form" of the sexual organs.

Citing cases of known physical hermaphrodites,[11] Ulrichs pointed out that, just as nature's "rule" is not always followed in the differentiation of the sexual organs, so too the differentiation of the sex drive may vary from the usual rule. He concluded:

> *What is present in germ can also develop. But each primary embryo bears in itself potentially developable testicles, penis, body cavity capable of growing into a scrotum, and along with this the germ of a potential psychical development of a feminine sex drive. Furthermore, creating Nature does not succeed in making every creature according to rule. That is the key to the riddle of Uranian [homosexual] love.*[12]

Ulrichs apparently accepted without question the idea that love directed toward a man must be a woman's love, and he saw it as a confirmation of his theory that he could detect "feminine" traits in himself and other homosexual males (for example, gestures, manner of walking, love of bright colors). He summed up his theory in a Latin couplet that precedes and explains the title of his second publication of 1864, *Inclusa:*

Sunt mihi barba maris, artus, corpusque virile;
His inclusa quidem: sed sum maneoque puella.[13]

[*Have I a masculine beard and manly limbs and body;*
Yes, confined by these: but I am and remain a woman.]

This idea later was expressed more clearly in the phrase *anima muliebris virili corpore inclusa* [a feminine soul confined by a masculine body].[14]

One consequence of Ulrichs' theory is that the homosexual man will feel a certain discomfort because of the confinement of his feminine soul in a masculine body, a discomfort he may be at a loss to explain. "For not everyone arrives at a consciousness of this female element. I myself, as mentioned, became aware of it only very late, and I might never have arrived at it had I not pondered the riddle of Uranian love or become acquainted with other Urnings."[15]

Ulrichs noted in 1864 that one of the first to refer to his writings in print was K. M. Benkert.[16] Benkert, who did not adopt Ulrichs' terminology, later coined the term "homosexual." This was never used by Ulrichs, however.[17] For his own terminology, Ulrichs turned to the speech of Pausanias in Plato's *Symposium:*

For we all know that Love is inseparable from Aphrodite, and if there were only one Aphrodite there would be only one Love; but as there are two goddesses there must be two Loves. And am I not right in asserting that there are two goddesses? The elder one, having no mother, who is called the heavenly Aphrodite—she is the daughter of Uranus; the younger, who is the daughter of Zeus and Dione—her we call common. . . . The love who is the offspring of the common Aphrodite . . . is apt to be of women. . . . But the offspring of the Heavenly Aphrodite is derived from a mother in whose birth the female has no part. . . . Those who are inspired by this love turn to the male.[18]

Ulrichs modified the names in this legend to create the nouns *Urning* and *Dioning* for homosexual and heterosexual males, respectively.[19] This terminology allowed the addition of German feminine endings to form *Urningin* and *Dioningin* for their female counterparts, that is, homosexual and heterosexual females. While this theory seemed adequate to explain his own self, further acquaintance with other Urnings showed more variety than he had anticipated and Ulrichs was forced to elaborate his theory even more. There were two main classes of Urnings, the *Mannlinge* and the *Weiblinge* (the masculine and the feminine), between which there was a "quite regular series" of intermediate types.[20] The Mannling has a feminine soul and sex drive, but otherwise is entirely masculine; the Weibling is masculine only in the gender of the body. (Ulrichs placed himself midway between these extremes.)

Ulrichs then considered the bisexual man, whom he termed *Uranodioning,* and distinguished two types, the "conjunctive" (those who have both tender and passionate feelings toward other men) and the "disjunctive" (those who have tender feelings toward other men, but passionate feelings only toward women).[21] Ulrichs admitted that his theory of the undetermined germ of sex drive in the embryo did not explain the existence of these two types, and so he suggested the possibility of there being two noncorporeal sex-drive germs in the embryo, one for tender love and one for passionate love, the direction of each being determined separately. He added, however, that care must be taken in classifying someone as a conjunctive Uranodioning, since closer inspection often has shown such apparent types to be in fact *virilisierte Mannlinge,* that is, Urnings who have, through forcing themselves or through habit, learned to act like Dionings.[22] Realizing, perhaps, that he was treading on dangerous ground here, Ulrichs hastened to add that this feat is not possible for all Urnings.

As counterpart to the virilisierte Mannling, there is the *uranisierter Mann* or *Uraniaster,* the man who acts like an Urning.[23] Ulrichs suggested that the usual causal factor of this condition is the lack of women—he had noted the phenomenon in prisons and military barracks—but did not rule out the possibility of individual choice. When one remembers that there also must be a classification of women parallel to that just described for men, and when one considers the mathematical possibilities for the varieties of physical hermaphrodites, the theory seems ready to collapse under the weight of its own complexities.

There were, however, more important factors operating against general acceptance of the theory. One was the current of thought that began in the eighteenth century and stressed the physical dangers of nonprocreative sex.[24] Masturbation, for example, came to be regarded in the nineteenth century as one of the prime causes of insanity.[25] Another factor was the accusation that Ulrichs was guilty of special pleading, since he himself was admittedly homosexual. For this last reason, Ulrichs sought out, and often mentioned, the interest of scientists in his theory, however tenuous their support may have been.

Ulrichs biggest coup was to gain the interest of Richard von Krafft-Ebing, who wrote to Ulrichs on January 29, 1879:

The study of your writings on love between men interested me in the highest degree, . . . since you . . . for the first time openly spoke about these matters. From that day on, when—I believe it was in 1866—you sent me your writings, I have devoted my full attention to this phenomenon, which at the time was as puzzling to me as it was interesting; it was the knowledge of your writings alone which led to my studies in this highly important field.[26]

This acknowledgment, however, came too late to comfort Ulrichs. By 1879 his theory of the congenital nature of homosexuality was being undermined by the developing medical (sickness) model of homosexuality of which Krafft-Ebing was the leading spokesman. Ulrichs complained:

My scientific opponents are mostly doctors of the insane. Thus, for example, Westphal, v. Krafft-Ebing, Stark. They have observed Urnings in lunatic asylums. They have apparently never seen mentally healthy Urnings. The published views of the doctors for the insane are accepted by the others.[27]

Ulrichs, who felt that he had discovered a basic truth about human beings, had thought at first, like many a reformer, that people needed only to have the truth revealed to them in order to accept it. That this did not happen was due, perhaps, not to a rejection of the explanatory aspect of his theory, but a prejudice against the logical conclusions that Ulrichs drew from it. Ulrichs was a lawyer and was quick to point out the implications of his theory, that homosexual activity—under certain restricted conditions, to be sure—was entirely natural and legal. Thus, since homosexual persons were by nature sexually attracted to members of the same sex, laws that proscribed "unnatural acts" did not apply to them, so long, of course, as the recipient of homosexual attentions freely accepted the advance. This last was a difficult point for Ulrichs, since he believed that homosexual individuals were seldom attracted to one another.[28]

Ulrichs was willing to admit, however, that some homosexual acts were the actions of depraved persons for whom the acts were not in fact "natural." His willingness to accept this possibility vitiated much of his legal argument, for, as it was impossible to distinguish natural from unnatural homosexual acts, there was no way to determine if an act was legal or illegal. The simple solution was to remove all legal restrictions on homosexual acts as such, while retaining age-of-consent laws, laws against the use of force, and so forth. This was in fact the situation in Hanover until its annexation as a province of Prussia in 1866.

Ulrichs objected to the Prussian invasion of his homeland, not only because he feared (correctly) that the Prussians would impose their antihomosexual laws, but also out of loyalty to the exiled King George V. Ulrichs turned political activist and twice was imprisoned for his outspoken views on political rights. In the course of his second arrest, in 1867, the police confiscated from his home a large collection of manuscripts on homosexual love, and the press used the occasion to ridicule him and his party.[29]

On his release from prison, Ulrichs was forced to leave Hanover. He moved to Bavaria, where homosexual acts were still tolerated by the law. There, on August 19, 1867, at the Congress of German Jurists in Munich, in an act that may be said to mark the beginning of the public homosexual emancipation movement in Germany, he spoke out for the rights of homosexual men and women.[30] Ulrichs was shouted down, but he was proud of his action, writing later that he wished to blaze "a trail to freedom."[31] The southward march of the strict Prussian laws was not to be stopped, however, and by 1872, following the unification of Germany, the antihomosexual statute had been extended to all parts of Germany. Ulrichs' final publication on "love between men," in 1879, described the disastrous effects of this legislation. Feeling himself driven from southern Germany, in 1880 Ulrichs sought a new homeland in Italy. Eventually he settled in Aquila, where he supported himself by teaching languages and publishing a Latin journal. He died there on July 14, 1895 and was buried beside the family tomb of his benefactor, the archeologist Niccolò Persichetti.[32]

The core of Ulrichs' theory, the congenital nature of homosexuality, was defended later by Havelock Ellis and others, but without the physiological basis that Ulrichs had posited for it. Probably no serious scholar thereafter entirely accepted the idea of an *anima muliebris virili corpore inclusa,* although the idea of a "feminized male brain" still persists in contemporary biology, and the "third sex" has remained a staple of popular fiction.

By 1891, an American professor had pointed out a basic objection to the unstated assumption underlying Ulrichs' theory: "There is an error in the view that feminine love is that which is directed to a man, and masculine love that which is directed to a woman. That doctrine involves a begging of the whole question."[33] It seems not to have occurred to Ulrichs that a man could love another man, and so he was led to the somewhat circular argument that a man could love another man only if the lover really had a feminine soul, and that his having a feminine soul was proved by his loving another man. Ulrichs knew from experience that a man can truly, honestly, and naturally love another man sexually. To conclude that this love was feminine, based on the assumption that a man could not love another man, was indeed "begging the question."

Strictly speaking, Ulrichs' "third sex" theory stood outside the mainstream of the developing medical explanations of homosexuality. These were in essence attempts to justify society's condemnation of homosexual women and men, while Ulrichs sought to exonerate homosexuality. Ironically, Ulrichs' view that the homosexual male is not a "true" man has survived as one of the stereotypes used in the repression of male homosexuality. When proposed by Ulrichs, however, it was a progressive notion, having a liberating effect not only for Ulrichs but for many of his "nature comrades" as well. His "third sex" theory has been abandoned—indeed, modern gay liberationists seem less and less concerned about the etiology of homosexuality—but Ulrichs' role as a pioneer of the movement for gay liberation cannot be denied. As we approach the centenary of his death, we may recall the dedication of the collected edition of his writings on the subject, reprinted in 1925 on the centenary of his birth: "To the eternal memory of . . . Karl Heinrich Ulrichs, the great self-sacrificing champion of the emancipation of same-sex love from legal persecution and social ostracism."[34]

NOTES

1. Alan P. Bell and Martin S. Weinberg, *Homosexualities: A Study of Diversity Among Men and Women* (New York: Simon & Schuster, 1978), p. 195.

2. Vern L. Bullough, "Homosexuality and the Medical Model," *Journal of Homosexuality* 1 (1974): 99.

3. Karl Heinrich Ulrichs, *Forschungen über das Rätsel der mannmännlichen Liebe,* 12 vols. in one (Leipzig, 1898; reprint ed., New York: Arno Press, 1975), 7:3.

4. Information on Ulrichs' family is taken from the records of the Evangelical Lutheran Church, Aurich, Federal Republic of Germany.

5. From the autobiographical statement included in Niccolò Persichetti, *In Memoriam Caroli Henrici Ulrichs, Ephemerides Cui Titulus 'Alaudae' Auctoris, Sylloge* (Rocca San Casciano, Italy: privately published, 1896), p. 5.

6. Gustav Mayer, *Johann Baptist von Schweitzer und die Sozialdemokratie, ein Beitrag zur Geschichte der deutschen Arbeiterbewegung* (Jena: Gustav Fischer, 1909), p. 69.

7. Ulrichs, 3:18.

8. Magnus Hirschfeld, "Vier Briefe von Karl Heinrich Ulrichs (Numa Numantius) an seine Verwanten," *Jahrbuch für sexuelle Zwischenstufen* 1 (1899):56.

9. Ulrichs, 7:25-73.

10. Garland E. Allen, "Edmund Beecher Wilson," in *Dictionary of Scientific Biography,* 16 vols., ed. Charles C. Gillispie (New York: Scribners, 1970-80), 14:431. Priority questions are discussed in Stephen G. Brush, "Nettie M. Stevens and the Discovery of Sex Determination by Chromosomes," *Isis* 69 (1978): 163-72.

11. Ulrichs, 1:16-19.

12. Ibid., 4:77-78.

13. Ibid, 2:4.

14. Ibid., 7:3.

15. Ibid., 2:87.

16. Ibid., 4:7. Ulrichs refers to K. M. Benkert, *Erinnerungen an Charles Sealsfield* (Leipzig: Ahn, 1864), p. 74.

17. The term "homosexual" appears to have been used for the first time in K. M. Benkert [Kertbeny], *Paragraph 143 des preussichen Strafgesetzbuches vom 14.4.1851 und seine Aufrechterhaltung als Paragraph 152 im Entwurf eines Strafgesetzbuches für den Norddeutschen Bund. . .* (Leipzig, 1869); reprinted in *Jahrbuch für sexuelle Zwischenstufen* 7 (1905): 1-66.

18. *The Dialogues of Plato,* trans. Benjamin Jowett, 2 vols. (New York: Random House, 1937), 1:309.

19. Ulrichs, 1:21.
20. Ibid., 7:35.
21. Ibid., 7:45.
22. Ibid., 7:51.
23. Ibid., 7:56.
24. Vern L. Bullough and Martha Voght, "Homosexuality and Its Confusion With the 'Secret Sin' in Pre-Freudian America," *Journal of the History of Medicine* 28 (1973): 147.
25. Gail Pat Parsons, "Equal Treatment for All: American Medical Remedies for Male Sexual Problems, 1850-1900," *Journal of the History of Medicine* 32 (1977): 62.
26. Ulrichs, 12:108.
27. Ibid., 12: 122.
28. Ulrichs also underestimated the number of homosexual males, setting the figure for Germany at one man in 500.
29. Ulrichs, 9:15.
30. Hubert Kennedy, "Karl Heinrich Ulrichs: Pioneer of Homosexual Emancipation," *The Body Politic,* March 1978, pp. 23-25 and April 1978, pp. 24-26.
31. Ulrichs, 6:13. The phrase refers to the Swiss national hero, Arnold von Windelried, who, at the victorious battle of Sempach in 1386, led the charge that broke the Austrian ranks. He fell with the legendary cry: "A trail to freedom!"
32. Magnus Hirschfeld, *Die Homosexualität des Mannes und des Weibes* (Berlin: Louis Marcus, 1914), p. 967.
33. Havelock Ellis and John Addington Symonds, *Sexual Inversion* (London, 1897; reprint ed., New York: Arno Press, 1975), p. 274. This professor has been identified as James Mills Peirce, mathematics professor and first dean of the Graduate School of Harvard University. See Hubert Kennedy, "The Case for James Mills Peirce," *Journal of Homosexuality* 4 (1978): 179-84.
34. Ulrichs, 1:3.

INVERTS, PERVERTS, AND MARY-ANNES
MALE PROSTITUTION AND THE REGULATION OF HOMOSEXUALITY IN ENGLAND IN THE NINETEENTH AND EARLY TWENTIETH CENTURIES

Jeffrey Weeks, BA, MPhil

ABSTRACT: The paper examines the relationship between patterns of male prostitution and the changing definitions (and regulation) of homosexual behavior in the late nineteenth and early twentieth centuries. A series of problems is explored. First, an attempt is made to delineate the changing patterns of legal and ideological control in the nineteenth century. This leads to a discussion of the second problem, the ways in which the social and legal context dictated the close relationship between the homosexual subcultures and the cash nexus represented by the prostitution relationship. The third problem concerns the ambivalent nature of the "prostitution," the complex self-concepts that developed, and the factors inhibiting the development of a distinctive subculture of male prostitution. The differences between female and male prostitution are discussed. The paper concludes by underlining the ambivalence of "male prostitution."

THE PROBLEM

It is significant that writings on male prostitution began to emerge simultaneously with the notion of "homosexuals" being an identifiable breed of persons with special needs, passions, and lusts. The early studies of male prostitution by F. Carlier, head of the morals police in Paris in the 1860s, were also the first major quantitative studies of homosexuality.[1] Havelock Ellis, Iwan Bloch, Magnus Hirschfeld, and

---

Jeffrey Weeks is Lecturer in the Sociology of Human Sexual Relations at the University of Kent at Canterbury, England.

The research on which this paper is based has been funded by the British Social Science Research Council. I should like to thank Mary McIntosh, Ken Plummer, and John Marshall for helpful comments.

Sigmund Freud also commented on the prevalence of homosexual prostitution. "Xavier Mayne," who wrote on the homosexual subculture in the early part of this century, suggested that male was no less frequent than female prostitution in major European cities. In 1948, Alfred Kinsey noted that male prostitutes were not far inferior in number to females. In the 1960s, D. J. West suggested that homosexual males' "inclination to such an outlet with prostitutes" was greater than that of heterosexual males, who usually were married and consequently had less pressing sexual urges as well as less time or opportunity to consort with prostitutes.[2] Although the existence of male prostitution is mentioned frequently, it has been studied less often. Most of our information is anecdotal and impressionistic.[3] As late as the mid-1960s, a writer on the subject could complain that the literature on boy prostitutes was scant when compared with studies of female prostitution.[4] A study of homosexual prostitution could illuminate the changing images of homosexuality and its legal and social regulation, as well as the variability of sexual identities in our social history and their relationship to wider social structures.

Iwan Bloch, writing in 1909, suggested that a discussion of male prostitution in E. A. Duchesne's *De La Prostitution dans la Ville d'Alger depuis la Conquete,* published in Paris in 1853, was:

> *. . . an expansion of the idea of prostitution which is, as far as my knowledge goes, found here for the first time. Naturally, in earlier works we find allusions to men who practice pederasty for money, but the idea of "prostitution" had hitherto been strictly limited to the class of purchasable women.*[5]

Bloch pinpoints the need to locate studies of prostitution within their specific social conditions and discriminates between promiscuity in earlier cultures and modern forms of prostitution, for the social meanings ascribed to the two behaviors are usually quite different.

Much recent work has stressed the vital importance of distinguishing among behavior, role, and identity in any sociological or historical approach to the subject of homosexuality.[6] Cross-cultural studies, as well as studies of schoolboy sex play, prison homosexuality, and sex in public places, show that homosexual behavior does not give rise automatically, or even necessarily, to a homosexual identity. Homosexual roles and identities are historically constructed.[7] Even if the homosexual "orientation" were given in a fixed minority of the population, as some recent writers suggest,[8] the social definitions and the subjective meaning given to the orientation can vary enormously. The mass of typologies and categorizations in the works of Krafft-Ebing, Albert Moll, Havelock Ellis, Magnus Hirschfeld, and others at the beginning of the century was an early attempt to grapple with this fact. Historians and social scientists alike have failed to fit everyone who behaves in a homosexual manner within a definition of "the homosexual" as a unitary type. Even those categorized as "homosexuals" often have had great difficulty in accepting the label. If this is the case for the clients of male prostitutes (the "steamers" or "punters," "swells" or "swanks"), how much more true is it for the prostitute himself who must confront two stigmatized identities—that of the homosexual and that of the prostitute? There is no legitimizing ideology for homosexual prostitution similar to that which condones heterosexual prostitution even when condeming the female prostitute. A number of studies have suggested that many males who prostitute themselves regard themselves as heterosexual and devise complex strategies to neutralize the significance of their behavior.[9] Our knowledge of this phenomenon is speculative, however, limited to particular classes of people, such as delinquents, and we do not know how attitudes change historically or in a particular lifetime. More generally, there is the problem of what constitutes an act of prostitution. One of Oscar Wilde's pickups in the 1890s, Charlie Parker, who eventually gave evidence against him, commented: "I don't suppose boys are different to girls in taking presents from them who are fond of them."[10] On a superficial level this is true, but the association with a stigmatized sexual activity has shaped profoundly the contours of male prostitution. These deserve serious examination.

This essay does not pretend to be an exhaustive study of the patterns of male prostitution. The necessary detailed empirical research still has to be done. Rather, the intention is to examine some of the practical and theoretical problems attendant upon this research and to make specific reference to evidence from the late nineteenth and early twentieth centuries. There are three broad areas of concern. First, we must pay closer attention than hitherto to the specific social circumstances that shaped concepts of, and attitudes toward, homosexuality. Second, the close, indeed symbiotic, relationship between forms of prostitution and the homosexual subcultures has to be recognized and analyzed. Third, the nature of the prostitution itself, the self-concepts it led to, the "way of life" it projected, and its differences from female prostitution must be articulated and theorized.

THE SOCIAL AND LEGAL CONTEXT

Certain types of subcultural formations associated with homosexual activity have existed in Britain for centuries, at the courts of certain monarchs (where the royal "favorite" can be seen as analogous to the "courtesan"), in the theatrical profession from the sixteenth century, or in developing urban centers, such as London and Bristol, from the seventeenth century.[11] Forms of prostitution undoubtedly existed within these subcultures and became more complex as the subculture expanded in the nineteenth century. Well into the present century the lineaments of the subcultures were much less well-defined in Britain, even in London, than in such places as Paris and Berlin, and as a result the evidence of prostitution is less concrete.[12] Different legal practices and moral traditions have had highly significant effects. In Britain, in contrast to France, homosexual behavior per se (not just prostitution) was regarded as a problem. Contemporary foreign observers had no doubt that male prostitution was as rife in England as elsewhere,[13] but its visibility was minimal. Much of our evidence for British prostitution is consequently sporadic, often the result of zealous public morality drives or of spectacular scandals.

Police, legal, and medical attitudes were manifestly confused. When the two "men in women's clothes," Ernest Boulton and Frederick Park, were arrested in 1870 for indecent behavior (for cross-dressing in public), they were immediately and without authorization examined for evidence of sodomy and eventually charged with conspiracy to commit such acts. The police, who had been observing the two men for over a year, often in notorious haunts of female prostitution, were of the opinion that Boulton and Park were male prostitutes. Indeed, some of the letters exchanged between Boulton, Park, and other defendants mentioned money. It is obvious, however, from the transcripts of the trial (before the Lord Chief Justice, in Westminster Hall) that neither the police nor the court were familiar either with male homosexuality or prostitution.[14] It is not even clear whether the men were charged with *male* prostitution. The opening remarks by the Attorney General hinted that it was their transvestism and their soliciting men *as women* that were the core of the crime.[15] A Dr. Paul, who examined them for sodomy upon their arrest, had never encountered a similar case in his whole career. His only knowledge came from a half-remembered case history in Dr. Alfred Swaine Taylor's *Medical Jurisprudence.*[16] The unclaimed body of one Eliza Edwards in 1833 had turned out on inspection to be the body of a twenty-four-year-old male: "The state of the rectum left no doubt of the abominable practices to which this individual had been addicted."[17] The implication was that sodomy might itself be an indication of prostitution, but even Dr. Taylor, who also gave evidence in the case, had had no other previous experience, and the other doctors called in could not agree on what the signs of sodomitical activity were. The Attorney General observed that "it must be a matter of rare occurrence in this country at least for any person to be discovered who has any propensity for the practices which are imputed to them."[18] The only "scientific" literature to which the court had recourse was French. Dr. Paul had not heard of the work of Tardieu, who had investigated over two hundred cases of sodomy for purposes of legal proof, until an anonymous letter informed him of its existence[19]. The Attorney General suggested that it was fortunate that there was "very little learning or knowledge upon this subject in this country."[20] One of the defense counsellors was more bitter, attacking Dr. Paul for relying on "the newfound treasures of French literature upon the subject—which thank God is still foreign to the libraries of British surgeons."[21]

It is striking that as late as 1871 concepts both of homosexuality and of male prostitution were extremely undeveloped in the Metropolitan Police and in high medical and legal circles. Neither was there any comprehensive law relating to male homosexuality before 1885. Prior to that date, the only relevant law was that concerning buggery, dating from the 1530s, and notionally carrying the maximum of a death sentence until 1861. Other male homosexual acts generally were subsumed under the heading of conspiracy to commit the major offense.[22] Proof was notoriously difficult to obtain, however, and it was ostensibly to make proof, and therefore conviction, easier that Henry Labouchère introduced his famous amendment to the Criminal Law Amendment Act of 1885. He claimed, though the substantiating evidence for this appears no longer to exist, that it was a communication from W. T. Stead about homosexual prostitution in London that prompted Labouchère to act.[23] The amendment defined "acts of gross indecency" between two men whether in *public* or *private* as "misdemeanors," punishable by up to two years of hard labor. This in effect made all male homosexual acts and all homosexual "procuring" illegal.

The 1898 Vagrancy Act further affected homosexual activities by enacting that any male person who knowingly lived wholly or in part on the earnings of female prostitutes, or who solicited or importuned for immoral purposes, was to be deemed a rogue and a vagabond under the terms of the Vagrancy Acts. The latter clauses were applied almost invariably to homosexual offenses. By a further Criminal Law Amendment Act ("The White Slave Trade Act") in 1912, the sentence was set at six months' imprisonment, with flogging for a second offense, *on summary jurisdiction* (that is, without a jury trial), a clause which, as G. B. Shaw put it, "is the final triumph of the vice it pretends to repress."[24] It is not entirely clear why the soliciting clauses were in practice confined exclusively to men meeting each other for homosexual purposes. The Royal Commission on the Duties of the Metropolitan Police noted in 1908 that there was nothing in the Act to prevent the clauses being applied to men soliciting women for immoral purposes,[25] but in fact they never were, nor have the activities of men who solicit women for acts of prostitution ever been illegal. The 1928 Street Offences Committee recommended that no change take place in these provisions.[26]

Although obviously less severe than a death sentence or life imprisonment for buggery, the new clauses were all-embracing and more effectively applied. They had specific effects on the relationship between male prostitution and homosexuality. *All* male homosexual activities were illegal between 1885 and 1967, and this fact largely shaped the nature of the homosexual underworld in the period "between the Acts." In particular it shaped the relationship between those who defined themselves as "homosexual" and those who prostituted themselves; for instance, it increased the likelihood of blackmail and violence. It also affected the nature of the prostitution itself, certainly making it less public and less sharply defined. As observers noted at the time, the male prostitute had the professional disadvantage of being obliged to avoid the open publicity of solicitation available to female prostitutes. This had important consequences.

In terms of social obloquy, all homosexual males as a class were equated with female prostitutes. It is striking that all the major enactments concerning male homosexuality were drawn from Acts designed to control female prostitution (1885, 1898, 1912). The juncture of the two concerns was maintained as late as the 1950s, when a Departmental Committee (the "Wolfenden Committee") was established to investigate both.[27]

After the repeal of the Contagious Diseases Acts in the 1880s, female prostitution was subject to a peculiar "compromise" that sought neither outright repression nor formal state regulation.[28] Prostitution was frowned upon, and the female prostitute was an outcast increasingly defined as a member of a separate caste of women,[29] but prostitution was "tolerated" as fulfilling a necessary social need. Beyond this was the distinction, which social purity campaigns sought to emphasize, between the sphere of public decency and that of private behavior. There were periods, particularly in the early decade of the twentieth century, when the advocates of social purity did reach toward straightforward repression, but by and large the compromise held.

On a formal level, the compromise never applied to male homosexuality. Even the sodomy provisions were applied to private as well as public behavior,[30] and after 1885 the situation was even more explicit. In practice, of course, enforcement varied between different police areas, depending on local police chiefs, the power of watch committees, and, over time, on the general social climate and the effectiveness of social-purity campaigns. There were also difficulties in the legal situation. Juries often refused to convict under the 1885 Act, and police often preferred not to prosecute if "public decency" were reasonably maintained.[31] Even after 1885, the government's legal officers preferred caution. In 1889, the Director of Public Prosecutions noted "the expediency of not giving unnecessary publicity" to cases of gross indecency. At the same time, he felt that much could be said for allowing "private persons—being full grown men—to indulge their unnatural tastes in private."[32]

When the law was applied, however, it was applied with rigor, particularly against males who importuned. Figures are difficult to come by, for until 1954 statistics for prosecution of male solicitation always were published with those for men living off immoral earnings, but one observer has suggested that the law was the cause of even greater misery than the 1885 Act.[33] It was enforced through summary jurisdiction, and, compared to the forty-shilling fine imposed on female prostitutes before 1959, the maximum sentence of six months' imprisonment and the associated stigmatization ground hard on homosexual males.

Given the social restrictions on forms of sexual contact, the demand for special services, and, in the case of homosexuality, the continuing difficulties of leading an openly homosexual life, there is undoubtedly at all times a market for prostitution. Given the legal situation since the end of the nineteenth century and the simultaneous refinement of hostile social norms, homosexual activity was potentially very dangerous for both partners and carried with it not only public disgrace but the possibility of a prison sentence. This also fed into the marked for prostitution and dictated much of the furtiveness, guilt, and anxiety that was a characteristic of the homosexual way of life.

In the diaries of Roger Casement, the Irish patriot executed in 1916, notes on his work for the colonial service lie cheek by jowl with descriptions of pickups, the price he paid for them, the size of their organs, and the occasional cry of despair. When he heard of the suicide of (the homosexual) Sir Hector Macdonald, Casement called for "saner methods of curing a terrible disease,"[34] but the surrounding entries joyfully extol his own recent adventures:

December 6, 1903
Very busy on report with typer. Did 6,000 words today and revised a lot. Dined at Comedy Restaurant alone. First time there in life. Porter good, excellent dinner, French chef, then walked. Dusky depradator huge, saw 7 in. in all. Two beauties.

December 7, 1903
. . . Awful mistake. Dine with Cui B and Mrs. C., jolly dinner, strolled. Dick, West End, biggest and cleanest, mui mua ami.

December 8, 1903
Busy all day and then to Robertson's at 30, Hemstall Road. Home by Marble Arch. D.W.14. C.R.£1. Drizzle, home tired and to bed. Bertie walked part of way.[35]

The frequency of encounters varied from thirty-nine in the 1903 diary to several hundred in 1911.[36] These adventures were completely hidden from friends and colleagues but evidently were a central part of his life, entering into his regular financial accountancy. The 1911 ledger, for instance, contains brief accounts of all activities and financial transactions, including payments for boys. Casement was exceptional in recording such (ultimately damning) details, but his life cannot have been unique. Indeed, there are striking parallels with the anonymous author of the Victorian sexual chronicle, *My Secret Life,* who also wrote of having a secret homosexual life, hidden from respectable friends and colleagues: "Have all men had the strange letches which late in life have enraptured me?"[37] Casement might well have asked the same question, for he seems to have had no sustained contact with a subculture or with other homosexual men except through casual prostitution.

THE HOMOSEXUAL SUBCULTURE

A sexual subculture can fulfill a number of complementary functions: alleviating isolation and guilt, schooling members in manners and mores, teaching and affirming identities.[38] The most basic purpose of the homosexual subculture in the nineteenth and early twentieth centuries, however, was to provide ways to meet sexual partners. Until comparatively recently, very few people found it either possible or desirable to incorporate sexual mores, social activities, and public identity into a full-time homosexual "way of life." Perhaps the only people who lived wholly in the subculture were the relatively few "professionals," the chief links between the world of aristocratic homosexuality and the metropolitan subculture of Molly houses, pubs, fields, walks, squares, and lavatories.

As early as the 1720s, these meeting places had been known as "markets," corresponding to the contemporaneous heterosexual use of the term "marriage market."[39] This does not differ much from Evelyn Hooker's description of the modern American gay bar scene as free markets in which the buyer's right to enter is determined solely by having the right attributes and the ability to pay.[40] By the 1870s, any sort of homosexual transaction, whether or not money was involved, was described as "trade." One defendant in the Boulton and Park scandal wrote to the other, "I will confess that I give you reason to think that I care for nothing but trade and I think you care too little for it as far as I am concerned."[41] In this world of sexual barter, particularly given the furtiveness, the need for caution, and the great disparities of wealth and social position among the participants, the cash nexus inevitably dominated.

Despite the wide social range of the subculture, from pauper to peer, it was the ideology of the upper classes that seems to have dominated, probably because there was a much more clearly defined homosexual identity amongst men of the middle and upper middle class and because these men had a greater opportunity, through money and mobility, to make frequent homosexual contacts.[42] A related phenomenon was the widely recognized upper-middle-class fascination with crossing the class divide, a fascination that shows a direct continuity between male heterosexual and male homosexual mores.[43] J. A. Symonds might have disapproved of some of his friends' compulsive chasing after working-class contacts,[44] but it was undoubtedly an important component of the subculture. The Post Office messenger boys of the Cleveland Street scandal and the stable lads, newspaper sellers, and bookmakers' clerks in the Wilde trial illustrate a few of the many sections of the working class involved.

The moving of class barriers, the search for "rough trade," or Wilde's "feasting with panthers" could become the defining tone. Lasting partnerships did develop, but in a world of relatively easy sex, promiscuity was a temptation, despite the dangers. Middle-class men generally had nonsexual relationships with friends, sex with casual pickups. One respondent of mine who found it difficult to have sex with friends of his own class had a fascination with the Guards and "suffered," as he put it, from "scarlet fever":

I have never cared for trading with homosexuals . . . I always wanted to trade with men. But of course, mine's always been prostitution . . . I don't say I never went with homosexuals because I did. But I would say that as a rule I wanted men.[45]

The desire for a relationship across class lines (the product, perhaps, of a feeling that sex could not be spontaneous or "natural" within the framework of one's own class), interacted with a desire for a relationship with a "man," a real man, a heterosexual. E. M. Forster wanted "to love a strong young man of the lower classes and be loved by him" and finally developed an ambiguous relationship with a policeman. Edward Carpenter proclaimed his love for the poor and uneducated in obviously erotic tones: "The thick-thighed, hot, coarse-fleshed young bricklayer with the strip around his waist." J. R. Ackerley sometimes felt that "the Ideal friend . . . should have been an animal man . . . the perfect human male body always at one's service through the devotion of a faithful and uncritical beast."[46]

There are very complex patterns recurring here. On the one hand was a form of sexual colonialism, a view of the lower classes as a source of "trade." On the other were an often sentimental rejection of one's own class values and a belief in reconciliation through sexual contact. As J. A. Symonds put it, "The blending of Social Strata in masculine love seems to me one of its most pronounced and socially hopeful features."[47] With this went a common belief that the working class and the Guardsmen (notorious from the eighteenth century and throughout Europe for their easy prostitution) were indifferent to homosexual behavior.[48] One regular customer of the Guardsmen observed: "Young, they were normal, they were working class, they were drilled to obedience."[49] They also were widely available:

The skeptic has only to walk around London, around any English garrison centre, to stroll around Portsmouth, Aldershot, Southampton, Woolwich, large cities of North Britain or Ireland to find the soldier prostitute in almost open self-marketing.[50]

With the guards, the money transaction was explicit. In the rarefied atmosphere of the "Uranian" poets, money would change hands but ideology minimized its significance. The Uranians worshipped youth, spoke of the transience of boyhood, and delighted in breaking class barriers.[51]

These class and gender interactions ("working-class" equals "masculine" equals "closeness to nature") were to play important roles in the rituals of prostitution, affecting, for instance, the stance adopted by the "prostitute" and the behaviors he was expected to tolerate.[52]

THE NATURE OF PROSTITUTION

The exchange of money could create a host of different symbolic meanings for both parties, while the uncertainty of both could make the transaction itself very ambiguous. It was not always easy, for instance, to distinguish among extortion, blackmail, and a begging letter. The giving of gifts could have the same complex inflection. Oscar Wilde's gift to his contacts of a dinner at Kettner's and a silver cigarette box (varying in cost from £1 to £5) could be interpreted either as payment for services about to be rendered or as tokens of friendship. A working-class man like George Merrill, Edward Carpenter's long-time companion, was able to recount quite unself-consciously his liaison in the 1880s with an Italian count who gave him presents, flowers, neckties, handkerchiefs, and money, which Merrill usually sent home to his mother.[53] In this sort of situation, the significance attached to the transaction could be quite complex, with the money and gifts often playing a quite secondary role.

Even when the commercial element was quite unambiguous, complex mechanisms could be adopted to mask the exchange. A client easily could adopt a self-saving attitude: "I seemed always to be pretending . . . that the quid that usually passed between us at once (the boys were always short of cash) was not a *quid pro quo* but a gift.''[54] Joe Ackerley has told of his nightly search for an ideal comrade and of his numberless pickups (Guardsmen and policemen). He writes, however:

The taint of prostitution in these proceedings nevertheless displeased me and must, I thought, be disagreeable to the boys themselves . . . I therefore developed mutually self-saving techniques to avoid it, such as standing drinks and giving cash at once, without any suggestive conversation, leading the boy free to return home with me if he wished, out of sexual desire or gratitude, for he was pretty sure to know what I was after.[55]

Payment could also be a necessary ritual to alleviate guilt:

There's a famous place behind a pub—in Camberwell, which was very interesting. And there was a—Army Captain there, who showed interest in me, and I in him. And he said, oh well, there are a lot of ditched houses over there, let's go round there. Which we did. And afterwards he pressed a ten shilling note into my hand. I said, I don't want this money. I don't take money, I enjoyed your company and so on. I said, I will not have it. He said, but you've got to have it. I said, I won't have it. And he went on and on. And eventually pressed it on—into my hand and ran. Now I think he got a thrill out of paying people. Most extraordinary.[56]

Fernando Henriques defined prostitution as ''any sexual acts, including those which involve copulation, habitually performed by individuals with other individuals of their own or the opposite sex, for a consideration which is non-sexual.''[57] A definition as all-embracing as this, however, is meaningless in the case of male prostitution. Terms like ''habitually'' and ''nonsexual'' are inappropriate where, as most commentators indicate, casual prostitution was the norm and casual pickups might evolve into ''companions,'' ''private secretaries,'' or ''personal assistants.'' An alternative definition suggests that activities be determined along a continuum between instrumentality and expressiveness and only those transactions in which the ''instrumental'' (i.e., the sexual services for money) is greater than the ''expressive'' (the degree of affection generated) be called prostitution.[58] The crucial question becomes: Would the transaction go on if goods and services were not exchanged?—a question involving self-concepts and identity as well as affection.

In a historical survey it is often very difficult to determine which actions are purely instrumental and which are affective. It is easier to describe the motivations and fantasies of the clients than to delineate the experiences and beliefs of those who prostituted themselves. Late-nineteenth-century theorists of the etiology of homosexuality looked to masturbation, bad parentage, congenital degeneracy, or corruption. A consensus developed among sexologists that, whatever one's moral views of homosexual behavior, there were essentially two types to distinguish: those who were inherently, perhaps congenitally, homosexual, "the inverts;" and those who behaved in a homosexual way from lust, "the perverts." Thoinot noted that "male prostitution finds as clients, on the one hand, *true uranists,* or the *passionates* as they are called in the language of the French police, and, on the other hand, libertines, old or young, disgusted with normal relations and impotent towards women."[59] This was an important distinction because it colored a great deal of public reaction. The Director of Public Prosecutions, reflecting on the affair of the Cleveland Street brothel in 1889, wrote that it was a duty "to enforce the law and protect the children of respectable parents taken into the service of the public . . . from being made the victims of the unnatural lusts of full-grown men."[60] The notion of the upper class corrupting the working class into vice is repeated in Labouchère's description of the boys named in the Cleveland Street affair as being "more sinned against than sinning." The constable in charge of the boys came to the conclusion that "they were ignorant of the crimes they committed with other persons."[61] The merging of homosexuality with the class question was recurrent in the press during the Cleveland Street scandal and continued through the 1950s.[62]

Alongside this view, and to some extent contradicting it, was the theory that the prostitute exhibited a characteristic predisposition toward corruption and sexual degeneracy, a characteristic sign of which was effeminacy. It is true that throughout Europe, from the eighteenth century on, those who prostituted themselves often displayed stereotyped "effeminate" characteristics and adopted female names,[63] but it is wrong to assume that male prostitutes were drawn from any particular type of person predisposed toward prostitution. Effeminate behavior can be as much an adopted role as inherent, and, as we have seen, the homosexual subculture stressed the desire for "manly" men. In fact, a variety of factors drew people into prostitution.

Writing of Berlin in the 1920s, Werner Pincton mentions two prostitute populations: an "outer ring" that fluctuated in numbers and composition and was caused by unemployment and want; and

> *the inner and more stable nucleus of this variable and non-coherent body . . . less driven by want or unemployment than by other circumstances, such as psychopathy, hysteria, mental instability, sexual curiosity, love of adventure and longing for luxuries.*[64]

Some of these categories ("psychopathy," "hysteria," "mental instability") conform to the view that prostitutes were "degenerate" or had been pushed into prostitution by emotional inadequacy or sex-role confusion. The other categories, however, suggest what appears to have been commonly the case: that the men had experienced a general and characteristic "drift into deviancy" (described as a "sliding down"[65]) that had varying, and certainly not predetermined, effects on their self-concepts and identities.

"Drift" has been identified as characteristic for both female and male prostitution, with "situational and cognitive" processes tending to be the dominant influences.[66] Whereas with female prostitution frequent sexual relations with men can lead to a woman's decision that her future transactions will be for money, the pattern is significantly different for male prostitutes. Here the dominant pattern seems to be one of chance contacts, accidental learning, or association with a subculture (such as that of the Guards) with a tradition of casual prostitution.

Youthful sex play frequently led to casual prostitution. Thickbroom, a boy messenger for the Post Office who was involved in the Cleveland Street affair, told how mutual masturbation in a water closet with Newlove, another messenger, had been followed by Newlove asking him, in Thickbroom's words, "if I would go to be with a man. I said no. He then said: you'll get four shillings for a time and persuaded me."[67] The messenger boys did not prostitute themselves frequently, and, were it not for the subsequent scandal, their involvement probably would have had minor impact on their lives. Sometimes, however, the decision could be more calculating. Charlie Parker recounted how he became involved with Alfred Taylor and Oscar Wilde. Taylor approached him:

passed the compliments of the day, and asked us to have a drink. We got into conversation with him. He spoke about men. Taylor said, "you could get money in a certain way easily enough if you cared to." I understood to what Taylor alluded and made a coarse reply . . . I said that if any old gentleman with money took a fancy to me, I was agreeable. I was agreeable. I was terribly hard up.[68]

These initial purposeful contacts could slide easily into a transitional career of blackmail and threat, but this was not a necessary development.

A third route to prostitution was through a world symbiotic with homosexuality, such as the Guards. A working-class recruit would soon learn how extra money could be made with little effort and with no risk of stigma by his fellows. Indeed, tradition and perennial shortage of funds among the Guards sanctioned these activities.[69] Subcultural support from peers was likely to militate against a Guardsman becoming a "professional." Sometimes a propensity for leading an explicitly homosexual life, a particular skill for learning the ways of the subculture, support from other prostitutes or homosexual men, or the willingness to recognize himself as a prostitute would turn a man to "professionalization," but "professionals" were very much in a minority among Guardsmen and nonmilitary youths alike.

The records of professional prostitutes are rare, which gives a particular interest to *The Sins of the Cities of the Plain* (1881),[70] the life story of

Jack Saul (a historical character who later—in 1890—gave evidence in the Euston libel case as part of the Cleveland Street brothel scandal). A choice piece of homosexual pornography, the book is purportedly Saul's autobiography and, despite its presumably fictionalized account, gives vivid insights into male prostitution. In the libel trial, Saul asserted proudly that he was still a "professional Maryanne:" "I have lost my character and cannot get on otherwise. I occasionally do odd jobs for different gay people."[71] These odd jobs, as he made clear in his cross-examination, were house cleaning for women on the beat, suggesting a commitment to a career as a professional, the ghettoization that could result from this choice of career, and its vagaries as age diminished charm. The life was by no means completely harsh, however, as this dialogue shows:

And were you hunted by the police?

No, they have never interfered. They have always been kind to me.

Do you mean they have deliberately shut their eyes to your infamous practices?

They have had to shut their eyes to more than me.[72]

The likes of Saul were few, however: His purported memoirs note that "We do not know of many professional male sodomites in London."[73]

THE LIFE

The professional organization that has been characteristic of female prostitution never arose within homosexual prostitution. Even in the larger European cities, such as Berlin and Paris, the "boy-houses" were rare, though numerous places of rendezvous existed under the guise of literary clubs and athletic societies.[74] In England, the Criminal Law Amendment Act of 1885 had been directed partly against brothels but was ambiguous in its application to homosexual haunts. The Director of Public Prosecutions complained to the Home Secretary in 1889 that he was "quite aware that although it is a legal offence to keep a bawdy house—it is not a legal offence to keep or frequent a house kept for the accommodation of sodomites."[75] Labouchère claimed in 1889 to have in his possession "a short list of houses, some in fashionable parts of the city which are every inch as bad; if not worse,"[76] but nothing seems to have followed from his threat to reveal them.

Such establishments had dozens of clients. Soldiers, MPs, peers, members of the National Liberal Club, a tailor, and a banker all frequented 19 Cleveland Street, for example. The boys were paid "sometimes a sovereign, sometimes half a sovereign; 4/- was kept by themselves and the rest given to Hammond or kept by Newlove.''[77] Jack Saul lived with Hammond for a while, and both earned their livelihood as ''sodomites:'' ''I used to give him all the money I earned, oftentimes as much as £8 or £9 a week.''[78]

Hammond lived a fully professional life as a ''madame,'' married a French prostitute, Madame Carolino, and lived with her thereafter. He also had a ''spooney-boy,'' one Frank Hewitt, who used to ''go with him'' and procure boys for the establishment.

Even within this twilight world there were subtle distinctions. Saul complained to Hammond of his allowing boys ''in good position in the Post Office to be in the house while I had to walk the streets for what is in my face and what is shame.''[79] Professional Mary-Annes with neatly printed calling cards like gentlemen's visiting cards[80] were scarcely the norm. More common contact would be the likes of Mrs. Truman, who received orders for Guardsmen at her tobacconist shop near the Albany Street barracks in Regents Park.[81] The Guards themselves also might take up an informal pimping role. One customer tells how he met one Guard several times:

. . . and then he said, well do you want anybody else . . . I can bring them along . . . So I said . . . have you got one with ginger hair . . . And then of course (he) procured me—oh—dozens. Dozens of them.

There were also widespread informal coteries.[82] Oscar Wilde made many of his contacts through his friend, Alfred Taylor, who lived in exotically furnished rooms in Little College Street near Westminster Abbey. The son of a wealthy cocoa manufacturer, Taylor became notorious for introducing young men to older men and as the center of a ''sort of secret society.''[83] Others, like John Watson Preston, who lived at 46 Fitzroy Street (near Cleveland Street), held openly transvestite parties, one of which was raided by the police. One such raid precipitated Taylor's first arrest.[84]

Similar arrangements continued into the 1930s:

I was introduced to somebody called Tommy . . . he had a flat. . . . And he used to have ''friends'' who used to call on him for tea, and he would invite his ''friends'' and pair them off. And—presents used to change hands . . . his clients were MPs, doctors, lawyers and professional gentlemen. . . . They paid him. . . . He paid the boy . . .

In London, however, most contacts would be made in the normal picking-up places and at ''watering holes'' (public lavatories), the occasional ''mixed'' pubs, the rare private clubs, the public walks, and parks. Some places, such as Picadilly Circus, were notorious, and here the more ''obvious'' or blatant young prostitutes might gather. Some of the more obviously effeminate prostitutes wore women's clothing and powder,[85] but most young men were more discreet. Discretion was indeed the hallmark of homosexual prostitution.

DEFINITIONS OF HOMOSEXUALITY

Picton's survey of 154 Berlin prostitutes revealed that approximately two-thirds spent between one and five years on the game, having started between the ages of seventeen and twenty-five. This admittedly very rough survey suggests that most men had quit the trade by their mid-twenties.[86] The routes out were numerous, from becoming a "kept boy" (either in a long-term relationship or in successive relationships), to integration into the homosexual world, or to a return to heterosexual family life. At least two of the boys involved in the Cleveland Street affair founded "modest but upwardly mobile family dynasties"[87] and lost all contact with the world of prostitution. The participants' self-concepts, as homosexual and as prostitute, were likely to determine how long a man remained a "Mary-Anne." Historically specific definitions are all-important here.

Most discussions of homosexuality have been dominated by an essentialism that presupposes a given, and unproblematic, homosexual "condition" and identity. From this have developed the confusions of typologies and categorizations: invert, pervert, bisexual, degenerate, and so on. There are three possible ways to address the task of definition. The first would be to suppose that all those who take part in homosexual behavior are themselves "homosexuals," even if the concept of "the homosexual" is not known to them or, as in some cultures, does not exist. This is plainly unsatisfactory. The second approach is to assume that the willingness to practice homosexuality, whatever one's self-concept, indicates an "unconscious" or latent homosexuality, which is generally repressed. This neo-Freudian approach is widely credited among self-identified "homosexuals" themselves. As one respondent put it, "I don't see once you've been to bed with a man how you can possibly say you're straight again." This may or may not be the case, but in fact it merely displaces the problem from the social construction of sexual ideologies to the individual level. The third approach, and the one that offers the most satisfactory entree to historical work, would concentrate on the social level and would recognize the ways in which sexual meanings and identities are historical constructs. A human identity is not a given in any particular historical situation but is the product of different social interactions, of the play of power, and sometimes of random choices. The homosexual orientation may be strong, but its significance depends on a host of factors that change over time.

Jack Saul regarded himself as a "sodomite," a term not necessarily coextensive with "homosexual." In his memoirs he reports that one of his clients was "not an actual sodomite. He likes to play with you and then 'spend' on your belly."[88] The distinction would be strange to the present century, but in 1890 the term "sodomite" was related to an act; "homosexual" implied a type of person, a member of a "species."[89]

An individual who could identify as "a homosexual" was more likely to be absorbed into the homosexual subcultures, to develop friendship networks and relationships (whether as "kept boy" or as partner), and to use his homosexuality as a way to rise in the world. One respondent, who took pride in having been "passed from hand to mouth" in the 1930s, moved from a poor working-class background in the North of England to the center of the metropolitan subculture as the companion of a gregarious member of the London intelligentsia: "I was never kept in the background . . . he wore me like a badge." The respondent was fully prepared to adapt himself to his new ambience, adopting a new accent and learning to "entertain": "You weren't just taken . . . out because you were pretty . . . you weren't taken out the second time because you were just a pretty face." Such a person is likely to be able to cope with a wider range of sexual demands than one who is anxious to preserve a male and heterosexual self-image. (A Guardsman, for example, might charge extra for taking an "active" role in anal intercourse ["taking a real liberty"] but would baulk at taking a "passive" role.[90]) Reiss's classic study of delinquent youth has shown the sort of norms that may govern casual transactions. First, because the boy must make it clear to his partner and to himself that the relationship is solely a way to make money, the boy must not actively pursue his own sexual gratification. Secondly, the sexual transaction must be limited to specific sexual acts (for example, no buggery) or sexual roles ("active"). Thirdly, the participants must remain emotionally neutral for fear of endangering the basis for the contract. Violence can be avoided as long as these rules are maintained but could erupt if they were threatened.[91]

A variety of self-definitions is possible: as homosexual, as homosexual prostitute, as a prostitute but not homosexual, or as neither homosexual nor prostitute. One respondent, who admitted to having been maintained by a friend, was highly indignant at having been described in a book as a "well-known male prostitute." Another interviewee, who as a Guardsman had had a large number of homosexual experiences and had followed these by a lifelong friendship with a homosexual man, was careful to explain that he was neither homosexual nor bisexual, but a "real" man who did it for the money.[95]

The general impression that emerges from the nineteenth and early twentieth century is that the more casual the prostitution, the less likely was the individual to identify himself as homosexual or as a prostitute in the absence of any firm public categorization. Conversely, the longer the person stayed in the homosexual subculture the more likely he was to accept its values and to identify himself as primarily homosexual. In each case the important factor was not an inherent propensity but the degree to which the man's activities and self-concepts were supported by the subculture. Prostitution flourished among the Guardsmen and among the messenger boys of Cleveland Street precisely because the ideology operating in both networks acted to sustain the men's existing self-images as heterosexual "trade."

CONCLUSION

It is difficult to define homosexual prostitution, dependent as it is on changing definitions of homosexuality and shifts in the homosexual subculture. Clearly, there was a vast difference between the casual act of prostitution in a public lavatory for a small amount of money and the conscious adaptation of homosexuality as a "way of life." The experiences are related, however, not so much by the fact of the sexual acts as by the experience of homosexuality as a stigmatized category. This opprobrium demanded strategies of adaptation and techniques of avoidance. In this regard, male prostitution was strikingly different from the experience of female prostitution, for once the barrier to the initial act of prostitution has been crossed, the female prostitute could enter a world of values that served to support the choices she made and to reinforce the identity she was adopting. There was no comparable subculture of homosexual prostitution. For the young man who prostituted himself, the choices were effectively between retaining a conventional self-concept (and hence adopting neutralizing techniques to explain his behavior to himself and to others) or accepting a homosexual identity with all its attendant dangers in a hostile society.

Once the choice had been made, however, full integration into the nonprofessional homosexual subculture could take place. In this there were advantages unavailable to the female prostitute. The asymmetry of relationship between the female prostitute and client was permanent, and the stigma of prostitution was lasting. In the homosexual world the patterns and relationships were inevitably more ambiguous. The "deviance" of prostitution was supplementary to the "deviance" of homosexuality.

NOTES

1. F. Carlier, *Rapport d'un Officier de la Police Municipale de Paris* (Paris: 1864) and *Les Deux Prostitutions* (Paris: 1887). For a comment on Carlier's work see Vern L. Bullough, *Sexual Variance in Society and History* (New York: John Wiley & Sons, 1976), p. 638.

2. Xavier Mayne, *The Intersexes: A History of Similisexualism as a Problem in Social Life* (privately printed, 1908); Alfred C. Kinsey, Wardell B. Pomeroy, and Clyde E. Martin, *Sexual Behaviour in the Human Male* (Philadelphia and London: W.B. Saunders Co., 1948), p. 596; D.J. West, *Homosexuality* (Harmondsworth, England: Penguin Books, 1968), p. 127.

3. For example, see Simon Raven, "Boys will be Boys: The Male Prostitute in London," in H.M. Ruiteenbeek, *The Problem of Homosexuality in Modern Society* (New York: E.P. Dutton & Co., 1963).

4. Michael Craft, "Boy Prostitutes and their Fate," *British Journal of Psychiatry* 12 (1966): 111.

5. Iwan Bloch, *The Sexual Life of our Time* (London: William Heinemann, 1909), p. 313.

6. See for example Mary McIntosh, "The Homosexual Role," *Social Problems* 16, no. 2 (1968): 182-92; Kenneth Plummer, *Sexual Stigma: An Interactionist Account* (London: Routledge & Kegan Paul, 1975); Jeffrey Weeks, *Coming Out: Homosexual Politics in Britain from the Nineteenth Century to the Present* (London: Quartet, 1977).

7. For a useful summary of cross-cultural evidence see Randolph Trumbach, "London's Sodomites: Homosexual Behavior and Western Culture in the 18th Century," *Journal of Social History* 2, no. 1 (Fall 1977): 1-33. McIntosh's "The Homosexual Role" is the classic statement on the construction of homosexual roles.

8. See, for example, F.L. Whitham, "The Homosexual Role: A Reconsideration," *The Journal of Sex Research* 13, no. 1 (February 1977): 1-11. It is also implied in Trumbach, "London's Sodomites."

9. A.J. Reiss, "The Social Integration of Queers and Peers," in Ruitenbeek.

10. H. Montgomery Hyde, *The Trials of Oscar Wilde* (Harmondsworth, England: Penguin Books, 1962), p. 172.

11. For discussions of subcultural formations see Trumbach, "London's Sodomites," and McIntosh.

12. On France see Carlier, *Les Deux Prostitutions* (Paris, 1887); Abraham Flexner, *Prostitution in Europe* (New York: 1914), p. 30, comments on the German situation; Mayne has a survey of the European legal situation relating to homosexuality.

13. See, for example, Carlier, *Les Deux Prostitutions,* p. 454; Jacobus X, *Crossways of Sex: A Study in Eroto-Pathology,* 2 vols. (Paris: Charles Carrington, 1904), 2:195; Werner Picton, "Male Prostitution in Berlin," *Howard Journal* 3, no. 2 (1931).

14. The transcripts of the trial in 1871 are preserved in London in the Public Record Office: DPP 4/6. This section is based on these transcripts.

15. Public Record Office: DPP 4/6, transcript for Day 1, p. 193.

16. Ibid., transcript for Day 2, p. 256.

17. Alfred Swaine Taylor, *Medical Jurisprudence* (London: 1861), p. 657.

18. Public Record Office: DPP 4/6, transcript for Day 1, p. 21.

19. Ibid., transcript for Day 2, p. 276. The work of A. Tardieu is referred to in Arno Karlen, *Sexuality and Homosexuality* (London: Macdonald, 1971), pp. 185, 217.

20. DPP 4/6, transcript for Day 1, p. 82.

21. Ibid., transcript for Day 3, p. 299.

22. On the legal situation see H. Montgomery Hyde, *The Other Love* (London: Mayflower Books, 1972), p. 17; Edward J. Bristow, *Vice and Vigilance: Purity Movements in Britain Since 1700* (Dublin: Gill and Macmillan, 1977), p. 29; Weeks, Chapter 1.

23. See Henry Labouchère's parliamentary statement, quoted in *The Times,* 1 March 1890. For discussion of Labouchère's motives see F.B. Smith, "Labouchère's Amendment to the Criminal Law Amendment Bill," *Historical Studies* 17, no. 67 (October 1976).

24. Shaw is quoted in Ian Gibson, *The English Vice: Beating, Sex and Shame in Victorian England and After* (London: Duckworth, 1978), p. 164; see also p. 160. George C. Ives,

The Continued Extension of the Criminal Law (London: 1922) gives a useful description of the legal developments.

25. Report of the Royal Commission on the Duties of the Metropolitan Police, Cmnd. 4156, 1908, 1, p. 119.

26. For a comment on this recommendation see *Howard Journal* 2, no. 4 (1929): 334.

27. For a discussion of the social and political conjunctures in which these enactments took place see Deborah Gorham, "The 'Maiden Tribute of Modern Babylon' Re-examined: Child Prostitution and the Idea of Childhood in Late-Victorian England," *Victorian Studies* 21, no. 3 (Spring 1978); Bristow, Chapters 4 and 5; Weeks, Chapter 1.

28. Abraham A. Sion, *Prostitution and the Law* (London: Faber & Faber, 1977), p. 33; Bristow, p. 54.

29. cf. Judith R. Walkowitz and Daniel J. Walkowitz, " 'We are not beasts of the field': Prostitution and the Poor in Plymouth and Southampton under the Contagious Diseases Acts," *Feminist Studies* 1, nos. 3-4 (1973); Judith R. Walkowitz, "The Making of an Outcast Group: Prostitutes and Working Women" in Martha Vicinus, ed., *The Widening Sphere* (Bloomington: Indiana University Press, 1977).

30. *Report of the Committee on Homosexual Offences and Prostitution,* Cmnd. 247 (London: HMSO, 1957), p. 39.

31. cf. Havelock Ellis, *The Task of Social Hygiene* (London: Constable, 1912), p. 272.

32. Director of Public Prosecutions to Metropolitan Police Commissioner, 20 July 1889; Director of Public Prosecutions to Attorney General, 14 September 1889; Public Record Office: DPP 1/95/1.

33. Michael Schofield, *Sociological Aspects of Homosexuality* (London: Longman, Green & Co., 1965), p. 200.

34. Casement Diaries, 17 April 1903. Public Record Office: HO 161/2.

35. Ibid.

36. cf. H. Montgomery Hyde, *The Trial of Sir Roger Casement* (London: William Hodge, 1964), p. clv.

37. "Walter," *My Secret Life,* 11 vols. (Amsterdam: privately printed, 1877), 1:14.

38. Plummer, p. 147.

39. cf. Trumbach, "London Sodomites."

40. Evelyn Hooker, "The Homosexual Community" in J.H. Gagnon and W. Simon, *Sexual Deviance* (London: Harper & Row, 1967), p. 174.

41. Public Record Office: DPP 4/6 transcript for Day 6, p. 243, Hurt to Boulton.

42. cf. J.R. Ackerley, *My Father and Myself* (London: Bodley Head, 1966); Tom Driberg, *Ruling Passions: The Autobiography of Tom Driberg* (London: Jonathan Cape, 1977).

43. As revealed, for instance, in the volumes of *My Secret Life.* See also Leonore Davidoff, "Class and Gender in Victorian England: The Diaries of Arthur J. Munby and Hannah Cullwick, " *Feminist Studies* 1, no. 5 (1979).

44. As described in Phyllis Grosskurth, *John Addington Symonds: A Biography* (London: Longmans, 1964).

45. This is from one of a series of interviews conducted with homosexual men over sixty, which is part of a Social Science Research Council funded project on the organization of the homosexual subsculture in England. The researchers were Mary McIntosh and Jeffrey Weeks. The research was carried out between April 1978 and July 1979. All unreferenced quotations come from these interviews.

46. E.M. Forster, *The Life to Come and Other Stories* (Harmondsworth, England: Penguin Books, 1975), p. 16; Edward Carpenter quoted in Timothy d'Arch Smith, *Love in Earnest* (London: Routledge & Kegan Paul, 1970), p. 192; Ackerley, p. 218; see also Anomaly, *The Invert, and His Social Adjustment,* 2nd ed. (London: Bailliere, Tindall & Cox, 1948), p. 179.

47. H.M. Scheuller and R.L. Peters, eds., *The Letters of John Addington Symonds* (Detroit: Wayne State University Press, 1969), 3: 808.

48. See for example, the views of Havelock Ellis, *Sexual Inversion* (New York: F.A. Davies, 1936), p. 22; Havelock Ellis and John Addington Symonds, *Sexual Inversion* (London: Wilson & Macmillan, 1897), p. 9.

49. Ackerley, p. 135.

50. Mayne, p. 220.

51. On the worship of youth see d'Arch Smith; Brian Taylor, "Motives for Guilt-free Pederasty: Some Literary Considerations," *Sociological Review* 24, no. 1 (February 1976); George C. Ives, *Obstacles to Human Progress* (London: George Allen & Unwin, 1939), p. 200; Michael Davidson, *The World, the Flesh and Myself* (London: Mayflower-Dell, 1966), p. 88.

52. cf. Paul Gebhard's comments, quoted in Robin Lloyd, *Playland: A Study of Boy Prostitution* (London: Blond & Brigg, 1977), p. 195:

> In female prostitution the prostitute rarely or never reaches orgasm and the client almost invariably does; in male prostitution the prostitute almost invariably reaches orgasm, but the client frequently does not.
>
> . . . . The homosexual male ideally seeks a masculine-appearing heterosexual male, and the prostitute attempts to fit the image. Consequently the prostitute can do little or nothing for or to a homosexual client lest he betray a homosexual inclination of his own and ruin the illusion.
>
> This cannot be taken as a general statement of the situation but it does undoubtedly express one type of experience.

53. See Edward Carpenter's "Memoir" of George Merrill, Edward Carpenter Collection, Sheffield City Library, Sheffield, England.

54. Ackerley, p. 215.

55. Ackerley, p. 136.

56. Interview with Gregory, January 1979.

57. Fernando Henriques, *Prostitution and Society: A Survey: Primitive, Classical and Oriental* (London: Macgibbon & Kee, 1962), p. 17.

58. M. Brake and K. Plummer, "Rent Boys and Bent Boys" (unpublished paper, 1970).

59. L. Thoinot and A.W. Weysse, *Medico Legal Aspects of Moral Offences* (Philadelphia: F.A. Davis, 1911), p. 346.

60. Quoted in L. Chester, D. Leitch, and C. Simpson, *The Cleveland Street Affair* (London: Weidenfeld & Nicolson, 1977), p. 73.

61. H. Montgomery Hyde, *The Cleveland Street Scandal* (London: Weidenfeld & Nicolson, 1976), p. 28.

62. See *Reynolds Newspaper,* 12 January 1890; *The Referee,* 24 November 1889, for comments on the involvement of working-class boys in the Cleveland Street Scandal; and Peter Wildblood, *Against the Law* (Harmondsworth, England: Penguin Books, 1957), p. 80 for a similar view in the 1950s.

63. See, for examples, the contents of Carlier, *Les Deux Prostitutions,* p. 323.

64. Werner Picton, p. 90.

65. Ibid., p. 91.

66. Nanette J. Davis, "The Prostitute: Developing a Deviant Indentity," in James M. Henslin, *Studies in the Sociology of Sex* (New York: Appleton-Century-Crofts, 1971), p. 297.

67. Public Record Office: DPP1/95/3, File 5.

68. Quoted in Hyde, *The Trials of Oscar Wilde,* p. 170.

69. See Ackerley, p. 135; Raven, p. 280.

70. *The Sins of the Cities of the Plain, or the Recollections of a Mary-Anne,* 2 vols. (London, 1881).

71. Saul's deposition, Public Record Office: DPP1/95/4, File 2.

72. See the report in the *Star,* 15 January 1890.
73. *Sins of the Cities of the Plain* 2: 109.
74. Mayne, p. 430.
75. Quoted in Chester et al., pp. 46-47.
76. *Truth,* 21 December 1889, p. 49.
77. Public Record Office: DPP 1/95/3, File 4, transcript of trial, p. 6.
78. Public Record Office: DPP 1/95/4, Saul's deposition.
79. Ibid.
80. Ibid.
81. *Sins of the Cities of the Plain* vol. 2, quoted in Chester et al., p. 57.
82. F. Carlier, *Les Deux Prostitutions,* p. 317.
83. Hyde, *The Trials of Oscar Wilde,* pp. 60, 125, 162.
84. Rupert Croft-Cooke, *The Unrecorded Life of Oscar Wilde* (London and New York: W.H. Allen, 1972), p. 141.
85. For a colorful example of a male prostitute arrested in female clothes see the reference in Mayne, p. 443. See also Quentin Crisp, *The Naked Civil Servant* (Harmondsworth, England: Penguin Books, 1977), p. 26.
86. Werner Picton, p. 90.
87. L. Chester et al., p. 225.
88. Saul's deposition, Public Record Office: DPP 1/95/4, File 2.
89. cf. Michel Foucault, *The History of Sexuality,* vol. 1: *Introduction* (London: Allen Lane, 1979), p. 43; see also Jeffrey Weeks, p. 14.
90. Simon Raven, p. 280.
91. A.J. Reiss, pp. 264-71.

"STIGMATA OF DEGENERATION"
PRISONER MARKINGS IN NAZI CONCENTRATION CAMPS

Erwin J. Haeberle, PhD, DA

ABSTRACT: The persecution of homosexual men, transvestites, and "race defilers" in Nazi Germany carried the traditional religious and psychiatric stigmatization of sexual nonconformists in Europe to its logical extreme. The system of prisoner markings in Nazi concentration camps and its stigmatizing function are described.

There is a long tradition in Europe and America of branding men who engage in same-sex erotic behavior as wicked, dangerous, and inferior, and of referring to them only in negative terms. In medieval and early modern times the motive for this verbal stigmatization was mostly religious. When a man was called a sodomite or bugger (a corruption of Bulgar), he was thereby defined as an enemy of the people because, as everyone knew, sodomy (the sin of Sodom) and buggery (the heresy of Bulgaria) were aberrations from the path of righteousness and insults to God that invited His retribution. By ostracizing and persecuting sodomites and buggers, the faithful duly protected themselves.

In the nineteenth century, when psychiatrists began to convert sins of the flesh into mental diseases ("sexual psychopathies"), the originally religious terms "aberration," "perversion," and "deviation" came to be used as elements of a medical diagnosis. This process is observed most easily in the work of an influential French psychiatrist who had begun his academic training as a student of theology, Benedict Augustin Morel (1809-1873). In analogy to the Bible, Morel assumed the past existence of a perfect man or *"type primitif"* (Adam) who, after some external and internal corruption (the Fall), became susceptible to various negative influences. The resulting general enfeeblement produced several less perfect, but still relatively healthy, human races and a number of "degenerative" genetic lines that would grow weaker with each generation and finally die out: "Degenerations are deviations

Dr. Haeberle is Director of Historical Research, The Institute for Advanced Study of Human Sexuality, San Francisco, California 94109.

Journal of Homosexuality, Vol 6(1/2), Fall/Winter 1980/81

from the normal human type, which are transmissible by heredity and which deteriorate progressively toward extinction."[1] It was the task of psychiatry to recognize the symptoms of degeneration in individuals and to take appropriate (mostly palliative) measures. As the medical historian Zilboorg summarized it:

> *. . . Morel's attention was absorbed by the problem of degeneration. In 1857 his magnum opus appeared, a volume of seven hundred pages entitled* Traité des dégénérescences physiques, intellectuelles et morales de l'espèce humaine. *He viewed mental disease primarily as a "result of hereditary weakness." Degeneration was a hereditary phenomenon, of course, and Morel developed a detailed method of discovering the great variety of "stigmata of degeneration" to be found among the mentally sick. These were mostly physical signs—various malformations—but also various intellectual and moral deviations from the normal.*[2]

In the same year, 1857, another Frenchman, Ambroise Tardieu, published his *Étude médico-légale sur les attentats aux moeurs,* which purported to be a scientific study of same-sex eroticism in France. Tardieu claimed to have discovered physical evidence for an inclination toward "pederasty." Pederasts were depraved individuals and differed not only morally but also anatomically from other men. Active pederasts had an underdeveloped, tapered penis, resembling that of a dog; the anus of a passive pederast, even before any sexual activity, was naturally smooth, lacking in radial folds.[3]

Under the influence of Morel, such alleged characteristics were soon regarded as "stigmata of degeneration," and for the rest of the nineteenth century "experts" all over Europe tried to find, list, and classify more and more of these stigmata for diagnostic purposes. In the opinion of most psychiatrists, "degeneration" remained the major and rarely questioned cause of sexual nonconformity. Even in 1906, when Iwan Bloch tried to escape the narrow psychiatric assumptions about sexual behavior by introducing the new, broader concept of *Sexualwissenschaft,* or sexology, the infamous "stigmata of degeneration" continued to haunt his mind:

> *We distinguish physical and mental* stigmata degenerationis. *To the former belong . . . malformations, such as asymmetry of the skull, narrowness of the palate, hare-lip, cleft palate, anomalies of the teeth and the hair, . . . abnormal and morbid states of the genital organs and genital functions, and more especially malformations of the ear, such as Morel's ear (the complete or partial absence of the helix or antihelix). . . . The mental degenerative phenomena comprise all that are known as "bizarre or abnormal" characters. . . . These phenomena comprise peculiar disturbances of the harmony of the spiritual life, characterized by lack of balance between emotion and intellect, as well as by an abnormal irritability and undue reaction to stimulation.*[4]

Bloch, however, had developed serious doubts as to the meaning of these stigmata. Indeed, he had reservations about the whole idea of degeneration and stated that "perversions" could be found also among the healthy. Homosexuality, for example, might simply be one of many "vicious habits," like excessive smoking.[5] Furthermore, even in mentally disordered persons, the "stigmata of degeneration" might be traced not to genetic but to various social causes, such as bad conditions of life or deficient nourishment, as illustrated by the rachitic bandy legs of English factory workers. To prove degeneration, therefore, one had to place much more stress upon the mental stigmata, that is abnormalities of the spiritual personality.[6]

Within a few years, it became obvious that even such critical reservations could not save Morel's theory. Bloch's individual doubts gave way to widespread skepticism and finally to open rejection. Especially after Sigmund Freud had replaced the whole notion of hereditary degeneration with that of an individual, largely unconscious life history, the search for the old physical stigmata was abandoned by all serious scientists.

Nevertheless, the idea of progressive degeneracy and of its physical manifestations lived on in sexual folklore and among various reactionary political movements. After the First World War, the Nazi movement in Germany especially clung to the belief in "degenerates" and inferior races. In popular Nazi propaganda (such as in Julius Streicher's *Der Stürmer*), the "racially inferior" Jews always were portrayed with various exaggerated "stigmata of degeneration" (misshapen heads, crooked noses, drooping lower lips, bent legs, and so on) in order to create the image of a sickly, sexually "perverse" enemy. Because the Nazis did not believe that the Jews would die out by themselves, however, Hitler decided to have them killed.

The eventual mass murder of European Jews could not proceed without some preparation. In the absence of anatomical stigmata, since Jews did not look like the stereotype of Nazi propaganda, they had to be identified. A process of governmental stigmatization was set in motion. First, all Jews were legally forced to adopt the additional first names "Israel" (for males) or "Sara" (for females) as a means of calling attention to their outcast state. Then, for the same reason, their passports were stamped with a big "J." In 1941, they were forced to wear a yellow star on their clothing, and finally, one year later, even the doors of their apartments had to display the star. In short, what once had begun as a French psychiatric theory turned into German political practice. The "stigmata of degeneration" turned from alleged inborn physical malformations into concrete, outward marks of bureaucratic identification. Worst of all, unlike Morel's imaginary "degeneration," this bureaucratic process did indeed single out its victims and literally moved them "progressively toward extinction."

In the Nazi view, the "degenerate" Jews with their inferior genetic heritage would infect even the healthy Nordic races if allowed to do so. Therefore, as early as 1935, Hitler's government passed a special "Law for the Protection of German Blood and German Honor," which proscribed sexual intercourse between Jews and non-Jews as "race defilement." Offenders were sent to concentration camps together with other sexual "degenerates," such as transvestites and homosexual males.[7]

Inside the camps, all prisoners were stigmatized with special markings that both justified their imprisonment and indicated the nature of their offenses. As Eugen Kogon, a political prisoner and survivor, later described it in his classic study of the camps:

> *Who belonged in a concentration camp, according to the Gestapo? Above all,* four groups *of people: political adversaries, members of "inferior races" and "inferiors from the standpoint of race-biology," criminals, and "asocials."* . . .
>
> *All groups of prisoners in the concentration camp had to wear external markings which were sewn to their clothing, namely a number and triangle of a certain color on the left side of the chest as well as on the right trouser leg.* Red *was the color of the political prisoners. . . . The other colors and designations were as follows:* green *for criminals . . .* violet *for Jehovah's witnesses,* black *for asocials,* pink *for homosexuals, at times* brown *for gypsies. . . . Jews wore an inverted yellow triangle underneath their red, green, black, or other markings, forming a star with six points. The so-called* race defilers, *Jews or non-Jews, . . . received an inverted black triangular outline over their yellow or green triangles. . . .*
>
> *In the case of* foreigners, *the first letter of their nationality was printed on the triangle: "T" for Tchech, "F" for French, . . . and so on.*
>
> *Members of penal companies had a black, dollar-sized dot between the lower point of the triangle and the number. Those suspected of escape attempts had red-and-white targets painted on both chest and back. . . .*
>
> *Colors, markings, and special designations—in this respect the whole concentration camp was a crazy farm. Occasionally there were veritable rainbow constellations: For example, there once was a Jewish Jehovah's witness as a race defiler with penal colony dot and escape target!*
>
> *It must be emphasized that the markings were no absolute guarantee that the prisoner truly belonged to the category. . . . Indeed, occasionally it happened that, rightly or wrongly, markings were changed.*[8]

In the original German edition of this book, Kogon provided a color chart illustrating the system of markings. The expensive color printing was dropped in the later English-language edition, however, and thus it has been almost inaccessible to the general American reader. For this reason, an adaptation and slight simplification of Kogon's chart is provided here. (The present version omits the prisoners' numbers, which appeared below the triangle, but groups the various color categories together in a more methodical fashion.) It will be observed that Jewish prisoners always wore a double stigma, and that homosexual inmates were assigned the "effeminate" color pink. One should also be aware of the divisive intent behind these markings, which were introduced not merely for the convenience of the camp administration but also to set one group of prisoners against the other. Here again, the homosexual men became victims of long-standing general prejudice:

> *Inside the concentration camp, mere suspicion was enough to label a prisoner as homosexual and thus to expose him to denigration, general suspicion, and special dangers. On this occasion it must be stated that the homosexual practice was widespread in the camps. However, the prisoners only ostracized those who had been marked by the SS with a pink triangle.*[9]

The fate of the various prisoner groups is a subject for specialized study; so, too, is a detailed history of religious, psychiatric, and political stigmatization. Nevertheless, the Nazi system of prisoner markings can serve as a sobering reminder of the vicious tendency inherent in all negative labeling of human beings.

NOTES

1. Quoted in Franz G. Alexander and Sheldon T. Selesnick, *The History of Psychiatry* (New York: Harper & Row, 1966), p. 162.
2. Gregory Zilboorg, *A History of Medical Psychology* (New York: W.W. Norton, 1941), p. 402.
3. See Arno Karlen, *Sexuality and Homosexuality: A New View* (New York: W.W. Norton, 1971), p. 186.
4. Iwan Bloch, *The Sexual Life of Our Time* (New York: Allied Book Co., 1908), p. 664 (translation of *Das Sexualleben unserer Zeit*).
5. Ibid., p. 662.
6. Ibid., p. 665.
7. H. Timpke, in *Studien zur Geschichte der Konzentrationslager* (Stuttgart, 1970), p. 18.
8. Eugen Kogon, *Der SS-Staat* (Frankfurt/M., 1946), pp. 46, 50f. (The quote has been translated from the German edition. The American edition of this work is entitled *The Theory and Practice of Hell* (New York: 1950).)
9. Ibid., p. 263.

THE PINK TRIANGLE
THE PERSECUTION OF HOMOSEXUAL MALES IN CONCENTRATION CAMPS IN NAZI GERMANY

Rüdiger Lautmann, Dr. phil. Dr. jur.

ABSTRACT: Having analyzed the fragmentary records of Nazi concentration camps, the author reports on the number and treatment of male homosexual prisoners. The total number of inmates officially defined as homosexual is estimated at about 10,000, although the number incarcerated varied greatly from camp to camp and as the war progressed. Pink-triangle prisoners had low social status, often were isolated from other inmates, and, as compared to political prisoners and Jehovah's Witnesses, more frequently were given the most difficult work assignments and less frequently were assigned to light duties. They had a higher death rate and a lower survival rate upon release. Suicide rates were not significantly different from those of the other inmate groups studied. Pink-triangle prisoners were not subjected to exceptionally cruel treatment in all camps and at all times, however, and were not the only group of prisoners subjected to extreme abuse.

INTRODUCTION

This century's most extreme form of antihomosexual repression occurred in Germany between 1933 and 1945, when the Nazis attempted to assure the male domination of society by strictly regulating masculine sexual behavior. Sanctions against homosexual males were tightened to the utmost degree (lesbianism was passed over as being of no consequence) and a kiss or an embrace became a felony. The death penalty was demanded for members of the SS caught in homosexual activity. For the civilian, a record or conviction of homosexuality led to the concentration camp.

This article is a condensed version of material from Professor Lautmann's book, Seminar: Gesellschaft und Homosexualität *(Frankfurt, 1977). Dr. Lautmann is Professor of Sociology, 2800 Bremen, Schubertstrasse 22, West Germany.*

This article is an attempt to reconstruct the situation of homosexual men in the concentration camps—a subject that hitherto has not been researched by historians or sociologists. Our research group spent several weeks sifting material in the archives of the International Tracing Service in Arolsen, Hessen, where all extant documents concerning the victims of the Nazi government are preserved. The names and data on all concentration-camp prisoners registered as being homosexual were examined, including individual data (prisoners' I.D. cards, fact sheets, lists of personal belongings, administrative data, infirmary sheets, work squad lists, death notices, medical records, and so on). Also examined were group data (log books of identification numbers, arrival entries, change of station, and transport lists) for the concentration camps Buchenwald, Dachau, Flossenbürg, Mauthausen, Groß-Rosen, Mittelbau, Natzweiler, Neuengamme, Ravensbrück, Sachsenhausen, Stutthof, and for a few of the earlier camps. Only the material for the first four camps has been preserved intact. We collected data concerning 1572 pink-triangles. According to the experts of the International Tracing Service, only in the camps just mentioned were pink-triangles to be found in more than insignificant numbers. We may fairly claim, therefore, to have made a complete survey of all identifiable homosexual prisoners in Nazi concentration camps. The comparable material was gone through for Jehovah's Witnesses (N = 751) in Buchenwald, Dachau, Flossenbürg, Mauthausen, Natzweiler, Neuengamme, Ravensbrück, Sachsenhausen and in a few earlier camps, and a sample was taken for political prisoners (N = 219) in Buchenwald and Dachau. Jehovah's Witnesses and political prisoners are used in this study as control groups for the homosexuals incarcerated in those camps.

Although hundreds of group-data files and several thousand personal-data documents were reviewed, the overall data remain somewhat sparse and incomplete: The administration of the concentration camps had been interested in no more than the name, age, and reason for detention of the prisoners; profession, marital status, place of residence, remaindering agency, and fate were not always registered. In addition, even these meager data exist for only some of the camps, or for certain periods in their existence, for many documents were systematically destroyed during the Third Reich.

A further source of our study were memoirs written by survivors of the camps soon after their liberation; some 100 volumes were studied. Even in this literature homosexual inmates have the status of a neglected, peripheral group; little is said about them and not always in the friendliest of tones. Those who were the subject of these observations—the prisoners with the pink triangles—no longer were able to speak for themselves: Most of them had died, either in the concentration camps or, broken in health and spirit, in the three subsequent decades. With two exceptions, none of them ever managed to reach print. What one might be able to learn from private discussions remains branded by the heavy burden of embittered memory: One must remember that the world in which the former inmates lived after 1945 remained hostile to them. This is why, in spite of announcements of the research project, so few interviews were conducted.

One possible way to deal with the emotions aroused by the phenomenon of the concentration camps is to exaggerate. In effect one sweeps actual events under the table by evoking a picture of the utmost in horror, a superlative of terror to which (supposedly) no other group was subject. By this method one summons up a picture of hundreds of thousands of homosexual men whose fate was the hardest of all to bear, who had a kind of monopoly on systematic persecution. Such pictures distort what actually happened and what could be repeated.

Studying the prisoners with the pink triangle demands a more integrated approach, abandoning exaggerated figures and simplistic slogans; it requires paying attention to the macro-structure of the concentration camps and all their inmates, to the fate of individuals and small groups, as well as to the position and function of the camps in society as a whole.

SENTENCING TO CONCENTRATION CAMPS

The Third Reich began its persecution of homosexual men immediately after the Nazi seizure of power. In the fall of 1933, homosexuals and pimps arrived at Concentration Camp Fuhlsbüttel as a new category of prisoner. In a top-level meeting of the Hamburg City Administration on November 13, 1933, the Head of Police was also asked to "pay special attention to transvestites and to deliver them to the concentration camps if necessary."[1]

The police set to work to destroy the homosexual subculture, performing raids that are described as exotic events in memoirs of the period. Not only were the public places scrutinized, but individuals were as well. Our interviewee J.R. was arrested in 1934, while spending the night at home with his lover, and was sentenced to six weeks' imprisonment. After this, he was detained for two years in Concentration Camp Dachau. One day in 1936 the rumor spread through Concentration Camp Dachau that in nearby Munich one such raid had been carried out. "A few days later a few hundred of these unfortunate creatures joined us in the camp. . . ."[2] In the summer of 1936 many raids took place in Hamburg and other locales. On one night alone in Concentration Camp Fuhlsbüttel, "80 homosexuals were brought in. . . . Nearly every day a few arrived.''[3] Such massive checks might possibly have had the aim of "cleaning things up" for the Olympics. In Concentration Camp Mauthausen on June 29, 1939, fifty-two homosexuals were brought in. The memoirist Heger, involved sexually with a fellow student who was the son of a high Nazi official, was ordered to report to the Gestapo in Vienna in 1939. He was sentenced to six months' imprisonment but spent the duration of the war in various concentration camps.

Directives defining "when someone was to be taken into preventive custody," (the official terminology for referral to a concentration camp) were sent down from the Reich Main Security Office, the head of the SS-Administration on April 4, 1938 (in the case of morals charges: to take effect immediately), and July 12, 1940 (" . . . all homosexuals who have *seduced* more than one partner are after their release from prison to be placed in preventive custody.") In an edict of March 21, 1942, R. Heydrich, a prominent Nazi official, decreed that the prevention of abortion and homosexuality would serve the purposes of maintaining racial purity. "It would contradict our best interests, were foreign . . . ethnic groups . . . aided in maintaining themselves." Suspects belonging to "foreign ethnic groups" were not only to be disciplined, but, according to the edict, removed from the territory of the Reich. In accordance with the idea of "racial purity," which was an attempt to keep the Fatherland free from taint, the persecution of homosexuals took place largely within the confines of the Reich. For this reason our research refers only to concentration camps located within Germany.

The legal justification for the persecution of homosexuals was Paragraph 175 of the Penal Code, which proscribed homosexual acts between males above twenty-one. "Seduction," defined as homosexual acts with minors from fourteen to twenty or with a dependent, was covered in paragraphs 174 and 176. Reference to these crimes, however, is relatively rare in the documents. A sample of the 250 inmates for whom documentation is more or less complete is shown in Table 1.

If one realizes that in the case of sex between people who are of-age and therefore not in a dependent relationship, there can hardly be a question of "seduction" as defined in the Penal Code, then for nine out of ten pink-triangle prisoners even the SS's own official criteria were not met. In many cases, the simplest evidence of a sexual act was missing.[4] On the other hand, the figures prove that collision with the courts and a sentencing to a conventional prison were for many homosexual men the first step toward a concentration camp—an irrevocable step. Those who could avoid prison generally escaped referral to the lethal camps. This is demonstrated by camp data and by

TABLE 1

PREVIOUS CONVICTIONS OF PINK-TRIANGLE PRISONERS

	%	n
Conviction according to paragraphs 174 and 176	10	26
Conviction according to paragraph 175 alone	76	189
No conviction according to paragraphs 174, 175 or 176	5	13
No data	9	22
	100	250

various court records: A considerable percentage of all pink-triangle prisoners had been convicted previously for homosexuality, but the total number of pink-triangle prisoners was much less than the 10,000 men convicted for homosexuality *each year* during the Nazi era. One can assume that in the Third Reich the same circles were spared conviction as traditionally enjoyed this privilege: highly-placed homosexual men. In 1937, Himmler issued an Exception to General Policy, according to which "the incarceration of an actor or an artist on the ground of unnatural vice required [Himmler's] express permission," a measure from which several prominent theater people profitted.

The total number of the inmates with the pink triangles will never be ascertained, for the documentation on them was kept too unreliably. This is in spite of the fact that the inmates were subjected to roll-calls, which often lasted for hours each day, regardless of the weather. To estimate figures, we consulted the head-counts that were taken sporadically and that have been only partially preserved, in which the approximate number and categories of prisoners present on a given day were recorded. On the basis of forty such counts (from seven camps between 1938 and 1945 and, as far as possible, taken from the data at three-month intervals) the following tentative and approximate estimates can be drawn.

The number of homosexual inmates incarcerated at any given moment in any given concentration camp varied (just as, for example, the number of political prisoners also varied). At times there were only a few—sometimes less than ten—but very rarely were there none at all. From one to eight pink-triangles were registered in Buchenwald on February 16, 1938; in Mauthausen on September 28, 1939; in Natzweiler on September 30, 1942; and in Sachsenhausen on April 30, 1943. At other times or in other camps, up to a few hundred pink triangles were reported. The highest figures known to us at present include the following: 150 in Dachau in March and September of 1938;

194 in Buchenwald on January 2, 1945; and "a few hundred" in Neuengamme. From 1933 to 1939, before construction on the camps had been completed, and when they were not yet filled to capacity, the percentage of homosexual prisoners was more striking: perhaps one percent of the total inmate population. Initially, in some of the smaller, more isolated camps, higher percentages occurred—one can speak of five to ten percent (which might be the reason for the occasional overestimation of the total figures). During the war the camps expanded rapidly and the percentage of homosexual inmates became somewhat lower; within the territories of the Reich one finds only one or a few pink-triangles among 1000 other inmates. Conservatively interpreting the evidence uncovered up to this time, we may hazard the following estimations: Immediately following the Nazi seizure of power, at any given moment, there was a total of several hundred homosexual prisoners in the concentration camps; later the figure would be around 1000. The total number of officially-defined homosexual prisoners ever incarcerated in the camps was about 10,000 (but it could be as low as 5,000 or as high as 15,000).

The documents studied told little about the social background of the various inmate groups, but did show small differences according to age grouping. Political prisoners dominated up to age twenty-eight, homosexual prisoners from age twenty-nine to thirty-four, and Jehovah's Witnesses from age thirty-five to fifty-four. The median age for homosexual prisoners was thirty-seven. Presumably these figures indicate the median age at which individuals engaged in the proscribed activities.

In the matter of religious affiliation, the data varied widely (see Table 2). It is to be expected that the Jehovah's Witnesses belonged to neither of the two main religious groups (Protestant and Roman Catholic), but the religious differences between homosexual and political prisoners are open to interpretation.

Only the data on prisoners' professions permitted conclusions as to socioeconomic positions (see Table 3). We used a three-strata model, with "lower-class" corresponding to manual laborers; "middle-class"

TABLE 2

RELIGIOUS AFFILIATION OF THE PRISONERS

	Protestant (%)	Catholic (%)	Other/Non-Religious (%)	Total (%)	N
Homosexual prisoners	63	27	10	100	241
Political prisoners	35	34	31	100	86
Jehovah's Witnesses	3	1	96	100	100

PRISONER MARKINGS IN NAZI CONCENTRATION CAMPS

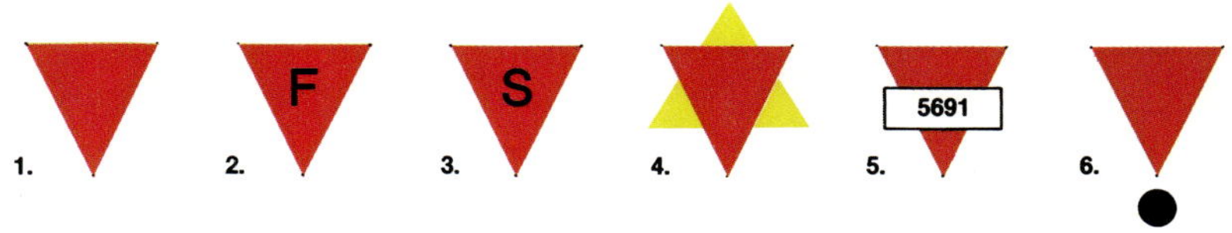

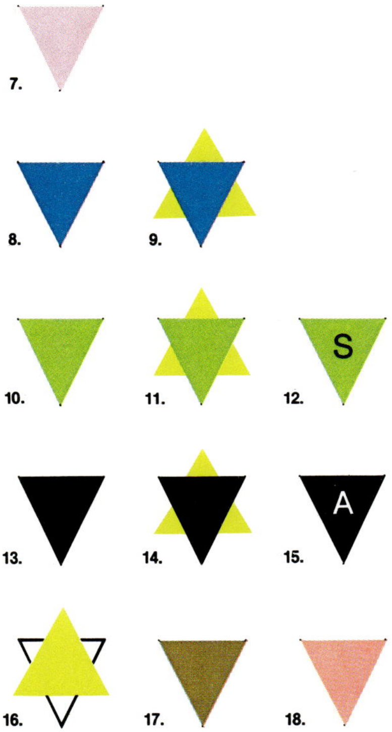

1. Political Prisoner (German)
2. Political Prisoner (French)
3. Political Prisoner (Spanish)
4. Political Prisoner (Jewish)
5. Political Prisoner (Special)
6. Political Prisoner (Penal Company)
7. Jehovah's Witness
8. Emigré
9. Emigré (Jewish)
10. Convict (in Protective Custody)
11. Convict (Jewish)
12. Convict (in Security Custody)
13. "Asocial" Prisoner
14. "Asocial" Prisoner (Jewish)
15. Labor Disciplinary Prisoner—"Loafer"
16. Race Defiler (Jewish)
17. Gypsy
18. Homosexual

Erwin J. Haeberle 1980 (after Kogon: **The Theory and Practice of Hell**)

TABLE 3

SOCIAL STATUS OF THE PRISONERS

	Lower (%)	Middle (%)	Upper-Middle to Upper (%)	Total (%)	N
Homosexual prisoners	52	16	32	100	883
Political prisoners	74	9	17	100	203
Jehovah's Witnesses	73	11	17	101	612

to nonmanagerial employees, lower and middle civil servants, and those self-employed on a small scale; and "upper-middle-class to upper-class" to managerial employees, higher civil servants, priests, and the medium- and high-scale self-employed. More than for the other two control groups, the homosexual prisoners represented the

THE DAILY LIFE OF HOMOSEXUAL INMATES

Prisoners arriving in a concentration camp embarked on a life that had very little resemblance to anything they had known previously. Many memoirs touch on this. The SS asked everyone, man for man, the reasons they had been convicted. A priest described an arrival in Dachau on September 12, 1941:

"One was there on account of paragraph 175. He was cuffed to and fro, had to confess his crime in a loud voice to everyone, describe in detail exactly what he'd done and how, and then they fell upon him again, cuffing and kicking. One could see their cruel pleasure and sadism plainly."

Another writer made the following observation in Neuengamme: Upon the delivery of a fresh convoy of prisoners, "the heads of the Jews and the homosexuals were shaved completely bald, so that they could be recognized. Nearly without exception, upon arrival they were beaten in their cells. . . ." This comes from Dachau in the beginning of 1936: "They were particularly picked on by the SS, humiliated in the most degrading fashion and corporally punished at every opportunity." In Sachsenhausen on April 19, 1940, during the arrival procedure, "A man who, as developed from his records, had been convicted according to paragraph 175 twenty years ago but had concealed this fact up to now, was then and there beaten to death." A former inmate recalls how, immediately after arrival in Natzweiler, he was brutally mistreated by an SS Sergeant, merely on account of his pink triangle.[5]

Two things should be kept in mind whenever reports of special incidences are cited: Homosexuals were not in all places and at all times exceptionally badly treated and they were not the only category of inmate subject to extreme degradation. Equally vulnerable were other groups, such as the Jews and, later, the "Non-Aryans."

Homosexual prisoners were always marked. In the first years there were varying symbols; among others these included yellow bands with an "A" (which sometimes was translated as "Arschficker"—ass-fucker); large, round, black dots; and a large 175 drawn on the inmate's back. In the course of time, a pink cloth triangle sewn to the clothing was introduced. Prisoners of other categories wore triangles of various colors (red for political prisoners, green for criminals, violet for Jehovah's Witnesses, yellow for Jews, and brown for gypsies). Of one camp it is reported that the pink triangle was appreciably larger than any other insignia and sometimes was augmented with a yellow bar to increase its visibility and distinguish it from other triangles.[6] Slang preserved in various memoris shows that categorization of homosexual inmates also occurred on the verbal level, both in articles about the concentration camp and in official papers, where they were referred to as "Homos," "175-ers," "warmer Bruder" (queer), "Sittenstrolch" (faggot), "schwules Arschloch" (queer asshole), or "Arschficker" (ass-fucker).

The housing of homosexual prisoners was handled differently at various concentration camps. Occasionally it was recorded in the files or elsewhere that homosexual inmates were housed in special blocks, barracks, or quarters reserved for them alone; this is true of Dachau, of Sachsenhausen from 1939-1940 and from 1944-1945, and of Flossenbürg from 1940-1941. In Sachsenhausen this was conceived of as "isolation" and was so designated. In other camps and at other times such segregation did not occur, for example in Sachsenhausen in the initial years as well as in 1943, and in Flossenbürg after April 1941. This either has been reported explicitly or can be deduced from the absence of contrary information. Sometimes the SS took advantage of segregation where it was practiced. Rudolf Hoess, onetime Block Leader in Dachau, reports in his memoirs: "At my suggestion all homosexuals were grouped together. They were assigned a Room Elder who knew how to take care of them."[7] Despite the solicitous tone, what is actually meant is that the homosexual inmates, once grouped together, could be subject to special repressions in addition to the already generally fearful conditions in the camps. Heger mentions the existence in Flossenbürg of "special rules for the gay wing of [his] block" and reports of Sachsenhausen in 1940:

"we were only permitted to sleep in a night-shirt with our hands outside the blanket. . . . The windows were covered with inch-thick ice at the time. Whoever was discovered sleeping

in their underpants—there were checks nearly every night—received the punishment of being taken outdoors, doused with several buckets of water, and being forced to stand there for an hour or so.''[8]

It is important to remember, however, that homosexual prisoners were not always segregated in isolated living quarters, and when they were this did not necessarily always result in increased repression on the part of the SS. The inmate R.K., who as a wearer of the pink triangle was in "isolation" in Sachsenhausen in 1940 and, after three years in Neuengamme, returned there in 1943, reports:

"The particularly bad situation of the 175-ers in Sachsenhausen had been ameliorated, at the time they were all in the 'Main Camp.' . . . Only in the last winter of 1944/45 were the 175-ers again grouped apart, but not treated worse."

Any group-forming or contact between homosexual inmates immediately raised the suspicion of the guard personnel. Hoess claims to ave observed that "Whenever they found the opportunity they were l over each other. No matter how physically far gone they were, they rsevered in their vice."[9] We found only one isolated report ocumenting "the existence of any kind of comradeship" among omosexual inmates (interviewee J.R.). The homosexual population equently must have been too small in numbers to have organized utual aid, for example, by engaging in barter. Possibilities for comunication with inmates of other categories also were limited, on the e hand because of the personal discredit that might result for a isoner of another category seen to associate with a homosexual inmate, and on the other hand because of the occasional formal suspenn of all contact privileges.[10] Of course this situation mirrors the cial status of all homosexual men in the Germany of the time, but in e camps their stigmatization was exacerbated to a perilous degree.

Besides mutual contact and communication with fellow prisoners of her categories, social integration in the concentration camps involved third aspect, that of contact with the outside world. Under conditions f extreme stress, such as incarceration, family ties are an important ource of security. Obviously the homosexual prisoner, as compared to mates in other categories, was less often in the position to receive pport from a conjugal family. This can be deduced by comparing the ta on marital status and number of children with our control group e Tables 4 and 5). The prisoners with the pink triangles were three five times less often married (or widowed) than the others and nearly twice as often without children. Divorced prisoners were counted as single, for the reason that, after the completion of divorce proceedings, contact with the wife's family usually was suspended. Nothing has been transmitted concerning the prisoners' continuation of contacts with parental family or with friends and acquaintances. It is safe to

TABLE 4

INTEGRATION IN A CONJUGAL FAMILY

	Married, Widowed (%)	Single, Divorced (%)	Total (%)	N
Homosexual prisoners	16	84	100	705
Political prisoners	51	49	100	202
Jehovah's Witnesses	74	26	100	597

assume that a pink-triangle prisoner could expect to hear nothing more from his former friends and acquaintances, if they themselves were homosexual and had to consider their own safety. Our interviewee, J.R., relates that after his release from Dachau in 1936 he was "avoided by a part of his gay acquaintances."

Prisoners of all categories had to work. They were forced to perform the most grueling physical labor, which only occasionally had any rational purpose and at times was completely senseless, for example, transferring mountains of gravel or sand from place to place. Heger reports how pink-triangle prisoners were required to move the snow in front of their block from the left to the right of the camp street in the morning, and in the afternoon to return the same mass of snow to its original position, carrying it in their coats and shovelling it with their bare hands.[11] The work assignments varied from camp to camp and from one period to another, and even within the same camp and in the same period, were so totally different in nature that it is impossible to describe general rules. During the course of the war, however, efforts were made to transform the rationale of the camps from the custodial and rehabilitative to the productive, and to utilize the work of the prisoners in an economically rational way.[12] As a consequence there were attempts to avoid deliberate mistreatment and to raise nourishment and health conditions to the physical minimum. This, however, hardly affected the death rates.

TABLE 5

NUMBER OF CHILDREN

	None (%)	One Child (%)	More than One (%)	Total (%)	N
Homosexual prisoners	82	9	9	100	601
Political prisoners	50	19	31	100	185
Jehovah's Witnesses	44	17	39	100	500

A perhaps extreme example of a work commando, and one that had the reputation among the prisoners of being a liquidation squad, was one outside-work commando at Buchenwald. This bore the name "Dora" and later became the Concentration Camp Mittelbau. We base the following description on the research of Bornemann and Broszat on the "inferno of this onetime underground camp."[13]

In a massif in the southern Harz Mountains, a mile-long tunnel system was excavated by some 10,000 prisoners, mostly foreigners. The V-2 rockets were produced here. The prisoners performed the heavy construction work of excavation—digging, laying explosives, leveling floors, pouring concrete, laying rails—and all at forced speed. In the winter of 1943-1944, when there was no barrack, they had to sleep at the work sites. They slept on the ground in four tunnels. These were 130 yards long with a diameter of 12 1/2 yards, open at only one end, and therefore poorly ventilated. The prisoners had only a few lamps and were without toilet facilities or running water. Later there were four-tier bunk beds three-and-a-half yards long and designed to hold four inmates per tier. There were two work shifts. When one crew departed, the other returned to occupy the bunks. In this way the capacity of each sleeping tunnel was doubled from 1000 to 2000 men. The low temperatures, as well as the moist air resulting from the exhalations of a thousand men, promoted colds, tuberculosis, and physical deterioration. The prisoners were mustered daily (later weekly) in roll calls that involved standing in formation for hours outdoors. The work itself took place in a particularly toxic environment of stone-, plaster-, and cement-dust. The result was a fearful increase in misery and mass deaths during the winter of 1943-1944. Although the youngest and healthiest prisoners were selected for Dora, 3000 died in a few months and a further 3000 had to be removed as no longer fit for work. Transportation decreased their survival chances still further.

In the contingent of German prisoners who were sent to Dora, the homosexual men were disproportionately represented: twice as many as political prisoners and five times as many as Jehovah's Witnesses, as far as we can tell from data on the work commandos (see Table 6).

TABLE 6

INMATES IN CONCENTRATION CAMP BUCHENWALD
LISTED WITH DORA

	%	N
Homosexual prisoners	11	839
Political prisoners	3	191
Jehovah's Witnesses	1	671

A series of reports shows that the pink-triangle inmates in other camps as well were intentionally placed in the most taxing work commandos, for example in the gravel pit of Dachau in 1934-1936.[14] In Dachau they were also given the task of pulling the street-roller. This was a five-ton iron roller used for leveling streets and was filled with water to attain the necessary weight. This work was thought of as "absolute slave labor."[15] In several books the clay pit of the brick works in Sachsenhausen is described in great detail: All the camp's homosexual inmates worked here.[16]

In spite of all the reports on the allotment of particularly grueling or dangerous work to pink-triangles, such as picking up unexploded bombs after the air raids on Hamburg,[17] we must not forget that inmates from other categories also were used in this way and actually formed the large majority of these commandos. What is more, much of the work by all inmates was undertaken in similarly unthinkable conditions. The assignment to work commandos changed from time to time, and many pink-triangle prisoners also succeeded in getting less taxing work; indeed, at times, they got the "soft" jobs (cf. our interviewee, J.R., who worked in Clothing Issue in Dachau in 1936). A great deal of luck must have been operating here, for the "group" of homosexual inmates was anything but organized, unlike the political and criminal prisoners, who fairly consistently were successful in getting the good jobs and retaining them for members of their own groups. This is reflected in the quantitative results of our research. Among the types of work commandos, we differentiated between hard and light duties. The latter included kitchen, laundry, administration, and other indoor duties that afforded a chance for health and prolonged life. As shown in Table 7, compared with our control groups, the homosexual prisoners were eight times less likely to obtain the light duties. Work assignments often had little to do with the actual qualifications of the inmates. The homosexual men tended to have worked in nonmanual occupations (commerce, public services) before internment, as may be deduced from current research and from studies of the previous occupational

TABLE 7

ASSIGNMENT TO LIGHT DUTIES
(MANY INMATES ARE LISTED MORE THAN ONCE)

	Listed		Total No. of Inmates
	n	%	
Homosexual prisoners	9	0.6%	1,572
Political prisoners	10	4.6%	219
Jehovah's Witnesses	44	5.9	751

TABLE 8

PREVIOUS OCCUPATION

	Manual (%)	Desk-Jobs (%)	Total (%)	N
Homosexual prisoners	56	44	100	850
Political prisoners	77	23	100	198
Jehovah's Witnesses	81	19	100	590

status of "perverts" convicted in 1936.[18] The majority of the personal records we studied contained records of former employment (see Table 8). It is no longer possible to say, however, whether these were falsified with an eye for increasing survival chances, as often was done by experienced inmates or inmates given some advance warning.

In addition to the hardship of executing the assigned task, the work commandos involved a second aspect that was relevant to survival: surveillance by the guards and Kapos. After his arrival in Concentration Camp Natzweiler, our interviewee Dr. J.L. and another pink-triangle were kicked and beaten constantly by the SS and the Kapos: "In the first weeks of my stay in the camp, I often felt I was the sole whipping boy everybody could vent their aggression on." Natzweiler's Block Elder arranged transferral to another commando. In the Sachsenhausen work squads, the pink-triangle prisoners were for years the objects of scarcely checked aggression from the SS. The otherwise hesitant interviewee H.N. reports: "It's indisputable that many of them were tortured, shot, and beaten to death on their work commandos." Heger describes the construction of a firing range that the SS put into use before its completion, utilizing the homosexual inmates working in the earthworks there as living targets.[19] The behavior of Rode, the Commandant of Concentration Camp Fuhlsbüttel, who otherwise was concerned about making conditions more humane in his camp, can be cited as a further example of the special treatment imposed on homosexual prisoners. According to reports, Rode "was filled with an unspeakable rage" by them and they "were required to perform all duties in double-quick—until they dropped. If there was no work to be done, they had to play 'sports'."[20]

It is reported of several camps and for several periods that the prisoners with the pink triangle received more brutal extra punishments than did the other groups.[21] In Dachau, for example, a homosexual inmate who had made waves with his "effeminate," "queen"-like behavior, got the "tree," that is, he was hung from a pole with his hands behind his back.[22] In Sachshausen all those previously convicted under paragraph 176 spent their first three months in the stockade company.[23] We reviewed the material still extant from the so-called "Special Section" at Buchenwald for the period July 1938 to March 1940 and found data on differentiated treatment for our control group, as shown in Table 9.

Not all SS men participated in the cruelties against homosexual inmates, however; some kept themselves at a distance, and some actually tried to prevent incidents of abuse. Also, the status of a "K-inmate" (an inmate subject to special procedures), although encountered relatively seldom in our research among the Jehovah's Witnesses (0.5%), was comparatively frequent among political (3.7%) and homosexual (3.9%) prisoners. The position of homosexual inmates as whipping boys finally improved in the beginning of the 1940s, when they no longer occupied the lowest level of the internal camp status hierarchy. At that time they were relieved from their former position by the Jewish and Eastern European prisoners, who apparently were disliked more and regarded as more dangerous by the surveillance personnel.

SURVIVAL AND DEATH

The basic question for every concentration-camp inmate, especially after the war started, was: *Can I survive or must I die?* In the face of the total number of deaths in the camps, the details of living conditions just presented might seem less important; but we must recall that the difference between life and death also depended on the prison conditions as encountered by the individual. Survivors of the camps were those who were released (a frequent event before the war, but after the beginning of the war limited to special cases), those who escaped (in which only a few succeeded), and those who were liberated after the war (which an appreciable number of the German, non-Jewish inmate population experienced). On April 14, 1945, SS leader Himmler had cabled the directive: "No inmate may fall into the hands of the enemy alive," but this was scarcely obeyed. In any event, because of the illnesses and damages they had suffered during their incarceration, many inmates did not live long after their liberation. "Survival" for most of the inmates included a reduced life expectancy under the shadow of permanent physical and psychic damage.

The total number of concentration-camp deaths never will be known; in particular, the fate of the homosexual prisoners remains uncertain. For 28% (N = 1572) of the homosexual prisoners, as opposed to 19% (N = 751) and 16% (N = 219) of the political prisoners, there is no certain information on the nature of the termination of imprisonment. It is not rare, however, despite the paucity of available information, to uncover detailed reports of the greater probability of

TABLE 9

REFERRAL TO THE SPECIAL SECTION IN BUCHENWALD
(1938-1940)

	Referral Procedure	Duration (Average)	N
Homosexual prisoners	Automatic for all; no further explanation	Unlimited	93
Political prisoners	For 1 out of 10; some reason given	For 144 cases: 2.7 months For 62 cases: unlimited	206
Jehovah's Witnesses	Automatic for all, but only after first arrival	3 months	191

death for men of the pink triangle. Such data come from heterosexual inmates, who had a wider perspective on conditions in the camps. Independent of each other, two authors report of Dachau: "The inmates with the pink triangles never lived long, they were exterminated by the SS with systematic swiftness;" and "In general these unfortunate creatures did not survive long."[24]

In Sachsenhausen, E. Büge, a political prisoner who worked in the Political Section of the camp, kept a diary that has been preserved. For the period between April 1940 and June 1942 he records that 395 homosexual inmates had died (with a frequency increasing yearly). The ultimate death toll is not known; on April 30, 1943, only six men were still alive. H. Lienau, another political prisoner, also reports: "The SS could count themselves satisfied if by nightfall a few of the 175-ers had been picked off: but when in January 1943 the number of homosexuals eliminated in one day reached the sum of twenty-four, the Commandant's Office became somewhat disquieted. A pause then ensued."[25]

At certain times and places the pink-triangles were left alone, for example in Concentration Camp Neuengamme, and since absolutely no data are available from certain camps with regard to the treatment of homosexual prisoners (for example, for Concentration Camp Flossenbürg or Mauthausen),[26] one may assume that in these camps homosexual prisoners ran no more risks than did other groups. Such conclusions must be made cautiously, however, for the smallness of the homosexual group made it difficult for others to observe them and accordingly diminished access to the particulars of their fates.

This reduced visibility is apparent in three letters we received from ex-inmates of Buchenwald, in response to our request for information. We had distributed extensive questionnaires through several organizations of ex-concentration-camp inmates. As remembered by these three, there were never more than two or three dozen homosexual prisoners in Buchenwald and they never received any "special" treatment. According to our research this was probably true for long periods of time, but it is overshadowed by certain temporary developments. For example, the number of pink-triangle inmates exceeded 100 in 1942, again in 1943, and rose at the beginning of 1945 to nearly 200. As regards the severity of treatment, in the period between the end of 1939 and the end of 1941, when the figures indeed hovered around thirty, there were twenty-six dead, which allows one to deduce an extraordinarily high death rate.

Of the survival-threatening factors to which the inmates were subjected, the homosexual prisoners appear to have been particularly vulnerable to physical mistreatment by the surveillance personnel (SS and Kapos) and at times to the dangerous transports. Every prisoner was afraid of the transports. After all, he had to leave a place he had grown accustomed to and embark on a dangerous journey, often lasting days, which more often than not cost him his health or life. In a sample of the "Change of Station" lists, three times we came upon records of between twenty-seven and forty homosexual inmates who were "transferred" from Buchenwald to other camps. In the transports, homosexual prisoners formed the "highest percentage, as the camp had an understandable tendency to eliminate those who were viewed as its least important or valuable elements, and those who were viewed as distinctly worthless."[27] The only hope for avoiding transport lay in entertaining good relations with the inmates most influential in the self-policing activities of the camps; yet this, as a rule, was a possibility denied the homosexual prisoner. There is even a report from Sachsenhausen that homosexual inmates were made the special targets of transports to the gas ovens.[28]

On the other hand, there is no indication that homosexual men chose suicide more frequently than others, although R. Hoess, in his memoirs (which include hair-raising descriptions of the instability presumed to be found "in these soft natures") might lead one to believe that many committed suicide.[29] In the 393 documents we uncovered where cause of death is listed, suicide by homosexual men occurs only three times, no more frequently than the rate (1%) for political prisoners and Jehovah's Witnesses.

The death rates for our three categories (ascertained on the basis of official registration) and the rates of release are shown in Table 10. The death rate for homosexual prisoners (60%) was half again as high as for political prisoners (41%) and Jehovah's Witnesses (35%). Correspondingly, upon liberation the political prisoners and Jehovah's Witnesses remaining in the camps (41% and 57% respectively) showed a higher survival rate than the homosexual prisoners (26%). Reprieve and release were quite rare, least frequently for the Jehovah's Witnesses (8%) and slightly more frequently for the homosexual (13%) and political (18%) prisoners.

TABLE 10

DISPOSITION OF PRISONERS
SO FAR AS KNOWN

	Dead (%)	Liberated (%)	Released (%)	Escaped (%)	Total (%)	N
Homosexual prisoners	60	26	13	0.4	99	1,136
Political prisoners	41	41	18	0.6	101	181
Jehovah's Witnesses	35	57	8	0	100	609

Those pink-triangle inmates most threatened with death were the very young and the older prisoners. Only for inmates between twenty-one and thirty were chances of survival at all good. These tendencies are shown in Figure 1. How much survival depended on adapting to conditions in the camps is shown by the correlation between length of incarceration and the nature of the termination of imprisonment. As shown in Table 11, among the homosexual inmates who were in the concentration camps for one year or less, four out of five died, whereas for those who were imprisoned for longer than two years, three out of four survived.

FIGURE 1

NATURE OF THE TERMINATION OF IMPRISONMENT

RELATIVE TO AGE FOR THE PINK-TRIANGLE INMATES

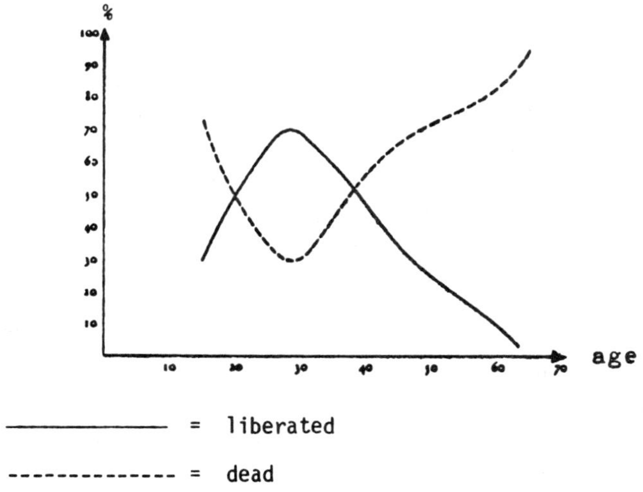

TABLE 11

NATURE OF TERMINATION OF IMPRISONMENT FOR THE PINK TRIANGLE, RELATIVE TO LENGTH OF INCARCERATION

	Dead (%)	Released/ Liberated (%)	Total (%)	N
Up to 1 year	79	21	100	541
1-2 years	43	57	100	203
More than 2 years	25	75	100	263

THE SOCIAL RANK OF THE PINK TRIANGLE

The reasons for the different fates of the various categories of prisoner can be explained sociologically in terms of the stratification system of the camps and in terms of social control.[30]

In the memoirs, as well as in more recent studies by homosexual authors, one often reads that the homosexual inmates were the worst off of all prisoners in the concentration camps. Taking into account the personal involvement of these authors and considering accepted methodological standards for the gathering of historical data, one hesitates to rely exclusively on such sources. The data base remains precarious, as most of the "noninvolved" authors either say nothing about matters of social stratification in the camps or remain silent on the matter of the pink triangle. Concise and accurate information confirming that the lowest rank was occupied by homosexual prisoners is available, however, for Concentration Camp Fühlbuttel, where, together with pimps, they figured in the lowest of three ranks, that is below the political prisoners and criminals.[31] In Buchenwald, from 1938 to 1942 "they belonged to the lowest caste of the camp precisely at the worst period."[32]

Other fragmentary information indicates a consistently low, if not the lowest, position in the hierarchy of the camps: Mocked and placed at a disadvantage because of the color of their triangle, the homosexual inmates found themselves on the level accorded the most contempt, at least when compared with nonforeign, non-Jewish inmates. Even when an individual succeeded in raising himself, his success would have to be attributed to his personal initiative and qualities, rather than to a sudden reassessment of the status of his triangle. In this fashion Heger became a subforeman, then foreman, and in the end even a Kapo, after having been for years the lover of influential inmates.[33] The literature we reviewed contained a few additional references to homosexual individuals who "made it" to higher positions in the camps: a prison doctor in Sachsenhausen, Kapos and foremen in Dachau, a Block Elder in Dora, as well as a Kapo in Auschwitz.[34] These isolated cases, however, scarcely made much of a dent: of 1572 pink-triangles, a Kapo was listed only once; of 219 red-triangles, twice.

The prisoner's position within the stratification of the camp was of great relevance to his daily life, for it determined the quality of his chances for work, shelter, food, medical care, and time off. Among the inmates, the "VIPs" and the "middle class" enjoyed the best work conditions, obtained extra rations, and in this way could avoid the much-feared transports. As opposed to this group, the "masses" were subjected to the normal prison conditions without being able to work against them. Only those with some pull with the VIPs had relative security in dangerous situations. According to the Buchenwald inmate VIP, Kogon:

> *Hundreds of valuable people could only be saved by juggling with the work sheets, in part by secretly removing their names from lists of those designated for death-transports, in part by smuggling them into work-squads operating outside the camp when their life in the base-camp was endangered.*[35]

In anomic situations the acquisition of power and privileges can proceed only via group organization. The homosexual prisoners, generally bereft of power and largely disorganized, remained at the bottom of the camp stratification. Their social position explains their liquidation.

NOTES

1. H. Timpke, in *Studien zur Geschichte der Konzentrationslager* (Stuttgart, 1970), p. 18.
2. H. Burkhard, *Tanz mal Jude,* 2nd ed. (Nürnberg, 1967), p. 68.
3. P. Zylmann, "Report 1938" (Forschungsstelle hamburg), p. 24.
4. H. Lienau, *Zwölf Jahre Nacht* (Flensburg, 1949), p. 69.
5. S. Hess, *Dachau—eine Welt ohne Gott* (Nürnberg, 1946), p. 62; H. C. Meier, *So war es* (Hamburg, 1946), p. 46; Burkhard, p. 69; A. Weiss-Rüthel, *Nacht und Nebel* (München, 1946), p. 51—cf. H. Heger, *Die Männer mit dem rosa Winkel* (Hamburg, 1972), pp. 33f.; Interviewee Dr. J. L.
6. Heger, pp. 32f.; E. Kuster, *Weltreise nach Dachau* (Bad Wildbad, 1947), p. 162.
7. R. Hoess, *Kommandant in Auschwitz* (Stuttgart, 1958), p. 77 (English edition: New York, 1961).
8. Heger, pp. 36, 57.
9. Hoess, p. 78.
10. cf. Heger, p. 37.
11. Ibid., p. 39.
12. cf. M. Broszat in *Anatomie des SS-Staates* (Olten, 1965), 2: 149-52 (English edition: New York, 1968).
13. M. Bornemann and M. Broszat in *Studien.*
14. Interviewee J. R.
15. Hoess, p. 77; Burkhard, pp. 37, 39.

16. L. D. Classen von Neudegg in *Humanitas* (1954): 58.
17. Interviewee R. K.
18. cf. M. Dannecker and R. Reiche, *Der gewöhnliche Homosexuelle* (Frankfurt a.M., 1974), pp. 318-22; cf. A. Hurst, "Die Homosexualität" (Jur. Diss., Freiburg, 1949), p. 158.
19. Heger, pp. 51-53.
20. Zylmann, p. 24; Timpke, pp. 21f.
21. E. Gostner, *1000 Tage im KZ* (Mannheim, 1946), pp. 40, 70f; cf. Lienau, p. 70; witnesses' statements in H.G. Dam and R. Giordano, eds., *KZ-Verbrechen vor deutschen Gerichten* (Stuttgart, 1962), pp. 170, 189; Heger, pp. 115-18; communication with interviewees R. B. and W. M.
22. Gostner, pp. 40, 70f.
23. Weiss-Rüthel, p. 87; communication with Interviewee R. K.
24. R. Schnabel, *Die Frommen in der Hölle* (Frankfurt a. M., 1966), p. 53; P. Berben, *Histoire du camp de concentration de Dachau* (Brussels, 1968), p. 19.
25. Lienau, p. 70.
26. G. Rabitsch in *Studien,* p. 154.
27. E. Kogon, *Der SS-Staat,* 1946 (München, 1974), p. 264—English edition: New York, 1950.
28. Lienau, p. 165.
29. Hoess, pp. 78f.
30. For a systematic account of these aspects see R. Lautmann, *Seminar: Gesellschaft und Homosexualität* (Frankfurt, 1977) and R. Lautmann and E. Vismar, *Pink Triangle: The Social History of Antihomosexual Persecution in Nazi-Germany* (forthcoming book).
31. Zylmann, pp. 15-21; Timpke, p. 21.
32. Kogon, p. 262.
33. cf. Heger, pp. 57, 79f, 101.
34. cf. Classen von Neudegg, p. 163; B. Kautsky, *Teufel und Verdammte* (Zürich, 1946), p. 146; W. Hein, *Lebens-und-Arbeitsbedingungen der Häftlinge im KL "Dora-Mittelbau"* (Warschau, 1969), p. 39; report about E. W.
35. Kogon, p. 66; cf. P. d'Harcourt, *The Real Enemy* (London, 1967), pp. 142-55, 169f.

THE HOMOSEXUAL RIGHTS MOVEMENT IN THE UNITED STATES
A TRADITIONALLY OVERLOOKED AREA OF AMERICAN HISTORY

Salvatore J. Licata, PhD

ABSTRACT: In this short account, the homosexual rights movement in the United States, traditionally overlooked by historians, is presented as a minority movement. References are made to the European origins and the early efforts in America. The author sees eight stages in the growth of the movement. In Stage 1, from 1908 through 1945, there were sporadic individual attempts to defend the rights of homosexual men and women. In the years immediately following World War II, Stage 2 witnessed the dawning of a minority consciousness among gay people living in the cities. Stage 3, from 1950 to 1952, represented a search for identity. During the years 1952-1953, Stage 4, righteous indignation flared up within the movement. In Stage 5, from 1953 to 1960, the movement emphasized information and educational approaches. The decade of the sixties, Stage 6, brought civil-rights activism to the homophile movement. In Stage 7, beginning in 1969, gay liberation emerged. Finally, in Stage 8 (1973-1979), the movement and the government responded to each other through institutional channels. The 1970s ended with two major confrontations, giving the decade of 1969 to 1979 a unity and sense of accomplishment.

During the decade of the 1970s, hundreds of thousands of gay men and lesbians marched into the pages of American history. As if out of nowhere, there emerged an extensive minority defined solely by its members' sexual identity and composed of two very distinct segments. Gay men and lesbian women suddenly were visible in both rural and urban areas, but primarily in the inner cities. The social and sexual complexities within this subculture and the host of institutions it supported were evidence that a sizable homosexual minority had been in existence for longer than previously recognized. For reasons both personal and professional, American historians had chosen to ignore the presence of sexual nonconformity as a facet of American life. That is, it was ignored until homosexual mass militancy forced society and its historians to acknowledge the presence and impact of gay men and lesbians. This paper delineates the institutional attempts by homosexual Americans to organize for social and political reasons and explores the shifts and changes that occurred within the movement from its sketchy early history up through the well-documented 1970s.

Before examining the homosexual rights movement in America, however, it is necessary to make a few comments regarding earlier European efforts. The two countries that had the greatest influence on America were Germany and England. The Germans, most notably Karoly Maria Benkert and Karl Heinrich Ulrichs, began defending homosexual rights in the mid-nineteenth century. The first homosexual rights organization, the Scientific Humanitarian Committee (SHC) founded in 1897 under the leadership of Magnus Hirschfeld, introduced political organizing, publishing, and a host of other activities.[1] The Nazis ruthlessly eliminated the German movement during the 1930s. England's homosexual resistance relied on the literary contributions of Edward Carpenter, John Addington Symonds, and Havelock Ellis.[2] Strict censorship laws, however, and the inhibiting effects of the Oscar Wilde trials, hampered English efforts to organize formally after the German example. While the efforts of the Europeans might appear short-lived and their success minimal, in fact they provided inspiration and models for Americans who later attempted to develop a minority consciousness and to organize. What is more, the European pioneers provided a past, a history for homosexual resistance to oppression.

Since 1908, American homosexual rights efforts have developed rapidly, from isolated attempts by individuals into a movement recognized as a political and economic force. Politicians are beginning to court the gay community for votes, just as advertisers are targeting the increasingly important gay market. The history of this transformation can be divided into eight stages. In Stage 1, from 1908 to at least 1945, there were sporadic attempts to defend the rights of homosexual men and women. In the years immediately following World War II, Stage 2 witnessed the dawning of a minority consciousness among gay people living in the cities. Stage 3, from 1950 to 1952, represented a search for identity. During the years 1952-1953, Stage 4, righteous indignation flared up within the movement. In Stage 5, from 1953 to 1960, the movement emphasized information and educational approaches. The decade of the sixties, Stage 6, brought civil-rights activism to the homophile movement. In Stage 7, beginning in 1969, gay liberation emerged. Finally, in Stage 8 (1973-1979), the movement and the government responded to each other through institutionalized channels. Although each successive stage was characterized by the emergence of new commitments, new organizations, and often new leaders, frequently organizations and individuals from an earlier stage continued to operate in the next stage with little or no alteration in their strategies or philosophies.

STAGE 1: SPORADIC INDIVIDUAL ATTEMPTS (1908-1945)

The earliest attempts by Americans to defend the rights of homosexual people were sporadic and, with rare exceptions, were undertaken as individual efforts. It was necessary first to introduce the idea that homosexuality actually existed in North America, was not confined to isolated cases of sexual anomaly, and in fact was not uncommon in cities and jails. Throughout the twenties and later, attempts to organize homosexual men and women proved too daring for the times and seemed to confirm that only individual efforts would be tolerated. The efforts of individuals to defend the rights of homosexual persons continued into the post-World War II period and remains the strategy of many, even in 1980.

The first individual attempt was made by the writer Edward Prime Stevenson, who published his pioneering work, *The Intersexes: A History of Similisexualism as a Problem in Social life,* in 1908. This book included numerous accounts of the lives of homosexual men and women, whom he called "intersexes." Stevenson himself was almost certainly homosexual. He listed a number of American cities as having known homosexual activity, including St. Louis, San Francisco, Milwaukee, New Orleans, Philadelphia, Boston, Chicago, Denver, and New York.[3] In his attempts to research and publish his work, Stevenson encountered many obstacles. Not only did he need a physician's permission to read the European books on the subject, he finally had to have his book printed privately in Italy under a pseudonym, Xavier Mayne. His pioneering inquiry into the existence and status of American homosexuality gave a few people their first authoritative introduction to a surprisingly lively local subculture. American sexual nonconformity was in print at last.

Besides Stevenson, only the birth-control advocate Margaret Sanger and anarchists Emma Goldman and Alexander Berkman made any gestures in support of the rights of homosexual individuals.[4] The political, religious, and scientific communities in the United States echoed the most conservative sentiments emanating from Europe and labeled homosexuality a crime, a sin, or a sickness. Attempts by a few Europeans to stimulate humane treatment of Uranians, that is, "homosexuals," proved futile in the United States.

The first known attempt to organize the homosexual minority in America took place in Chicago during the 1920s. A German-American immigrant named Henry Gerber gathered about him a core of working-class homosexual men and tried to duplicate the successes he had seen in the Weimar Republic. Accordingly, he fashioned an organization called the Society for Human Rights (SHR), loosely modeled on Magnus Hirschfeld's Scientific Humanitarian Committee. The name Gerber chose was inspired by a contemporary German group, the *Bund für Menschenrecht.*[5]

On December 10, 1924, SHR received a charter from the State of Illinois. Its objectives were:

> . . . *to promote and to protect the interests of people who by reason of mental or physical abnormalities are abused and hindered in the legal pursuit of happiness which is guaranteed them by the Declaration of Independence, and to combat the public prejudices against them by dissemination of facts according to modern science among intellectuals of mature age. The society stands only for law and order; it is in harmony with any and all general laws insofar as they protect the rights of others, and does in no manner recommend any acts in violation of present laws, nor advocate any matter inimical to the public welfare.*[6]

Reflecting upon the Illinois charter years later, Gerber commented that "no one seems to have bothered to investigate our purpose."[7]

Despite Gerber's hope for a "mass" organization, the SHR never had more than ten members. Attempts to attract the active support of prominent Americans, such as Margaret Sanger, failed. This probably was due to potential members' fear of exposure as being homosexual or sympathetic to homosexuality; in Sanger's case, however, it was Gerber's personality that doomed mutual cooperation, for he could be exceedingly doctrinaire.[8]

The immediate strategy of the SHR was to concentrate on the statutes of Illinois pertaining to homosexuality. The Illinois sodomy law applied only to one sexual act, anal intercourse, and punished it with one to ten years. To argue for reform, Gerber wrote and financed two issues of a publication entitled *Friendship and Freedom.*[9] Gerber's bold plans collapsed, however, after the estranged wife of Al Meininger, vice president of SHR, turned over some of the organization's literature to a social worker, who gave it to the police. Early one Sunday morning, all of the SHR officers were jailed. Years later, Gerber recalled the headline in the Chicago *Examiner:*[10]

Strange Sex Cult Exposed

According to Gerber, the article claimed that SHR's literature "urged men to leave their wives and children."[11] The hearings and court proceedings illustrated the corruption inherent in Chicago's system of criminal justice. After a series of hearings in which insults were directed at Gerber and the other members, the charges against the officers of SHR were abruptly dismissed. Soon afterward, Gerber was fired from his job with the U.S. Postal Service.[12] His organization was destroyed and he himself was shattered financially and spiritually. His mistreatment by the Chicago police and the local press was aggravated by the realization that Chicago's sizable homosexual community had given him no support. He had expected too much from a group that feared to give even a little.

Dejected, Gerber packed his belongings and moved to New York City, where he reenlisted in the Army and served seventeen years at Governor's Island. In the years that followed, Gerber corresponded with two gay men who were later to be active in the post-World War II homophile movement: George Mortenson and Manuel Boyfrank. He toyed with the idea of redesigning SHR or even starting a new organization, but his cynicism ultimately rejected idealistic reform.[13] He had a brief association with the Mattachine Society of New York City in the mid-fifties, and in 1962 he wrote a revealing autobiographical article for *ONE* magazine. Shortly before his death in 1972, he translated for ONE, Inc. a one-volume homosexual encyclopedia by Magnus Hirschfeld.[14]

Henry Gerber's aspirations and energy stand in marked contrast to the complacency of closeted homosexual Americans in the years between the wars. This lonely, rebellious individual dared to dream, speak, and write of a better society. For his visionary attempts, Gerber earned respect from future leaders of the homosexual movement in the United States.[15]

In the 1920s and 1930s, homosexual men and women were forced to resort to underground clubs and other surreptitious methods of communication. Science-fiction clubs attracted some, who corresponded with one another through the personal columns of the clubs' newsletters. The personal ads of certain physique magazines functioned as a means of communication for males.

By the forties and fifties, individual efforts began to meet with success, encouraged by the development of Stage 2, to be discussed later. In California, a young lesbian who called herself Lisa Ben, an anagram for lesbian, published a lesbian-oriented periodical entitled *Vice Versa: America's Gayest Magazine.* She produced nine issues in Los Angeles between June 1947 and February 1948 but ended her germinal efforts because the work load proved too heavy.[16]

STAGE 2: THE DAWNING OF MINORITY CONSCIOUSNESS (1945-1950)

Stage 2 was characterized by a growing awareness that homosexual men and women constituted a distinct minority. This awareness was encouraged indirectly by the federal government during World War II, when by labeling certain citizens "homosexuals" it encouraged overt discrimination. The growing gay communities in the large cities responded with intermittent efforts to protect their members but were unprepared for the task. Stage 2 did increase self-recognition by the community, however.

World War II impacted with American society in many ways, among others by rapidly expanding the armed services and creating labor shortages in the wartime economy. The war efforts disrupted familiar, long-held social patterns for both men and women and for homosexual as well as heterosexual citizens. Hundreds of thousands of young men and women were given their first taste of freedom from parental supervision and from the social norms of their home towns. The frequent anonymity and psychological pressures inherent in wartime allowed, at times even encouraged, sexual experimentation and made it easier for some to discover their homosexuality.

Authorities in the armed services began to realize that large numbers of the enlistees and draftees were homosexual, and they discharged thousands during the war years. In the early war period, homosexual personnel were given a yellow, undesirable discharge, but by 1943-1944, a special blue, general discharge was being issued to those who had fought in the war effort. This blue discharge was neither honorable nor dishonorable and continued to be used until July 1947.[17]

The government's identification and labeling of thousands of individuals marked a new institutional position. For the first time, homosexual men and women became a statistically and socially designated minority. They still were despised and ridiculed, but their label gave them a minority status that some were content to adopt. The labeled "homosexuals" often found it uncomfortable or impossible to return to their parents and home towns, so many joined the postwar migration to the large cities, where homosexual men and women could congregate with other sexual nonconformists. In these gay ghettos, camaraderie fostered more openness and visibility. Some heterosexual residents, of course, felt threatened by the new life-styles and new faces, and their resentment often stimulated police harassment. This in turn acted as a catalyst to forge collective self-protection by gay people.

The earliest such collective effort occurred in Boston around 1943. Staged by a nameless group, public meetings featured notable speakers on sex research and the law, but nothing enduring resulted.[18] At the end of the war, a Quaker Emergency Committee was organized in New York City to assist gay males arrested in public places while seeking sexual contact. The Committee's forty members helped some 15,000 sex offenders in its three years of existence, but fear of exposure led to the organization's demise.[19] Another New York organization, the Metropolitan Veterans' Benevolent Association, was incorporated in 1948 and provided a host of social functions. Disagreement over its purpose led to factionalism and by 1954 it had disbanded.[20] (There were also efforts to restrain the emerging gay subculture. The George

W. Henry Foundation, created in 1948 by a group of doctors, lawyers, and clergy, aimed at "curing homosexuals."[21]) In Los Angeles, the Knights of the Clock were formed in 1949 to combat both homophobia and racism. The idea for such an organization came to a black gay male, Merton Bird, who saw the added difficulties faced by interracial homosexual couples. The only document from the Knights of the Clock to survive is an informal record of membership dues that indicates less than twenty members in 1950.[22]

STAGE 3: SEARCH FOR IDENTITY (1950-1952)

Stage 3 marks a period of increased discussion of what it meant to be homosexual, discussion aired publicly in print and privately among homosexual individuals. Academic research was implicitly in opposition to the stance taken by the new, inflammatory political trend. The confusion and publicity that resulted from this contradiction prompted small numbers of homosexual men and women to meet in private to talk over their personal search for identity. These meetings gave birth to an ongoing homosexual rights movement in North America.

In the postwar years, two outside factors had a profound impact on the homosexual minority in North America. The first was the publication of the Kinsey reports, which analyzed human sexuality in North America more thoroughly than ever before. *Sexual Behavior in the Human Male* (1948) and *Sexual Behavior in the Human Female* (1953) included two findings that surprised, even shocked, many: the extent of extramarital intercourse and the prevalence of homosexual activity. While conservatives and traditionalists attacked these findings, others were intrigued by their implications. The Kinsey reports gave a stamp of academic approval to homosexual acts, placing them in the realm of natural sexual response rather than among disturbing abnormalities.

Amidst this intellectual breath of fresh air came a heat wave of accusations and antihomosexual associations: McCarthyism. The second Red Scare was partly a reaction to liberalism in political and social behavior. Patriotism and anticommunism became issues of public morality, dominating the American consciousness and tyrannizing many independent thinkers and reformers. Deviation, whether sexual or political, was a cardinal sin. "Red-baiting" and "queer-baiting" forced people from government, employment, and home. Headlines read:[23]

Perverts Called Government Peril

By 1953, the State Department was credited with having fired 531 "Perverts, Security Risks." That same year, President Dwight

Eisenhower signed Executive Order 10450, which excluded from government employment persons guilty of "sexual perversion."[24] Homosexual Americans thus were classified as security risks. Not one political or pressure group protested these violations of civil liberties. While many contemporary historians investigated McCarthyism, few mentioned the plight of the homosexual "security risk."

Caught between the contradictory messages of the Kinsey reports and McCarthyism, it is understandable that homosexual individuals sought out others with whom to discuss the paradox. Their meetings gave rise to the modern homosexual rights movement in America, first in Los Angeles, but soon after in the San Francisco Bay Area, New York City, and Chicago.

In Los Angeles, a group of gay men met cautiously to discuss the problems faced by their minority. Henry Hay, Bob Hull, Dale Jennings, Charles Roland, and others had all been involved in the far-left labor-education movement in the film capital. Now they met semiprivately to discuss both the abstract and the immediately relevant issues of homosexuality. The popularity of these discussions required that the groups be split in half to accommodate the increasing audience. Eventually the founders fashioned an organization employing the cell-like secrecy of the communist model familiar to many from their days in the American leftist movement during the thirties and forties. The groups spread through Los Angeles and Long Beach, and by May 1953 meetings were being held in San Diego, San Francisco, Oakland, Berkeley, New York City, and Chicago.[25] While accurate figures on the number of people who attended these various discussion groups are lacking, the important thing to note is how quickly the movement spread to the large urban gay ghettos, proof that a gay communication network already existed surreptitiously but effectively in the large cities.

The founders named their organization the Mattachine Foundation (MF), in honor of medieval and Renaissance societies of "unmarried townsmen who never performed in public unmasked. . . ."[26] The early MF contained both heterosexual and homosexual men and women. Their group meetings aimed at sharing knowledge, exposing injustice, and reminding one another that they were the "world's largest minority."[27]

STAGE 4: RIGHTEOUS INDIGNATION (1952-1953)

From the discussion groups of Stage 3 came a new vocal anger. Entrapment and other examples of harassment were seen as ethical and legal violations of citizens' rights. The new movement made a decision to protest institutionalized harassment and to become involved in local politics. The political climate, however, stirred fears of reprisals from the outside. This led to the first American convention of homosexual men and women. Amidst accusations and resignations, the stormy convention chose retreat and retrenchment.

The decision to become involved in active protest followed the arrest of one of the MF's members. Dale Jennings had been falsely accused of solicitation by the Los Angeles Police Department. A Citizens' Committee to Outlaw Entrapment was formed by a core of MF members who distributed leaflets and protested the proceedings. After the defendant Jennings surprised the court by openly testifying he was homosexual but not guilty of the charges, the case was dismissed.[28] This was the nascent movement's first victory. The activists were ecstatic. The MF's next strategy was to change laws affecting homosexual individuals. When the MF sent questionnaires to candidates for local office, three Los Angeles candidates responded.[29]

Problems soon began to beset the MF. Because MF's lawyer had a history of defending leftist groups, a columnist in a Los Angeles newspaper accused the MF of having affiliations with subversive individuals, labeling it the "Homintern."[30] *Confidential,* a gossip magazine, also made exaggerated statements as to MF's size, assets, and aims.[31]

In addition, internal discontent beset the sprawling MF. Its loose structure, its rapid growth, and its early political aims bred distrust and divisiveness in the overwrought McCarthy era. New, middle-class opposition to the secrecy of the founders led to demands for an open, democratic organization. As a result, in April 1953 a constitutional convention was convened in Los Angeles, where a strong, vocal, and seemingly well-organized group demanded that the MF disassociate itself from leftism.[32] The dissidents wanted social and educational programs, but no overt political action. The Mattachine was struggling with the same major political and philosophical problems that faced the nation as a whole: whether to continue to build on progressive reform or to consolidate within the available institutions. News that Representative B. Carroll Reece (R.-Tenn.) was bringing a congressional committee to California to investigate tax-exempt foundations prompted the original leaders to resign and to destroy much of their original correspondence for fear it might be subpoenaed. The new leadership that emerged in the MF began a thorough housecleaning in 1954 and renamed their organization the Mattachine Society (MS) on March 23, 1954.[33] In the MS, political action was replaced with an emphasis on social support for the membership and education and information for the outside world. In San Francisco, Hal Call began editing a new publication, *Mattachine Review.* By 1957 the national headquarters of the MS had been relocated to San Francisco, under Call and Don Lucas.

STAGE 5: INFORMATION AND EDUCATION (1953-1960)

The movement's next stage, Stage 5, was a period of consolidated growth, a nurturing, cautious time. Its new priorities were to keep as many homosexual people as possible informed and to educate the heterosexual public about homosexual men and women and their mistreatment. The Big Three California homophile organizations published magazines and other printed materials as encouragement to their members and in order to air the homophile viewpoint. Faced with a government effort to inhibit homophile publication, ONE, Inc. responded successfully with indignant legal protest, keeping alive the tradition set in Stage 4. The movement was becoming more complex, however: A separate, lesbian wing emerged and a new homosexual religion was offered. The greatest victories during the information-and-education stage were certain legal reforms and the simple fact that the movement survived, and even grew, despite internal disruptions.

Aware that the MF was reaching only a very small number of people, a group evolved in October 1952 from one of the Los Angeles discussion groups. They formed themselves into a new organization devoted to publishing a magazine/newsletter specifically designed to give a more accurate picture of gay life in America. A young member, Guy Rousseau, remembering a quote by Thomas Carlyle, "A mystic bond of brotherhood makes all men one," came up with the name of the organization: ONE, Inc. *ONE* magazine began publication in January 1953 and continued to serve as one of the unofficial voices of the homosexual rights movement until 1972.[34]

In 1954 the movement met a serious challenge from the U.S. Postal Service. All homophile organizations used the mails to distribute their magazines and to keep in contact with their own chapters, with each other, and with the European and Japanese homophile organizations. In 1954, the entire October issue of *ONE* magazine was seized by the Los Angeles Postmaster as obscene material. The case slowly meandered up through the layers of judicial appeal. On January 13, 1958, the Supreme Court reviewed the case and unanimously lifted the ban on the October issue.[35] This decision gave the homophile movement its second important legal victory. By winning the right to mail its material, the movement not only facilitated its own survival but also helped quell fears that sex-research materials would be censored.

During the last half of the fifties, the movement addressed three areas of importance to its development: the increasing role women played in the movement, shifts in legal attitudes affecting homosexuality, and domination of the movement by a few California organizations.

Women, both heterosexual and homosexual, had been active from the earliest days of the MF. *ONE* magazine published the work of several lesbian contributors, and a number of women, including Ann Carll Reid, Eve Elloree, Alison Hunter, and Sten Russell, served in positions of authority. "The Feminine Viewpoint" was a regular feature of *ONE* magazine. Although these women participated in ONE, MF and MS, they wanted and needed more than mere collaboration in male-dominated organizations. Anticipating later feminist thinking, they felt a need for an all-women's organization within the homophile movement.

On September 21, 1955, four lesbian couples in San Francisco formed the Daughters of Bilitis (DOB) as an alternative to the limited social outlets then available to them.[36] The divergent intentions of the founders eventually caused a permanent split. The blue-collar couples wanted a secret, exclusively lesbian, social organization. The white-collar couples, led by Phyllis Lyon and Del Martin, eventually succeeded in moving the DOB into a middle-class activist stance—in the mid-fifties, this meant providing information and education about homosexuality. They published a magazine, *The Ladder,* and established chapters in Los Angeles and on the East Coast. After the blue-collar contingent left, the DOB pursued a course that led them into cooperation with the male members of the movement.

The presence of vocal lesbian spokespersons gave the homophile movement a diversity and level of awareness frequently lacking elsewhere in contemporary America. The problems lesbians encountered were somewhat different from those of homosexual males. Both faced stigmatization as well as economic and official government discrimination. Gay males, however, often had to worry about police vice details; lesbians, generally not as adventurous sexually, seldom were bothered by these tactics. On the other hand, lesbians faced problems with child custody and visitation rights more often than did gay men, made less money in the marketplace, and found fewer professional opportunities. These differences were significant enough to make lesbians prefer the DOB to the cosexual MS or ONE.

The year 1955 saw a major shift in attitudes of professional jurists toward homosexuality. The American Law Institute published its Model Penal Code, which recommended that all consensual relations between adults in private be decriminalized. Believing that "no harm to sexual interests of the community is involved in atypical sex practice(s)," the institute questioned the right of the state to interfere in the personal affairs of an individual where there was no harm involved.[37] In 1961, the State of Illinois enacted the Model Penal Code as part of a thorough reform effort. Its passage, however, did not make life appreciably more comfortable for gay people in Illinois during the sixties.

During the fifties, only a small number of men and women were willing to join a homophile organization. The actual number actively involved was never impressive: DOB had fifty-four members in 1957; the MS had 250 members in 1959, as did ONE, Inc. *ONE* magazine, the most successful publishing venture, was selling approximately 3600 copies monthly by the end of the decade.[38] Other publications included organizational newsletters to members, the more scholarly *ONE Institute Quarterly,* and the book *Homosexuals Today: A Handbook of Organizations and Publications.*

To encourage participation in the movement, the older organizations continued to establish branches or chapters in other cities. Having several chapters allowed the national offices of the Big Three (ONE, the MS, the DOB) to exert greater impact. ONE, Inc. remained cautious of expansion, but the DOB soon had affiliated chapters in San Francisco, New York City, Los Angeles, and Providence. The MS had chapters in San Francisco, New York City, Los Angeles, Denver, and Chicago, with a scattering of members in Detroit, Boston, Washington, and Phoenix.

Chapter problems plagued the MS, beginning with its first convention. An East-West rivalry emerged between the national chapter in San Francisco and the New York chapter (which had nearly fifty members in 1957).[39] At the 1959 Mattachine convention in Denver, the challenger in the San Francisco mayoral election attempted to link the incumbent mayor with the MS by wangling a political endorsement for the incumbent from the MS. The plan backfired and was a major news story in the local press of both San Francisco and Denver. The MS gained considerable news coverage in both cities, but some felt that the national leaders of the MS had been duped. A year later, at the 1960 convention in San Francisco, seating of delegates was a hot issue as control of the national organization appeared to be leaning toward the New York chapter, for the MSNY's membership was outdistancing the MSSF.[40] The national leaders, Hal Call and Don Lucas, responded by unilaterally dissolving affiliations among the chapters on March 12, 1961. Mattachine Societies everywhere became independent, allowing many to adopt more activist strategies while the MSSF continued in its traditional posture of emphasizing information and education.[41]

The Big Three dominated the movement in the fifties by virtue of their organizational abilities and the time, energy, and creativity they invested in their publications. Internal differences, whether personal or ideological, were often resolved by the exodus of prominent individuals or factions from a group. Chuck Rowland, for instance, created the Church of ONE Brotherhood in 1956, hoping it would satisfy the spiritual and emotional needs of troubled homosexual men.[42] The early movement had been marked by militant atheism. The church proved short-lived; indeed, the mortality rate of other break-away groups and new organizations was quite high everywhere.

The most important feature of the American homosexual rights movement during the fifties was that it survived and grew: The early fear of the MF founders, that a single mistake could doom an American homosexual rights movement indefinitely, had not come to pass. The breakup of the Mattachine chapter network was also significant and set the stage for new developments within the movement.

STAGE 6: CIVIL RIGHTS ACTIVISM (1961-1969)

During the sixties, people in the movement grew bolder, borrowing Negro civil-rights tactics of demonstration and protest to emphasize their conviction. Cooperation increased, first regionally and then nationally, as the number of organizations proliferated. Although gay demonstration served as a convenient symbol throughout the decade, the movement's growing political expertise achieved the greatest long-term impact. The most successful gay community was in San Francisco, which introduced many innovative programs. As the decade drew to a close, a number of homosexual organizations were created that would survive to play increasingly significant roles in the seventies.

The major focus of the homophile movement of the sixties was a shift to activism in pursuit of civil rights. While homophile traditionalists remained dedicated to the information-and-education approach, the liberal activists became the real leaders of the homophile movement and directed its policies.

The passage of the Civil Rights Bill of 1964 proved that civil rights activism was indeed an effective strategy—at least for Negroes. In 1965, small bands of gay demonstrators began picketing selected targets in Washington, D.C. and other cities. During the last half of the decade, demonstrating around Independence Hall in Philadelphia became an annual Fourth-of-July homophile event. The protesters aimed to call public attention to overt discrimination against homosexual persons by the various agencies of government. The picketers' numerical strength was hardly impressive when compared to the crowds produced by the contemporary Negro civil-rights movement, but if they could not turn out legions of people, the homophile leaders decided at least to challenge the stereotyped images that stigmatized homosexual men and women. Indeed, the homophile picketers' attire and behavior were meticulously supervised by Dr. Franklin Kameny, president of the Mattachine Society of Washington, D.C. (MSW).[43] Respectable, clean images pervaded the demonstration.

Dr. Kameny saw the MSW as the homosexual equivalent of the National Association for the Advancement of Colored People and the B'nai Brith's Anti-Defamation League. For its strategy, however, the MSW adopted the tactics of the Southern Christian Leadership Conference, which was dedicated to demonstrations and picketing. In 1962 Kameny met with representatives from the Pentagon to discuss the denial of security clearances to gay people. By calling press conferences to announce a person's homosexuality, thus removing the sting from any threat of disclosure, he later challenged the Pentagon's argument that homosexual men and women were extraordinarily subject to blackmail.[44] The Pentagon did not change its position, but some newspapers did publish the contradiction.

This shift from education and information to direct action was accomplished by the leaders of a number of organizations, including Barbara Gittings of the DOB-NY and Randy Wicker of the MSNY. Their priorities centered on eliminating discriminatory policies in the nation's institutions. In the late sixties, representatives from the MSNY testified before the City of New York's Human Rights Commission and were able to get the city to stop asking job applicants whether or not they were homosexual.[45]

In the eastern United States, leaders from New York, Philadelphia, and Washington, D.C. began to cooperate and formed a confederation called the East Coast Homophile Organizations (ECHO). It coordinated activities and gave that area a newly militant élan. ECHO focused attention on local, state, and national agencies, as well as the United Nations.[46]

On the West Coast, San Francisco's gay community created very innovative and activist organizations. A short-lived League for Civil Education (LCE) assisted in hundreds of legal cases involving gay civil rights. An offshoot group from LCE promoted the political career of the first openly gay candidate in the early sixties: Jose Sarria, a well-known local gay entertainer, entered the race for Board of Supervisors and polled a surprising 5600 votes.[47] This demonstration of the sizable homosexual voting bloc did not escape the attention of local politicians.

The premier organization of the sixties was the male-dominated Society for Individual Rights (SIR) of San Francisco. SIR provided a myriad of activities, including a publication *(Vector),* dances (the only ones in the city where same-sex couple dancing was allowed), social activities (from sports to theater), political education (Candidates' Night), and community service. By the late sixties, SIR claimed 900 members, and its expanded operation included a blood bank, VD education campaigns, a housing file, and a second-hand store called "Sirporium."[48]

Each year, the number of candidates appearing at SIR's Candidates' Night to answer questions and make commitments increased as the political clout of gay people grew. Toward the end of the decade, gay voters demonstrated the significance of a strategic gay swing-vote in the Hollywood-Silverlake area of Los Angeles.[49]

As SIR came to overshadow the MSSF, the DOB-SF changed to accomodate the new activist stance. The leaders of SIR, the DOB, and other local gay organizations cooperated and designed a program to educate liberal Protestant clerics in San Francisco. From their efforts emerged the Council on Religion and the Homosexual (CRH), which included representatives of the Methodist, Episcopal, Lutheran, and United Church of Christ denominations, as well as homophile leaders. On December 31, 1964, CRH hosted a fund-raising Mardi Gras New Year's Eve costume ball. Patrons of the event were blatantly harassed by the police, a clergyman was threatened with arrest, and three attorneys and a homemaker were actually arrested. It was a triumph for the gay community since, for once, heterosexual, respectable members of society witnessed, and in a few cases suffered, the heavy-handed treatment gay people often received from local police departments. The American Civil Liberties Union sprang to the defense of the CRH victims. Although the charges were dropped, CRH threatened a sizable lawsuit against city officials and published a "Brief of Injustices" that expose[d] a pattern of social, legal, and economic oppression . . . " and came down hardest on police abuse.[50] By making the homophile movement respectable in San Francisco, the CRH made the homophile voting bloc even more attractive to politicians. Nowhere else did the gay community achieve such compatibility with local institutions.

Another San Francisco organization, as successful as the CRH, was the Tavern Guild. The Tavern Guild effectively coordinated the resources of local gay businesses to combat the flagrant tactics of local police and of state alcoholic beverage investigators who harassed gay bars and gay patrons. The Tavern Guild's greatest asset seemed to be its financial flexibility, something no other homophile organization could match.[51]

Even San Francisco's young male street hustlers organized themselves under the name Vanguard in 1966, to deal with police problems and discrimination and to undertake suicide prevention.[52] While it flourished only briefly, Vanguard anticipated many of the characteristics of the next stage of the American homosexual rights movement.

San Francisco's gay movement was successful because the city was a small political unit and the local gay community was visible and growing rapidly. San Francisco's historic reputation for toleration of nonconformity helped but was not sufficient reason: The gay community succeeded because it recognized its potential and because the leadership audaciously exploited all possibilities.

In Southern California, the gay community attempted to duplicate the successes of San Francisco but found that the size of sprawling Los Angeles required much different tactics. Instead of a CRH, for example, Southern California's contribution to the gay religious struggle was a new church. Troy Perry, a gay Southern Baptist minister, founded the Metropolitan Community Church in 1968. By the end of the decade the MCC was ministering to some 300 persons in southern California. Under Perry's leadership, MCC demonstrated a lasting commitment to civil-rights demonstrations and to fasts in behalf of equality for gay people. Perry's similarities to the Rev. Martin Luther King, Jr. have not gone unnoticed.[53]

In 1967 gay demonstrators protested against the overzealous and sometimes violent actions of the Los Angeles Police Department. Coordinating the protests was PRIDE (Personal Rights in Defense and Education). PRIDE's major contribution to the movement was its newsletter, *The Advocate,* which eventually overshadowed its parent organization and became a private business run by Dick Michaels and Bill Rand.[54] *The Advocate* dominated gay news during the seventies, when the paper was moved to the San Francisco Bay Area by its new owner, David B. Goodstein.

It seemed logical and inevitable that the expanding ECHO should associate with the California efforts. In 1966, representatives from fifteen homophile organizations and publications met at the National Planning Conference of Homophile Organizations (NPCHO). This new confederation included delegates from the Midwest and South, as well as from the coastal cities, making NPCHO the first truly national gathering of American homophile leaders. Like ECHO, NPCHO was purely consultative in nature and wielded no authority over its members. It produced a number of brochures and pamphlets and sponsored a series of annual conferences. When NPCHO changed its name to the North American Conference of Homophile Organizations (NACHO), many hoped this signalled the beginning of a national federation, but others feared the sharing of dues and the delegation of authority to a few who presumed to speak for the entire movement.[55] With the support of the ACLU, NACHO established a National Legal Defense Fund (NLDF), which channeled money into gay-civil-rights cases with precedential possibilities, such as the homosexual alien case, *Boutilier v. Immigration and Naturalization,* 1969. *Boutilier* was appealed to the U.S. Supreme Court, unsuccessfully.[56]

To articulate the civil-rights resolve of the homophile movement was the purpose of the NACHO-sponsored Homosexual Bill of Rights.

This was passed in 1968 and established five basic rights:

1. *Private consensual sex acts between persons over the age of consent shall not be an offense.*
2. *Solicitation for any sexual act shall not be an offense except upon the filing of a complaint by the aggrieved party, not a police officer or agent.*
3. *A person's sexual orientation or practice shall not be a factor in the granting of renewal of federal security clearance, visas, and the granting of citizenship.*
4. *Service in and discharge from the armed forces and eligibility shall be without reference to homosexuality.*
5. *A person's sexual orientation or practice shall not affect his eligibility for employment with federal, state, or local governments.*

Another ten items were listed as areas in need of immediate reform, for example, prohibiting police from notifying employers of suspects arrested for homosexual offenses.[57]

The cross-fertilization of ideas between other causes and the homophile movement continued throughout the sixties. Unrest on the campuses affected gay students, particularly in New York City where the Student Homophile League (SHL) at Columbia University challenged homophobic attitudes in medical academia.[58] The SHL picketed the College of Physicians and Surgeons in the spring of 1968 after the academics refused to allow SHL members to sit on a panel about homosexuality or even to be admitted to the auditorium. Similar activities attested to the dedication of these young gay students to liberal activist principles.

The antiwar movement spawned a "Lavender contingent" of over 150 marchers at the 1967 antiwar demonstration in San Francisco. In 1966, homophile leaders had formed the Committee to Fight Exclusion of Homosexuals in the Armed Forces (CFEHAF). On the surface, the CFEHAF appeared to support the military and its efforts in Viet Nam, but in fact it offered any male, gay or heterosexual, an avenue of escape from the draft and acted as an information center for young men who suspected they might be homosexual, either seriously or conveniently. The CFEHAF coordinated a nationwide protest on May 21, 1966; the most successful rally was in San Francisco, with 300 to 500 in attendance.[59]

Throughout the sixties the homophile movement expanded its geographic representation and increased internal cooperation. There was progress in employment protection, religious tolerance, and political clout as the movement, adopting the slogan "Gay is Good," moved steadily into activism. The gay community as a whole, however, was generally unaffected by the movement's confidence and only rarely benefitted from its successes. Society's abhorrence and fear of homosexuality continued.[60] While there was greater visibility for American homosexuality in the sixties, it was still a sub rosa world that few talked about and fewer saw. Historians followed society's lead and avoided the controversial reality of sexual nonconformity in America.

STAGE 7: GAY LIBERATION (1969-1973)

The first gay riot heralded a new stage for the movement, one characterized by militant contempt for institutional American reform. Gay liberation borrowed ideas from the New Left and the counter-culture. Never before had so many homosexual Americans actively and openly supported the movement's efforts and events. To focus all these energies, there emerged a new organization concentrating only on gay issues. Lesbian separatism flourished and took that wing of the movement into close cooperation with, and sometimes even joining, the women's movement.

On June 27, 1969 a seemingly insignificant disorder in a Greenwich Village bar symbolically ushered in this next stage of the movement.[61] After the gay patrons of the Stonewall Inn were ejected from their bar by the local police, they erupted with unexpected outrage and rioted for at least four nights. The gay rioters utilized hit-and-run tactics reminiscent of guerilla warfare; the police responded with its special riot unit. This militancy proved contagious among growing numbers of young and dissatisfied members of the gay community who demanded personal respect and a thorough reorganization of society. A new organization, the Gay Liberation Front (GLF), became the prototype for groups across the nation. A fresh confidence and militancy began to permeate the social fabric of gay America. The Stonewall generation had been born.[62]

The Stonewall Riot marks the origin of a major division within the American homosexual rights movement. The older homophile wing of the movement continued but found itself increasingly under attack from the new wing, which represented the more radical desires of the young and rebellious "street gays." The differences between the two approaches were epitomized in the argument over a name for the movement. Like the black civil-rights movement, which rejected the word "Negro," the new gay militants refused to identify with "homophile" or "homosexual," associating these words with failure and stereotypes. Instead, the young radicals chose "gay," despite its obscure origins and the confusion over its acceptability for lesbians. During the 1970 NACHO meeting in San Francisco, gay radicals staged a coup that splintered the homophile group and created bitter resentment against all gay liberation fronts.[63] Eclipsed by the publicity given to the gay wing of the movement, the homophile faction lost some of its spokespersons and failed to attract sufficient replacements in the early seventies to maintain its dominance of the movement.

A significant difference between the homophile effort of the sixties and the gay liberation movement was the larger numbers of gay Americans attracted to the movement after 1969. Over 10,000 militant lesbians and gay men marched on Central Park in New York to celebrate the first anniversary of the Stonewall Riot. By the end of the seventies, gay pride events were occurring across the nation. The largest of these, the San Francisco Gay Pride Parade, drew hundreds of thousands of people.[64]

In a broad sense, gay liberation meant building a strong, supportive gay community. The philosophy of gay liberation encouraged all types of homosexual men and women to participate actively in the struggle for equality. Consciousness-raising sessions, originally developed by the women's movement, were used by gay liberation fronts to teach homosexual men and lesbians the politics of being liberated gay persons. California gay liberationists, expressing gay pride and nationalism in much the same way as black separatists had done earlier, made plans to establish a gay community in a wilderness area of California. Gay liberation also provided the impetus to introduce the gay movement and gay courses to college campuses from coast to coast.[65]

Important factors contributing to the success of gay liberation were the attitudes held by the young, by civil-rights activists, and by war protesters. The counterculture's rejection of long-held maxims, including those dealing with sex and promiscuity, created the supportive atmosphere necessary for large numbers of gay men and lesbians, as well as many heterosexual people, to redefine their personal concepts of morality and equality.[66] Protest was now respectable if not always safe, while nonconformity was chic if not always respectable. These social phenomena allowed and subtly encouraged homosexual men and women to come out publicly and to demand their rights.

The new militants were generally younger, poorer, and more antiestablishment than their homophile predecessors. They personified the New Left political philosophy but clothed it in street jargon. Not only were they angry, they no longer felt that their efforts were futile. They also differed from the homophile leaders in being willing to shout revolution in order to achieve equality.[67]

Many gay liberationists had been involved in nongay radical activities prior to gay liberation. Some had been in the Students for a Democratic Society (SDS), although, in retrospect, they deplored the homophobia and sexism they had witnessed there.[68] Gay liberationists acknowledged collective support for a number of New Left causes, including women's rights, protection of the environment, and equality for Third World peoples.[69] Gay liberation produced philosophical statements, such as Carl Wittman's particularly effective "Refugees from Amerika: A Gay Manifesto," printed in early 1970. Wittman indicted society for its treatment of homosexual men and women and declared spiritual independence for gay people.[70] Amidst the outpouring of gay liberation statements came a letter from Black Panther strategist Huey Newton, who urged the formation of working coalitions among his organization, gay liberationists, and women's liberationists.[71] This letter was the first significant support given the gay movement by a major black leader.

Although Newton's letter bolstered the Gay Liberation Front's prestige for a while, the issue of cooperation with the Black Panthers later provoked a divisive struggle within the gay movement. In New York City, the GLF was convulsed over this issue. Increasing Marxist-Leninist influence and a proliferation of cells foreshadowed a breakdown in the cohesion of gay liberation.[72] At the end of 1969, a group split away from the Gay Liberation Front and reformed as the Gay Activist Alliance, or GAA. Whereas the GLF actively supported many liberation movements, the GAA was a single-issue entity and concentrated exclusively on homosexual liberation. Where the Gay Liberation Front emphasized structureless, leaderless, collective decision making, the GAA adhered strictly to *Robert's Rules of Order* and a carefully hammered-out preamble and constitution. The GAA's stated goals were to end entrapment and harassment in gay bars, to guarantee fair employment and housing to gay people, and to abolish New York State Laws dealing with sodomy and solicitation.[73] By 1973, the Gay Liberation Front's hope for revolution had been overshadowed by the GAA's work for reform.

The GAA quickly became involved in the political process and petitioned and lobbied on behalf of homosexual civil rights in New York City. The GAA leaders learned to use the system and employed press conferences, voting blocs, and indeed all styles of political organizing and activity when necessary. The GAA's famous "zaps," or confrontations, zeroed in on such notables as New York City Mayor John Lindsay, gubernatorial candidate Arthur Goldberg, and Governor Nelson Rockefeller. Publications like *Harper's* and organizations like the New York City Fireman's Association were attacked for expressing antigay views.[74] The GAA developed support from liberal politicians, including Bella Abzug, and sought and won a tremendous amount of publicity for gay liberation. They acquired a gay social center, called the Firehouse, where their dances helped them build a treasury of over $10,000.[75] Advances by the GAA soon led to the proliferation of similar organizations across the United States.

As the gay movement grew, an early rift widened. Lesbian separatism emerged among gay women drawn to the women's movement as opposed to the male-dominated gay movement. Lesbians had constituted a strong minority within the homosexual rights movement throughout the fifties and sixties, but a theme of separatism and independent identity had always been discernible. The Daughters of Bilitis proved to be the only organization to respond successfully to these shifts. The DOB's founders, Phyllis Lyon and Del Martin, helped lead the way into the women's movement, particularly to the National Organization of Women (NOW). Rita Mae Brown, among others, fought the open homophobia of NOW's founder, Betty Friedan, and in 1971 NOW passed resolutions in support of homosexual rights.[76] The Houston Women's Year Conference confirmed that support. Some lesbians established women's caucuses within existing gay organizations open to both men and women, while others inaugurated new organizations, publications, and conferences open only to women.[77] An especially positive feature of lesbians' growing self-identity was their ability to attain positions of national leadership within both the homosexual rights movement and the women's movement. Lesbian separatism was a highly controversial issue, and some militant lesbians refused to speak with men. Dissension between homophile lesbians and lesbian separatists also occurred; nevertheless, the lesbian movement was more confident and more successful by the mid-seventies than ever in its history.

STAGE 8: INSTITUTIONAL RESPONSES (1973-1979)

By the mid-seventies, radicalism was being replaced by negotiation as the chief tactic of the movement. Building on the earlier militant successes, segments of the movement were even able to tap public funds for selected projects. The first group of openly gay politicians emerged. The psychiatric community partially acknowledged that homosexuality need not be a sickness. A backlash was inevitable and came from both coasts. The decade ended with gay victories and gay riots.

GAA's achievements prompted the creation, in 1973, of a more institutionally oriented gay organization, the National Gay Task Force (NGTF), in which older or more established gay people could participate. The GAA declined, partly because of a leadership drain to the NGTF. The National Gay Task Force attracted a lineup of East Coast luminaries both in and out of the movement, including Dr. Howard Brown, formerly New York City Health Commissioner under Mayor Lindsay; historian Dr. Martin Duberman; homophile leaders Dr. Frank Kameny and Ms. Barbara Gittings; and many others.[78] The National Gay Task Force utilized the highly politicized gay community and the increasingly sensitive support given to the movement by politicians and the mass media. Responding to a general national trend toward negotiation and away from radical confrontation, NGTF came to be regarded by many as the voice of the entire movement. Other organizations that had national significance in the seventies were the expanded Metropolitan Community Church and *The Advocate.*

The gay and lesbian movements witnessed a number of significant events during the seventies. The American Psychiatric Association removed homosexuality from its diagnostic manual of sicknesses in 1974 and indicated its support of protective legislation for homosexual civil rights.[79] However, as "ego-dystonic homosexuality," it again was listed, this time under "psychosexual disorders," in the revision (Diagnostic Manual III), considered for adoption in 1980. Gay caucuses developed within nearly all mainstream American religious denominations.[80] In politics, two openly gay delegates addressed the 1972 Democratic Party National Convention. An openly gay woman, Elaine Noble, was elected to the Massachusetts House of Representatives in 1974; and Minnesota legislator, State Senator Alan Spear, who publicly acknowledged his homosexuality in 1974, won reelection in 1976.[81] In San Francisco, District 5 (Castro/Haight) became known unofficially as the gay supervisorial district, successively electing openly gay candidates Harvey Milk and Harry Britt.

Federal, state, and local tax monies were allocated to gay service agencies in Los Angeles and Seattle in 1974, and in San Francisco federal funds supported academic research on homosexuality.[82] In less than a decade, the government of the United States had moved from a position of blanket discrimination against homosexual men and women to selective acceptance of homosexual personnel in some areas of government and support of some gay projects. Antidiscrimination ordinances protecting homosexual men and women were passed in cities from Seattle, Washington to Washington, D.C., while similar national legislation was introduced into Congress.[83] A 1977 Gallup poll found that 56% of those interviewed believed homosexual men and women should have equal rights in job opportunity; however, 65% objected to homosexual teachers in elementary schools.[84]

The movement in the mid-seventies faced a strong conservative reaction, which had the ironic effect of confirming the resolve of the highly politicized gay communities and fostering new coalitions between lesbians and gay men. The homosexual rights movement seemed to work best when meeting a specific target for which resources and personnel could be committed on a short-term basis. The antihomosexual campaigns of Anita Bryant and John Briggs, focusing on gay teachers, began with a string of gay defeats in local elections in Florida, Minnesota, Kansas and Oregon, but impressive gay victories in Seattle, Washington, and California more than offset these early losses. The antigay backlash continues, however, through the efforts of fundamentalist and conservative religious groups, anti-ERA and Pro Life associations, and other conservative forces.

Throughout the seventies, rising expectations, fed by gay advances in most facets of American life, helped create pride in a gay identity, realization of collective strength, and growing recognition of frustrations. The mixture of these elements produced gay riots. The decade of gay liberation ended with violent reactions by gay people on both coasts. The most significant of these occurred in San Francisco, where thousands of gay men and lesbians rioted following the lenient verdict in the Dan White murder case. Another angry reaction was in New York City, where gay protestors demonstrated against the filming of the movie *Cruising,* which they considered homophobic.

The violence that ended the seventies was far different from the Stonewall riot ten years earlier. Stonewall was a mini-riot responding to a routine police action. Frustrations long held back erupted unexpectedly that night. News of Stonewall spread chiefly through the gay grapevine, as the event received only minimal media coverage. In contrast, the San Francisco riot involved thousands of people and received national news coverage. Like Stonewall, however, the situation in San Francisco was one of delayed response. People did not riot immediately after the assassination of openly gay Supervisor Harvey Milk but instead waited for the city's institutions to act justly. When the jury handed in the most lenient verdict possible, betraying the collective expectations of San Francisco's gay community, the community reacted violently. From this series of events emergd a contemporary gay martyr, Harvey Milk, who may come to be honored in the eighties even more than he was in the seventies.

The achievements by the American homosexual rights movement have pushed forward the limits of acceptable sexual behavior for all people and have increased the acceptance of nonconformity and alternative life-styles by society and in general. The riots of the 1970s, however, confirm that much remains to be done by the American homosexual rights movement, including enactment of national civil-rights protection, elimination of discriminatory policies by agencies such as the U.S. Immigration and Naturalization Service, insurance of child-custody equality for homosexual parents, and provision for better protection from violence against gay men and lesbians. The movement must also address discrimination within the gay community against the poor, the old, the young, and the nonwhite, and must bridge the continued misunderstandings between the gay male and lesbian communities. The movement of the eighties has its work cut out for it, but it enters the decade with a history of solid achievement.

The eight stages of the movement have shown progress toward a positively self-identified minority (in particular, in Stage 1, 2, and 3). At first, the minority's recognition of oppression (Stage 4) was tempered by the limited opportunities for social change perceived as available in the political climate of the fifties. Consequently, in stage 5, homosexual men and women who worked for homosexual rights relied on publications to inform fellow gay people and to educate the heterosexual public. The successes of the Negro civil-rights movement provided the next phase (Stage 6) with models for protest and demonstration. When gay women and men spontaneously rioted in protest to public harassment (Stage 7), militancy expressed itself as gay liberation. The final stage (Stage 8) of the seventies was institutional interaction between the highly politicized gay and lesbian communities and America's public and private institutions. Together, the stages bear witness to the growing number of homosexual individuals supporting or participating in the aims of the movement and chart the continuing erosion of the legal and social barriers erected to harass homosexual people.

The success of each stage is difficult to evaluate in a short essay. Many questions surrounding the American homosexual rights movement remain to be investigated. Did the early leaders of Stage 4, who later left the movement during the next stage, seriously inhibit the movement's growth, or was their departure necessary for the long-term development of the movement? How similar were the aims and efforts of the GAA (Step 7) to those of the movement in Stage 6? A host of questions and demanding, fascinating research await those historians who have at last accepted sexual diversity as an integral part of the American historical pageant.

NOTES

1. Arno Karlen, *Sexuality and Homosexuality: A New View* (New York: W. W. Norton, 1971), pp. 186-87, 334; John Lauritsen and David Thorstad, *The Early Homosexual Rights Movement (1864-1935)* (New York: Times Change Press, 1974), pp. 6, 7, 9, 11, 14, 16, 25, 28-30, 40-42, 73; Jim Steakley, "The Gay Movement in Germany, Part One: 1860-1910," *The Body Politic,* no. 9 (1973): 12-16, "Part Two: 1910-1933," *The Body Politic,* no. 10 (1973): 14-18, and "Part Three: Homosexuals and the Third Reich," *The Body Politic,* no. 11 (1974): 1, 20-21; Christopher Isherwood, *Christopher and His Kind* (New York: Farrar, Straus & Giroux, 1976), p. 34.

2. See H. Montgomery Hyde, *The Love That Dared Not Speak Its Name: A Candid History of Homosexuality in Britain* (Boston: Little, Brown & Co., 1970); Brian Reade, ed., *Sexual Heretics: Male Homosexuality in English Literature from 1850 to 1900* (New York: Coward-McCann, 1970); Lauritsen and Thorstad, pp. 32-34, 83; Karlen, pp. 217, 221, 251.

3. Edward Prime Stevenson [Xavier Mayne], *The Intersexes: A History of Similisexualism as a Problem in Social Life* (Italy: Privately printed, 1908; reprint ed., New York: Arno Press, 1973), p. 646; Jonathan Katz, ed., *Gay American History: Lesbians and Gay Men in the U.S.A.: A Documentary* (New York: Thomas Y. Crowell, 1976), pp. 49-50.

4. James Kepner, "Who Founded America's Gay Movement?" *Entertainment West,* Summer 1974, p. 10; Katz, p. 377; Reb Raney, "Alexander Berkman in San Francisco," *Mother Earth* 10 (June 1915): 152.

5. Henry Gerber, "The Society for Human Rights—1925," *ONE,* September 1962, pp. 5-8.

6. Katz, pp. 385-87.
7. Gerber, "Society," p. 7.
8. Kepner, p. 10.
9. Katz, pp. 390, 632-33. No copy is known to exist and until recently one had to rely upon Gerber's own autobiographical article for documentation. James Steakley, however, located a photograph, probably taken in 1927, that included "Friendship and Freedom" among a collection of other homosexual emancipation publications (Katz, pp. 390, 633).
10. Katz, p. 391; Gerber, "Society," p. 7.
11. Gerber, "Society," p. 8.
12. Ibid., pp. 8-11; Katz, p. 391.
13. Gerber, "Society," p. 11; Kepner, p. 9; Katz, p. 633.
14. Kepner, p. 9.
15. There is an outside possibility that an earlier organization, called the Sons of Hamidy, existed around the turn of the century. According to two interviews given by an alleged former officer of the club, it operated informally and underwent reorganization in 1934. No other evidence of its existence has surfaced. See Marvin Cutler (pseud.), ed., *Homosexuals Today: A Handbook of Organizations and Publications* (Los Angeles: Publication Division of ONE, Inc., 1956), p. 88; Kepner, p. 3.
16. Interview with Lisa Ben, Los Angeles, 14 March 1976; "Vice Versa," May, July, August, September, October, and November 1947, and January and February 1948; *ONE Letter* 17, no. 2 (February 1972): 2; Cutler, p. 90.
17. Alfred C. Kinsey, Wardell B. Pomeroy, and Clyde E. Martin, *Sexual Behavior in the Human Male* (Philadelphia and London: W. B. Saunders Company, 1948), pp. 621-22; "Homosexuals in Uniform," *Newsweek,* 9 June 1949, p. 54; see also Colin J. Williams and Martin S. Weinberg, *Homosexuals and the Military: A Study of Less Than Honorable Discharge* (New York: Harper & Row, 1971).
18. Kepner, p. 3.
19. Donald Webster Cory (pseud.), *The Homosexual in America: A Subjective Approach* (New York: Greenberg Publisher, 1951), p. 56; Laud Humphreys, *Out of the Closets: The Sociology of Homosexual Liberation* (Englewood Cliffs, N.J.: Prentice-Hall, 1972), p. 50.
20. Cutler, pp. 89-90; Humphreys, p. 50; Katz, p. 635.
21. William Lambert, "Case of the Well-Meaning Lyncher," *ONE,* November 1953, p. 16; Cutler, p. 92.
22. "The Cloistered Loyal Order of Conclaved Knights of Sophistacracy" (ledger of members), June 1951 through June 1952; *ONE Letter* 19, no. 9 (September 1974): 2; interview with W. Dorr Legg, Los Angeles, 28 July 1975.
23. Katz, p. 92.
24. "State Department Fires 531," *ONE* 1, no. 7 (July 1953): 25; U.S., President, Proclamation, "Security Requirements of Government Employment," Federal Register 18, no. 82, 29 April 1952, p. 2489; see also E. Carrington Boggan et al., *The Rights of Gay People: The Basic ACLU Guide to a Gay Person's Rights* (New York: Avon Books, 1975), pp. 62-63.
25. Interview with Henry Hay, Los Angeles, 7 August 1976; Katz, pp. 401, 406-7, 512-14; *ONE Letter* 19, no. 9 (September 1974): 3; Cutler, p. 31.
26. Katz, pp. 406-7, 410-11, 412-14; Mattachine—What Does It Mean?" *Mattachine Review,* November/December 1955, p. 29.
27. "First Decade—1950-1960," *Mattachine Review* 6, no. 4 (April 1960): 26-27.
28. Ibid., pp. 24, 27; Jeff Winters, "Can Homosexuals Organize?" *ONE* 2, no. 1 (January 1954): 4; Katz, p. 415.
29. "Challenge and Response: A Report," *ONE* 1, no. 3 (March 1953): 9; Cutler, p. 30.
30. "Challenge," p. 10; Winters, pp. 4-8; Katz, pp. 416-17.

31. *The Mattachine Society Today: An Informal Digest* (Los Angeles: Mattachine, 1954), p. 1.

32. Katz, p. 417. Katz notes that other participants put the attendance figures between 110 and 160 (Katz, n. 131, p. 637). See also Damon Pythias, "Take It from Me!" *ONE* (March 1954): p. 17.

33. "Mattachine Society," *ONE* 2, no. 1 (January 1954): 9, 16, 18; *Interim*, August 1961, p. 6; Pythias, p. 17; Sidney Rothman, "Present Society," *ONE,* p. 7.

34. "How ONE Began," *ONE* 3, no. 2 (February 1955): 8-9; Cutler, p. 8; interview with Dorr Legg, Los Angeles, 17 July 1975; interview with James Kepner, Los Angeles, 10 September 1976; *ONE* 1, no. 1 (January 1953): entire issue.

35. "Editorial," *ONE* 5, no. 3 (March 1957): 4; *ONE Confidential* 3, no. 2 (Spring 1958): 4; *ONE Confidential* 3 (March 1958): pp. 12-16; "ONE's Victory at Supreme Court," *ONE* 6, no. 2 (February 1958): pp. 16-17.

36. Del Martin and Phyllis Lyon, *Lesbian/Woman* (New York: Bantam Books, 1972), pp. 238-42; "The Philosophy of the DOB," *The Ladder* 6, no. 9 (June 1962): 5; interview with Del Martin, San Francisco, 25 August 1975.

37. H.L.A. Hart, *Law, Liberty, and Morality* (Stanford: Stanford University Press, 1963), p. 15.

38. "Calling the Shots," *Mattachine Review* 5, no. 1 (January 1959): 18; *Interim,* December 1959, quotes 327 national members, but this does not tally with the accumulated figures, p. 12; *ONE Confidential* 4, no. 1 (Winter 1959): 17; *Interim,* December 1959, p. 10; Martin and Lyon, p. 242.

39. Edward Sagarin, "Structure and Ideology in an Association of Deviants" (Ph.D. dissertation, New York University, 1966), pp. 81-82.

40. *ONE Confidential* 4, no. 10 (October 1959): 2-3; interview with Hal Call, San Francisco, 26 August 1975; Wes Knight, "Smear Drive," *Mattachine Review* 5, no. 11 (November 1959): pp. 12, 24; interview with Dorr Legg, Los Angeles, 19 July 1975.

41. "Mattachine Organizational Shifts," *Mattachine Review* 6, no. 8 (August 1961): 26-27; Sagarin, pp. 82-87.

42. Public speech by James Kepner at the Twenty-fifth Anniversary Dinner of ONE, Inc., Hilton Hotel, Los Angeles, 30 January 1976; Cutler, pp. 104-5.

43. "Homosexuals Picket in Nation's Capital," *The Ladder* 9, nos. 10/11 (July/August 1965): 23; "Cross Currents," *The Ladder* 9, no. 8 (May 1965): 22; *Eastern Mattachine Newsletter* 10, nos. 8/9 (September/October 1965): p. 19.

44. *ONE Confidential* 9, no. 10 (October 1964): 11; Frank E. Kameny to ONE, Inc., 14 November 1962, in file of Homosexual Information Center, Los Angeles; Foster Gunnison, Jr., "The Homophile Movement," in *The Same Sex: An Appraisal of Homosexuality,* ed. Ralph W.Weltge (Philadelphia: Pilgrim Press, 1969), pp. 122-23.

45. "Cross Currents," *the Ladder* 13, nos. 1/2 (October/November 1968): 38; *Mattachine Midwest Newsletter,* January 1967, p. 8.

46. "East Coast Homophile Organizations—Report '64," *The Ladder* 9, no. 4 (January 1965): 4-5, 21-22.

47. "The List Grows," *The Ladder* 5, no. 12 (September 1961): 9; Roxanna B. Thayer Sweet, "Political and Social Action in Homophile Organizations" (Ph.D. dissertation, University of California, Berkeley, 1968), p. 116; Del Martin, "The Homophile Vote," *The Ladder* 6, no. 4 (January 1962): 4-5; interview with Bill Plath, San Francisco, 25 August 1975.

48. "SIR's Anniversary Party," *Vector* 1, no. 9 (August 1965): 1; "Kansas City Conference Finds Specific Immediate Reliable Goals," *Vector* 2, no. 4 (March 1966): 10; "Community Center Opens," *Vector* 3, no. 6 (May 1966): p. 1; interview with Bill Plath, San Francisco, 25 August 1975; Sweet, p. 120.

49. *ONE Letter* 14, no. 4 (April 1969): 10; *ONE Letter* 14, no. 5 (May 1969): 5-7.

50. *Mattachine Midwest Newsletter* 2, no. 4 (April 1966): p. 3; Kay Tobin, "After the Ball. . .," *The Letter*, February/March 1965, p. 4; Sweet, pp. 153-54; Council on Religion and the Homosexual, *A Brief of Injustices: An Indictment of Our Society in Its Treatment of the Homosexual* (San Francisco: Council on Religion and the Homosexual, 1965), p. 10.

51. Sweet, pp. 123-24; *Mattachine Midwest Newsletter* 2, no. 6 (June 1966): 3; interview with Bill Plath, San Francisco, 25 August 1975.

52. *ONE Confidential* 11, no. 7 (July 1966): 17; Del Martin, "History of San Francisco's Homophile Organizations," *The Ladder* 11, no. 1 (October 1966): 26.

53. Troy D. Perry and Charles L. Lucas, *The Lord Is My Shepherd and He Knows I'm Gay* (Los Angeles: Nash, 1972), pp. 56, 58, 67-69, 108-11; interview with Troy Perry, Los Angeles, 27 April 1977; Kay Tobin and Randy Wicker, *The Gay Crusaders* (New York: Paperback Library, 1972), p. 82; interview with Dorr Legg, Los Angeles, 8 August 1975; interview with James Kepner, Los Angeles, 1 October 1976; "Cross Currents," *The Ladder* 13, nos. 11/12 (August/September 1969): 4-5.

54. "Pickets Protest Police Sadists," *Vector* 3, no. 4 (March 1967): 20; *ONE Confidential* 12, no. 4 (April 1967): 6; *PRIDE Newsletter* 1, no. 1 (May 1966): 1 (*PRIDE Newsletter* became widely circulated in Los Angeles in 1967; in September 1967 it changed its name to *The Advocate*. Very few remember the original name, as the paper is always referred to as *The Advocate*); "President's Corner," *Vector* 2, no. 5 (April 1966): 5.

55. *Midwest Mattachine Newsletter* 2, no. 2 (February 1966): 5; "Kansas City Conference," *Vector*, p. 1; *New York Mattachine Newsletter* 12, no. 2 (March 1967): 3; "U.S. Homophile Movement Gains National Strength," *The Ladder* 10, no. 7 (April 1966): 5; Virginia O. Road, "Report on the Third North American Homophile Conference, 17-19 August 1967," *The Ladder* 12, no. 2 (January 1968): 25; *ONE Letter* 13, no. 6 (June 1968): 2-4; interview with Dorr Legg, Los Angeles, 8 August 1975; interview with James Kepner, Los Angeles, 1 October 1976; interview with Don Slater, Los Angeles, 19 August 1975; see also Gunniston, p. 126.

56. *National Legal Defense Fund* (San Francisco: National Legal Defense Fund, Inc., 1968), p. 1; "National Legal Defense Fund," *Vector* 3, no. 5 (April 1967): 9, 13.

57. "Cross Currents," *The Ladder* 13, nos. 1/2 (October/November 1968): 37.

58. *ONE Confidential* 9, no. 10 (October 1964): 11.

59. Interview with André Schamberger, Los Angeles, 2 July 1976 (Schamberger was a participant in, and has buttons and other memorabilia to confirm, the "lavender contingent"); "Armed Forces Day," *Vector* 2, no. 6 (May 1966): 3; interview with Don Slater, Los Angeles, 19 August 1975; "Homosexuals Protest Draft Exclusion," *Vector* 2, no. 7 (June 1966): 3.

60. In a 1965 Louis Harris survey, 70 percent of the people polled thought homosexual men and women were harmful to the nation, ranking them with prostitutes and Communists as the outcasts of society: "Cross Currents," *The Ladder* 10, no. 3 (December 1965): p. 12.

61. "Cross Currents," *The Ladder* 14, nos. 1/2 (October/November 1969): 40. There is some confusion as to the date, for the riot occurred past midnight on Friday, 27 June 1969. Therefore, 28 June is usually cited by gay liberationists: Donn Teal, *The Gay Militants* (New York: Stein & Day, 1971), p. 17.

62. Particularly helpful and informative works dealing with Stonewall and the gay liberation fronts are: Teal, *Gay Militants*; Karla Jay and Allen Young, eds., *Out of the Closets: Voices of Gay Liberation* (New York: Pyramid Books, 1972). See also Wallace Hamilton, *Christopher and Gay: A Partisan View of the Greenwich Village Homosexual Scene* (New York: Saturday Review Press, 1973); John Francis Hunter, *The Gay Insider, USA* (New York: Stonehill Publishing Co., Dell, 1972); and Humphreys.

63. *ONE Letter* 15, no. 9 (September 1970): 1, 4; Teal, pp. 309-10; Humphreys, pp.

103-9; *Mattachine Midwest Newsletter,* October 1970, p. 5.

64. Teal, pp. 322-33; Arthur Bell, *Dancing the Gay Lib Blues: A Year in the Homosexual Liberation Movement* (New York: Simon & Schuster, 1971), pp. 83-85; *ONE Letter,* June 1970, p. 41; *Mattachine Midwest Newsletter,* June 1970, p. 1; "The Big Parades," *The Advocate,* 10 August 1977, p. 7.

65. Hunter, pp. 120-38; "Notes on Gay Male Consciousness-raising," in Jay and Young, pp. 293-301; Teal, pp. 314-19; *ONE Letter* 17, no. 7 (July 1972): 1; J. Lee Lehman, ed., *Gay Student Syllabi* (Washington, D.C.: National Gay Student Center, 1976), pp. 1-12; Ron Schreiber, "Giving a Gay Course," in *College English* 36, no. 3 (November 1974): 316-23.

66. Theodore Roszak, *The Making of a Counter Culture: Reflections of the Technocratic Society and Its Youthful Opposition* (Garden City, N.Y.: Anchor Books/Doubleday, 1969), pp. 1-41.

67. Interview with Eben Clark, Los Angeles, 18 October 1976; Allen Young, "Introduction," in Jay and Young, pp. 6-31; one GLF flier captured the new free and defiant spirit in the following headline dated 24 July 1969 (Teal, p. 36): DO YOU THINK HOMOSEXUALS ARE REVOLTING: YOU BET YOUR SWEET ASS WE ARE!

68. Teal, pp. 50-51.

69. Ibid., pp. 52-53.

70. Carl Wittman, "Refugees from Amerika: A Gay Manifesto," *San Francisco Free Press,* 22 December 1969-7 January 1970.

71. Huey Newton, "A Letter to the Revolutionary Brothers and Sisters about the Women's Liberation and Gay Liberation Movements," in *The Homosexual Dialectic,* ed. Joseph A. McCaffrey (Englewood Cliffs, N.J.: Prentice-Hall, 1972), pp. 195-97.

72. Teal, p. 101.

73. Bell, pp. 18-19; Tobin and Wicker, p. 36; Del Whan, "Elitism," in Jay and Young, pp. 318-23.

74. Bell, pp. 24-25, 31, 48, 51, 55-56, 78, 138-39; Teal, pp. 122, 138, 140, 145-46, 239-46, 260, 266-67; Tobin and Wicker, pp. 39, 169, 191-92; *The Advocate,* 10 May 1972, p. 1.

75. "Arson—Theft Casts Doubt on GAA Survival," *The Advocate,* 6 November 1974, p. 2; Teal, p. 241; Tobin and Wicker, p. 38.

76. Martin and Lyon, pp. 203-302; Sidney Abbot and Barbara Love, *Sappho Was a Right-on Woman: A Liberated View of Lesbianism* (New York: Stein & Day, 1972), pp. 131, 134; *Mattachine Midwest Newsletter,* 2 March 1973, p. 10; "Minutes of the Fifth Annual Conference of the National Organization for Women," Los Angeles, 2 September 1971, p. 16; interview with Pat Danslow, Los Angeles, 7 January 1977.

77. Teal, pp. 58-59, 183; "Chronicle—The Lesbian Movement," *Lesbian Tide,* July/August 1976, pp. 24-25.

78. "Heavyweight National Gay Group Formed," *The Advocate,* 7 November 1973, p. 1.

79. Interview with Dr. Judd Marmor, Los Angeles, 2 August 1977; *The Advocate,* 2 January 1974, p. 1; see also Howard Brown, *Familar Faces, Hidden Lives: The Story of Homosexual Men in America Today* (New York: Harcourt Brace Jovanovich, 1976) and Teal, pp. 293-96.

80. "Gay Catholics Organize," *The Advocate,* 26 September 1973, p. 1; "Lutherans Join Tide, Form Caucus," *The Advocate,* 17 July 1974, p. 17; *Mattachine Midwest Newsletter,* June 1972, p. 4.

81. *ONE Letter* 17, no. 9 (July 1972): 5; "Openly Gay Woman Wins Primary," *The Advocate,* 9 October 1974, p. 1; Howard Erikson, "Legislator Comes Out," *The Advocate,* 1 January 1975; "Gay Candidates," *The Advocate,* 15 December 1976, p. 8.

82. Douglas Sarf, "Bonanza for Gays," *The Advocate,* 23 October 1974, p. 1; Sasha Gregory Lewis, "Center in Seattle Gets $120,000," *The Advocate,* 6 November 1974, p. 3.

83. "Oops, E. Lansing First with Hiring Law," *The Advocate,* 10 May 1972, p. 1; "New Seattle Law Protects Gay Jobs," *The Advocate*, 10 October 1973, p. 1; "D.C. Rights Bill Signed into Law," *The Advocate,* 19 December 1973, p. 1; Lars Bjornson, "Rights Bill Passed in Minneapolis," *The Advocate,* 24 April 1974, p. 6.

84. "Casting Our Fate to the Polls," *The Advocate,* 24 August 1977, p. 35.

HOMOSEXUALITY IN HISTORY
AN ANNOTATED BIBLIOGRAPHY

William Parker, PhD

Historians have given but scant attention to homosexuality in history. Some have felt that it is not a proper subject for historians to be concerned with. Others have argued that, because surviving source materials are so few and incomplete, a history of homosexuality, except for ancient Greece and recent centuries, cannot be written. The view that now is emerging, however, is that homosexuality is a valid and respectable subject for historians to deal with and that much historical work can be done with surviving materials.

In compiling this bibliography, I have selected those 123 books and articles, available in English, which I believe make a contribution to the history of homosexuality or illustrate the nature and quality of historical work now being done on the subject. I have accepted a particular work as "historical" if its author is a historian or if its subject matter or methodology is historical; however, since we lack a precise definition of history, there inevitably will be those who feel that some works included should have been omitted and that some works omitted should have been included.

To make it easier to use, this bibliography is divided into five sections: (1) *General works* that offer a survey of homosexuality in broad chronological and geographical terms; (2) *Specialized works* that focus on some period, person, topic, or interpretation; (3) *Documentary materials* that make readily available certain legal and historical documents, government reports, newspaper articles, and a few selections from writings by homosexual men and women; (4) *Biographies and autobiographies* whose authors frankly and fully discuss the role that homosexuality has played in their own lives or in the lives of their subjects; and (5) *Bibliographies* that can lead researchers to specific works on homosexuality in history and related subjects.

For persons interested in pursuing the historical aspects of homosexuality, the following suggestions may be helpful: First, use the text and notes of such thorough studies as Bailey (#1), Bullough (#2), Dover (#33), and Katz (#88) to track down specific source materials. Second, consult such standard reference guides as *America: History and Life; Disser-*

Journal of Homosexuality, Vol. 6(1/2), Fall/Winter 1980/81

tation Abstracts; Historical Abstracts; Humanities Index; New York Times Index; Newsbank; Readers' Guide; Social Science Citation Index; and *Social Science Index.* Third, become familiar with the contents of such gay periodicals (whether still being published or not) as *The Advocate, Body Politic, Christopher Street, Fag-Rag, Gay, Gay Community News, Gay Sunshine, In Touch, The Ladder, Mattachine Review, One,* and *Vector.* Fourth, consult those works that permit homosexual men and women to speak for themselves, for example, Nancy and Casey Adair, eds., *Word is Out: Stories of Some of Our Lives* (1978); Donald W. Cory (pseud.), *The Homosexual in America: A Subjective Approach* (1960); Karla Jay and Allen Young, eds., *Out of the Closets: Voices of Gay Liberation* (1972) and *After You're Out: Personal Experiences of Gay Men and Lesbian Women* (1975); Len Richmond and Gary Noguera, eds., *The Gay Liberation Book* (1973); and *Come Out: Selections from the Radical Gay Liberation Newspaper* (1970). Also consult those biographies that deal explicitly with the homosexual aspects of the lives of such persons as Gertrude Stein, Alice Toklas, Romaine Brooks, John Addington Symonds, Lytton Strachey, Emily Dickinson, Joe Orton, Montgomery Clift, Charles Laughton, and Tyrone Power.

If homosexuality in history is to be properly documented and assessed, American historians will have to accumulate and publish a large amount of specific data on all aspects of homosexuality for all periods of history, undertake oral history projects designed to preserve the information and experiences of persons and groups that might otherwise be lost, collect and publish primary-source materials on homosexuality for the ready access of all, translate important foreign-language materials into English, and critically examine existing theories about homosexuality to see whether they do or do not fit the historical data.

(The compiler of this bibliography has published a number of bibliographies of homosexuality, two of which (# 121 and # 122) are included here. He also has written a number of articles on homosexuality.)

GENERAL WORKS

1. Bailey, Derrick S. *Homosexuality and the Western Christian Tradition.* London: Longmans, Green, 1955. 181 pp.

Scholarly survey by an Anglican priest of the Christian attitude toward homosexuality. Careful attention is given to Biblical references, the legal tradition of the Roman Empire, the legislation of church councils, and the teachings of the Church Fathers of late antiquity and the whole of the Middle Ages. Bailey argues that the Sodom story does not deal with homosexuality, that the Christian tradition knew only "perversion" and not "inversion," that the charge of Christian persecution of homosexual men and women is a "gross and unwarranted exaggeration," that the Church never automatically branded homosexual persons as heretics, that the Church usually protected homosexual suspects from secular penalties, that there is no evidence that Hebrews or Christians or Roman emperors ever put homosexual men or women to death, that the Church is not responsible for society's harsh attitudes toward and treatment of homosexual males, and that severity against homosexual people is a product of the modern state. This work is important for the hundreds of source documents it cites for the ancient and medieval periods.

2. Bullough, Vern L. *Sexual Variance in Society and History.* New York: John Wiley and Sons, 1976. 715 pp.

The most important single work on homosexuality in history—a pioneer study of high quality. Bullough discusses in detail attitudes toward homosexuality and certain other forms of stigmatized sexual behavior as seen primarily in Western civilization. The work is divided into six parts: I. Background—the sources of Western attitudes in the ancient Near East, with special emphasis on the Hebrews; II. The European inheritance—the Greeks, Romans, and early Christians; III. Non-Western attitudes toward sex—Islam, India, and ancient China; IV. The Christian world—the Byzantine empire and Western Europe in the Middle Ages, the Renaissance, and the Reformation; V. New horizons and the New World—science and eighteenth- and nineteenth-century attitudes toward sex in Europe and America; VI. The twentieth century. Bullough says that for 2000 years Western culture has been "sex-negative" but that because of the recent sexual revolution it now has the potential for coming to terms with human sexuality. Through its text and footnotes, this study leads the reader both to the source materials and to their content.

3. Churchill, Wainwright. *Homosexual Behavior Among Males: A Cross-Cultural and Cross-Species Investigation.* New York: Hawthorn Books, 1967. 349 pp. Also in paperback: Englewood Cliffs, N.J.: Prentice-Hall.

Chapters 4, 7, 8, and 10 survey homosexuality from ancient times to the present in Europe, Africa, and Asia. The Greeks are seen as holding positive attitudes toward sex, and so also are the Romans until the Christians imposed a negative view. Much historical data are cited to show how laws from antiquity to the present have dealt with homosexuality and homosexual males.

4. Crompton, Louis. "Gay Genocide: From Leviticus to Hitler," in Louie Crew, ed., *The Gay Academic* (Palm Springs, Calif.: Etc. Publications, 1978), pp. 67-91.

For over a thousand years, Crompton says, Jews and Christians have pursued a policy of death for homosexuals, yet historians have been silent on the subject. Crompton says he has found evidence that over 200 homosexual men and women were in fact put to death. Also, he says, between 100,000 and 400,000 homosexual persons perished in Nazi Germany.

5. deBecker, Raymond. *The Other Face of Love.* Translated from the French by Margaret Crosland and Alan Daventry. New York: Grove Press, 1969. 209 pp. Also in paperback: London: Sphere Books.

Important and informative historical survey of homosexuality in the ancient Near East (Mesopotamia, Palestine, Egypt, and Asia Minor), in ancient Greece and Rome, in the Moslem world, in India and the Far East, in pre-Columbian America, and especially in the Christian world from the early Middle Ages to the present. The author uses art and letters to supplement the historical sources. Included are 172 pictorial illustrations.

6. Ellis, Havelock. "Sexual Inversion," in *Studies in the Psychology of Sex,* 2 vols. (New York: Random House, 1905), vol. 1, pp. 1-64 (chap. 1).

A still-useful survey of homosexuality in history, naming peoples and countries that have either tolerated or penalized homosexuality, listing famous persons believed to have been homosexual, and citing a number of specific historical sources providing information on homosexuality.

7. Fone, Byrne R. S. "Some Notes toward a History of Gay People," *The Advocate,* no. 259 (January 25, 1979): 17-19, and no. 260 (February 28, 1979): 11-13.

The author argues that the material for writing a history of gay people is available. In some periods—especially ancient Greece but also at times in the late Middle Ages, the Renaissance, and in the eighteenth and nineteenth centuries—the role and contributions of homosexuality to society not only are apparent, they are seen as "an aspect of a healthy society." At other times—especially during much of the Middle Ages and in the late nineteenth and early twentieth centuries—under the dominance of a hostile Christian Church supported by the state, the position of homosexual persons and their contributions to society are misrepresented or hidden.

8. Garde, Noel I. *Jonathan to Gide: The Homosexual in History.* New York: Vantage Press, 1964. 751 pp.

Biographical sketches, arranged in chronological order, of 303 men "who have been referred to" as homosexual or involved in occasional homosexual relationships. At the end of each sketch is listed the "responsible" printed work or works justifying inclusion of that person. Only a small part of each sketch, usually at the end, specifically concerns the subject's actual or alleged homosexual involvement. Informative but to be used with caution.

9. Graham, James. *The Homosexual Kings of England.* London: Universal Tandem Publishing Co., 1968. 92 pp. Paperback original.

Brief and superficial biographical sketches of William Rufus, Richard the Lion-Hearted, Edward II, Richard II, James I, and William III. No footnotes and no bibliography. Of limited value.

10. Hyde, H. Montgomery. *The Love that Dared Not Speak Its Name: A Candid History of Homosexuality in Britain.* Boston: Little, Brown, 1970. 323 pp.

Informative and comprehensive survey of homosexuality in Britain from King William Rufus to the present. Hyde discusses executions for homosexual acts (14 between 1608 and 1832), homosexual scandals (in the 1720s, 1811, 1800s, 1895), the homosexual witch-hunt of the 1940s and 1950s, the Wolfenden Report, and the law reform of 1967.

11. Karlen, Arno. *Sexuality and Homosexuality: A New View.* New York: W. W. Norton, 1971. 666 pp.

Part I (pp. 1-178) surveys homosexuality in history from the ancient Babylonians and Hebrews through the Victorian era. Part II (pp. 179-235) also includes miscellaneous historical data pertaining to the twentieth century. The author says that since the days of Justinian, a sixth-century Roman emperor, charges of homosexuality rarely have been made "until someone had a political or other ulterior motive for doing so." The absence of footnotes hinders checking the author's statements.

12. Mayne, Xavier (pseud. of Edward I. P. Stevenson). *The Intersexes: A History of Similisexualism as a Problem in Social Life.* New York: Arno Press, 1975. 641 pp. (Originally printed privately in 1908.)

A survey of homosexuality from earliest times to the twentieth century. Special attention is given to homosexuality among rulers; aristocrats; military and naval groups; athletes; and religious, ethical, and intellectual leaders.

13. Rattray Taylor, Gordon. "Historical and Mythological Aspects of Homosexuality," in Judd Marmor, ed., *Sexual Inversion: The Multiple Roots of Homosexuality* (New York: Basic Books, 1965), pp. 140-64 (chap. 8).

The author says the materials necessary for writing a detailed historical study of homosexuality do not exist; that in societies where deities are conceived of as mother-figures homosexuality is not deemed of much importance, whereas in societies where deities are conceived of as father-figures homosexuality is strongly condemned; and that only from the seventeenth century on is source material on homosexuality readily available.

14. Rowse, Alfred L. *Homosexuals in History: Ambivalence in Society, Literature, and the Arts.* New York: Macmillan, 1977. 346 pp.

An Oxford scholar and member of the British Academy surveys the lives and achievements of prominent homosexual men from the time of Richard the Lion-Hearted to the present. Englishmen, Frenchmen, Italians, Germans, Russians, and a few Americans are discussed. Rowse assumes a direct relationship between homosexuality and creativity. There are no footnotes or bibliography. Interestingly written and filled with a great wealth of detail.

15. Symonds, John A. *Studies in Sexual Inversion: "A Study of Greek Ethics" and "A Study of Modern Ethics."* New York: Medical Press, 1964. 191 pp.

These two essays, originally printed privately in 1896 and 1901 respectively, are among the earliest and most influential studies written in English on homosexuality in history. The essay on Greece, especially, contains much valuable historical and literary evidence.

16. Vanggaard, Thorkil. *Phallos: A Symbol and Its History in the Male World.* Translated from the Danish by the author. New York: International Universities Press, 1973. 231 pp.

The author, a psychiatrist, sees the phallos not merely as an erotic symbol but also, and more importantly, as a symbol of power and aggression in establishing rank order among nonhomosexual males. It is his thesis that there exists a "homosexual radical" (i.e., drive) that is found among heterosexual males and tends to establish a temporary hierarchical relationship between an older and a younger man. This drive, he says, has been suppressed by the Judeo-Christian legacy and by modern repression. The author also surveys homosexuality from antiquity to the present and provides information on Scandinavia not found elsewhere.

SPECIALIZED WORKS

17. Abbott, Sidney, and Love, Barbara. *Sappho Was a Right-On Woman: A Liberated View of Lesbianism.* New York: Stein and Day, 1972. Also in paperback: New York: Stein and Day.

Chapter 5 (pp. 107-134) provides a historical narrative of the contest in the National Organization for Women that led to the recognition of lesbianism as a legitimate concern of feminism.

18. Altman, Dennis. *Homosexual: Oppression and Liberation.* New York: Outerbridge and Dienstfrey, 1971. 242 pp. Also in paperback: London: Lane.

More important than his historical narrative are the author's observations on the meaning of gay liberation both for homosexual individuals and for society. The gay liberation movement could not have occurred, Altman (a Fulbright Scholar from Australia) argues, without the preliminary work of the black revolution, the women's movement, and the counterculture of recent years. Having become aware of their oppression and having achieved personal liberation through self-affirmation, homosexual men and women now want acceptance, not mere toleration. Before this can happen, Altman says, a complete transformation of society will be necessary. The end product, however, can be human liberation—a society in which such labels as black or white, masculine or feminine, and homosexual or heterosexual will be unnecessary.

19. Bell, Arthur. *Dancing the Gay Lib Blues: A Year in the Homosexual Liberation Movement.* New York: Simon and Schuster, 1971. 189 pp.

Valuable, well-written first-person account of the gay liberation movement in New York City (1969-1970). Special attention is given to the Gay Activists Alliance.

20. Bell, Arthur. *Kings Don't Mean a Thing: The John Knight Murder Case.* New York: William Morrow, 1978. 228 pp. Also in paperback: New York: Berkeley.

This book discusses (1) the murder of John Knight III, journalist and newspaper heir, in Philadelphia on December 7, 1975; (2) the sexual life of Knight and his association with homosexual hustlers and heterosexual pimps and prostitutes; and (3) the trials that resulted in the conviction of Salvatore Soli. The author, a journalist for *The Village Voice,* also discusses his own experiences as he worked on the story.

21. Bingham, Caroline. "Seventeenth Century Attitudes toward Deviant Sex," *Journal of Interdisciplinary History* 1 (1971): 447-68.

Discussion of the trial and execution of the Earl of Castlehaven (1631), along with two male accomplices, after their conviction for sodomy.

22. Bleuel, Hans P. "Ernst Roehm, A Taste for Men" and "Drowned in a Bog," in *Sex and Society in Nazi Germany,* translated from the German by J. Maxwell Brownjohn (Philadelphia: Lippincott, 1973), pp. 95-101, 217-25.

Discussion of homosexuality among the Nazis as represented by Ernst Roehm, a close associate of Hitler, and the Nazi campaign against it resulting in Roehm's murder and in the suggestion that homosexual persons be drowned in bogs as among the ancient Germans.

23. Bryant, Anita. *The Anita Bryant Story.* Old Tappan, N.J.: Fleming H. Revell, 1977. 156 pp.

Bryant's version of what led to the Dade County (Florida) campaign resulting in the repeal (June 1977) of an ordinance prohibiting discrimination against gay people. Contains some useful historical data, but the major emphasis is moral.

24. Bullough, Vern L. *Sex, Society, and History.* New York: Science History Publications, 1976. See pp. 1-16, 17-36, 74-92, and 161-72.

"Sex in History: A Virgin Field" (reprinted from *Journal of Sex Research,* 8(1972): 101-16) calls on historians to pursue serious research on sex and sexual attitudes because so much that has been written on the subject, especially on homosexuality, is inaccurate and based on unproved assumptions. "Attitudes toward Deviant Sex in Ancient Mesopotamia" (reprinted from *Journal of Sex Research,* 7(1971): 184-203) says the Sumerians institutionalized homosexuality as a form of religious prostitution, and the Persians, under the influence of Zoroastrianism, considered it the worst of sins and called for its punishment by death. "Heresy, Witchcraft and Sexuality" (reprinted from *Journal of Homosexuality,* 1(1974): 183-201) points out that, because medieval sources do not distinguish carefully between heresy, witchcraft, and homosexuality, historians find it difficult to deal with homosexuality in the Middle Ages. "Homosexuality and the Medical Model'' (reprinted from *Journal of Homosexuality,* 1(1974): 99-110) surveys eighteenth- and nineteenth-century medical attitudes toward homosexuality and finds in this period a shift in terminology from the moral to the pathological.

25. Burnham, John. ''Early References to Homosexual Communities in American Medical Writings,'' *Medical Aspects of Human Sexuality* 7 (August 1973): 36, 40-49.

Only in the early 1900s, as a result of vice raids, venereal disease, and the writings of psychotherapists and psychiatrists, did the American medical profession slowly learn that homosexual communities, often composed chiefly of male prostitutes and female impersonators, existed in such cities as New York, Washington, D.C., and Chicago.

26. Burton, Richard. ''Terminal Essay, Part IV, Social Conditions—Pederasty,'' in *The Book of the Thousand Nights and a Night,* 10 vols. (privately printed, 1886), vol. 10, pp. 205-54.

Burton says there exists a ''sotadic zone'' between the thirtieth and forty-third degrees, north latitude, within which homosexual and pederastic acts are popular and endemic.

27. Compton, Thomas. ''Sodomy and Civil Doom: The History of an Unchristian Tradition,'' *Vector,* Nov. 1975, pp. 23-27, 57-58.

Brief, clear, and informative survey of Christian hostility to homosexuality as seen in passages in the Old and New Testaments; the writings of early Church Fathers; the condemnations of Justinian, Charlemagne, and various Church councils; and town laws and prosecutions of the late Middle Ages and Renaissance.

28. Crompton, Louis. ''Homosexuals and the Death Penalty in Colonial America,'' *Journal of Homosexuality* 1 (1976): 277-93.

In tracing the legislative history of the statutes prescribing the death penalty for sodomy in the American colonies, Crompton shows that the laws were based on Biblical prohibitions and lasted until after the American Revolution, when fines or imprisonment were substituted. Crompton says two or three men were executed and two others may have been.

29. Crompton, Louis. ''What Do You Say to Someone Who Claims that Homosexuality Caused the Fall of Greece and Rome?'' *Christopher Street,* March 1978, pp. 49-52.

Argues that the myth of homosexuality causing the fall of Greece and Rome is based on ignorance and prejudice and that the edicts of Christian emperors (Constantius II, Theodosius I, and Justinian) established the tradition of persecution of homosexual men and women because they were associated with magic and paganism.

30. Daniel, Marc. ''A Study of Homosexuality in France during the Reign of Louis XIII and Louis XIV,'' *Homophile Studies: ONE Institute Quarterly,* nos. 14 and 15 (1961): 77-93 and 125-36, respectively. (Translated from the French by Marcel Martin.)

Precise, informative, and well-documented survey of homosexuality in seventeenth-century France. Special attention is given to the literary circle of Theophile de Viau, the royal court (including Louis XIII, several princes, and lesser nobles), a number of military commanders, and many clerics. Police reports provide information on the arrest and punishment of homosexual individuals from the lower class.

31. Daniel, Marc. ''Was St. Thomas [à Becket] a Homosexual?'' *Homophile Studies: ONE Institute Quarterly,* no. 19 (1963): 68-71. (Translated from the French by Marcel Martin.)

Concludes that critical research does not support Jean Anouilh's portrayal of Thomas à Becket and King Henry II of England as homosexual lovers.

32. D'Emilio, John. "Radical Beginnings, 1950-51," "Public Actions, Private Fears," and "Reaction, Red Baiting and Respectability" in "Dreams Deferred," *The Body Politic:* Nov. 1978, pp. 19-24; Dec. 1978-Jan. 1979, pp. 24-29; and Feb. 1979, pp. 22-27.

Precise and detailed discussion of the persons, events, and ideas that led to the formation of the Mattachine Society (1951) and its transformation from a radical to a conservative organization (1953). Among the specific subjects treated are: the leftist stance of the Mattachine founders, the organization's discussion groups, the group's decision to fight the arrest charges levied against one of its members, and the publication of ONE. The political and social climate of these years is presented effectively. This work is essential for any serious historical study of the gay liberation movement in the United States.

33. Dover, Kenneth J. *Greek Homosexuality,* Cambridge: Harvard University Press, 1978. 244 pp. Also in paperback: New York: Random House.

Thorough and sober study of Greek homosexuality between the eighth and second centuries B.C. as seen in the art and literature of the period. The author suggests, despite the traditional ideal, that the relationship between an older and a younger male may not always have been a sexless one. He also says homosexual relationships are found between adult males. Included are over 100 illustrations, mostly from vase paintings.

34. Duberman, Martin. "The Therapy of C. M. Otis, 1911," *Christopher Street,* Nov. 1977, pp. 33-37.

Uses the case of a homosexual male treated by a Boston psychiatrist in 1911 to illustrate how historians with perseverance can uncover unpublished material on homosexuality.

35. Eglinton, J. S. *Greek Love.* New York: Oliver Layton Press, 1964. 504 pp.

In this comprehensive and unusual work on the sexual and educational aspects of the relationship between men and boys, the author presents a wealth of material from both primary and secondary sources. Part II surveys the history and literature of boy-love in ancient Greece and Rome, the Middle Ages, and the period from the Renaissance to the present.

36. Evans, Arthur. *Witchcraft and the Gay Counterculture: A Radical View of Western Civilization and Some of the People It Has Tried to Destroy.* Boston: Fag Rag Books, 1978. 180 pp. Paperback original.

Evans points out that in primitive and prehistoric societies and religions, and in some ancient societies also, homosexual people had an important and accepted role as healers, prophets, shamans, and sorcerers; however, Evans argues, urbanism, industrialism, and patriarchal society, together with Christianity, turned against "the homosexual." Christianity chose to identify homosexuality with witchcraft and heresy and to persecute and exterminate homosexual men and women. The author says Western civilization is so corrupt that it needs to be overthrown and replaced by a new collective socialism.

37. Fisher, Saul H. "A Note on Male Homosexuality and the Role of Women in Ancient Greece," in Judd Marmor, ed., *Sexual Inversion: The Multiple Roots of Homosexuality* (New York: Basic Books, 1965), pp. 165-72 (chap. 9).

Fisher says that homosexual pederasty did not exist in the Homeric period when women enjoyed high status but did in later Greece when women's status had deteriorated. He suggests the social factor is important in explaining the change.

38. Flacelière, Robert. "Homosexuality," in *Love in Ancient Greece,* translated from the French by James Cleugh (New York: Crown Publishers, 1962), pp. 62-100 (chap. 3). Also in paperback: New York: Macfadden Books.

A distinguished French historian sees homosexuality among the Greeks as confined mostly to the prosperous and aristocratic groups, as associated with the comradeship of warriors and athletes, and as an educational relationship between an older man and a youth.

39. Foster, Jeanette H. *Sex Variant Women in Literature: An Historical and Quantitative Survey,* 2d ed. New York: Vantage Press, 1956. 420 pp. (Reprinted: Baltimore: Diana Press, 1975.)

Discussion of sex-variant women, primarily lesbians, as seen in literature from Sappho to the present, with emphasis on the classical period and the nineteenth and twentieth centuries. Some consideration is given to the personal lives of the authors, but major emphasis is on their imaginative writings. A useful bibliography of several hundred items is included.

40. Gearhart, Sally, and Johnson, Bill. "The Gay Movement in the Church," in Sally Gearhart and Bill Johnson, eds., *Loving Women/Loving Men: Gay Liberation and the Church* (San Francisco: Glide Foundation, 1974), pp. 61-88.

Summary of the support and resistance that homosexuality and gay liberation aroused within the Christian churches and associated groups during the 1960s and 1970s.

41. Gerassi, John. *The Boys of Boise: Furor, Vice, and Folly in an American City.* New York: Macmillan, 1966. 328 pp. Also in paperback: New York: Collier.

A journalist reports in detail on the homosexual scandal and witch-hunt in Boise, Idaho in the late 1950s. The author sees the incident as an example of legalized prejudice, political and personal vendettas, and human viciousness.

42. Gibson, E. Lawrence. *Get Off My Ship: Ensign Berg v. the U.S. Navy.* New York: Avon Books, 1978. 385 pp. Paperback original.

Precisely documented account of the ordeal of Ensign Vernon E. Berg III, who challenged the Navy's policy toward homosexual personnel. Gibson, Berg's companion, poignantly and incisively details the Navy's homophobia and misconduct from the time of their interrogation by agents of the Naval Investigative Service (July 22, 1975) to the recommendation of a board of officers (January 28, 1976) that Berg be separated under other than honorable conditions. An epilogue and table of chronology bring the story up to 1978. Five appendices contain pertinent documents.

43. Gilbert, Arthur H. "The 'Africaine' Courts-Martial: A Study of Buggery in the Royal Navy," *Journal of Homosexuality* 1 (1974): 111-22.

Careful treatment of the investigation and trial that led the British Navy (1815-1816) to hang four members of the ship's crew for buggery.

44. Goodich, Michael. "Sodomy in Ecclesiastical Law and Theory," *Journal of Homosexuality* 1 (1976): 427-34.

References to homosexual sodomy in the Middle Ages can be found in handbooks for penance, the writings of the Church Fathers, the canons of Church councils, and episcopal instructions to local clergy. Sodomy is discussed in terms of Biblical prohibitions, Roman and Visigothic legal precedents, and its association with magic and heresy. Sodomy in the Middle Ages often was regarded as a clerical vice.

45. Goodich, Michael. "Sodomy in Medieval Secular Law," *Journal of Homosexuality* 1 (1976): 295-302.

In the thirteenth and fourteenth centuries kings and lawmakers, closely associating sodomy with heresy, made secular law conform to Christian ideology. The government of Florence consistently sought to penalize and expel sodomites. So, too, did the Inquisition and lay confraternities associated with the mendicant orders.

46. Goodich, Michael. *The Unmentionable Vice: Homosexuality in the Later Medieval Period.* Santa Barbara, Calif.: American Bibliographical Center—Clio Press, 1979. 164 pp.

Extremely valuable and scholarly discussion of sodomy (with special emphasis on its homosexual aspects) and its relation to the larger subject of heresy, in the period from about 1000 to 1325. Goodich argues (1) that, beginning with the Gregorian Reform of the late eleventh century, the Western Christian Church sought to impose on society its views on sins against nature; (2) that the thirteenth-century scholastics (e.g., Thomas Aquinas) undertook to rationalize and systematize the Church's opposition to sexual sins; (3) that with the aid of the Inquisition the Church sought to enlist secular law and secular rulers in its campaign against sexual nonconformity; and (4) that it was not until the fourteenth century that the Church was willing to persecute sexual nonconformists. Goodich says that nobles, clerics, and townspeople were the groups most frequently charged with homosexual activities and that the harshness of the law was tempered by indulgences, remission, and penance. Examples of persecution and execution of homosexual men and women during the period covered are rare, he says. Goodich directs major attention to the Church's theoretical position as seen in the writings of clerics and in the ecclesiastical law, often supported by secular law. Largely due to the lack of information, less attention is given to the practical application of these condemnations to specific individuals; however, an appendix includes a translation of the trial record and confession of Arnold Verniole (1324) for heresy and for sodomy with teenage boys, offenses for which he received life imprisonment. This important work, together with its notes and bibliography, will be of greatest value to the specialist.

47. Gunnison, Foster. "The Homophile Movement in America," in Ralph W. Weltge, ed., *The Same Sex: An Appraisal of Homosexuality* (Philadelphia: United Church Press, 1969), pp. 113-28.

A historical summary of the homophile movement in the United States since World War II, with emphasis on the Mattachine Society and the Society for Individual Rights.

48. Harris, Bertha. "The More Profound Nationality of Their Lesbianism: Lesbian Society in Paris in the 1920's," in Phyllis Birkby et al., eds., *Amazon Expedition: A Lesbian Feminist Anthology* (New York: Times Change Press, 1973), pp. 77-88.

Lesbians (e.g., Natalie Barney, Romaine Brooks, Colette, Gertrude Stein, and Alice Toklas) created for themselves in Paris in the 1920s a Sapphic world intent on luxury, friendship, and pleasure. They also wrote some lesbian literature.

49. Humphreys, Laud. "Organizing for Change," in *Out of the Closets: The Sociology of Homosexual Liberation* (Englewood Cliffs, N.J.: Prentice-Hall, 1972), pp. 79-100 (chap. 5). Also in paperback: Englewood Cliffs, N.J.: Spectrum.

Tells why and how Mandrake, a gay organization in St. Louis, was formed. Some historical data on other gay organizations can also be found in other chapters.

50. Hyde, H. Montgomery. *The Cleveland Street Scandal.* New York: Coward, McCann and Geoghegan, 1976. 266 pp.

Comprehensive treatment of a homosexual scandal of Victorian England (1889-1890) and the three trials resulting therefrom. Hyde utilizes documents only recently opened to the public by the British government.

51. Lauritsen, John, and Thorstad, David. *The Early Homosexual Rights Movement (1864-1935).* New York: Times Change Press, 1974. 93 pp. Paperback original.
This pioneer work traces the rise and decline of the homosexual rights movement, which began in Europe in the 1860s and lasted until its suppression by Hitler and Stalin in the 1930s. Brief sketches of Karl Ulrichs, Magnus Hirschfeld, Sir Richard Burton, Walt Whitman, and Edward Carpenter are included. This work constitutes a significant contribution to the history of homosexuality.

52. Lea, Henry C. "Unnatural Crime," in *A History of the Inquisition in Spain,* 4 vols. (New York: Macmillan, 1922), vol. 4, pp. 361-77 (chap. 16).
Lea writes that between 1497 and 1723 at least twenty persons were burned at the stake for unnatural crime and that another forty-eight were "relaxed" (probably burned). In time, scourgings and assignment to the galleys came to replace the death penalty.

53. Legman, Gershon. *The Guilt of the Templars.* New York: Basic Books, 1966. 308 pp.
Legman argues that the Templars were "basically a homosexual warrior order," that their seal indicates pederasty, that homosexual rape was probably involved in their initiation practices, that they probably engaged in homosexual orgies, and that their homosexuality was "part and parcel" of their resistance to medieval Christianity. All these assertions are open to question.

54. Licata, Salvatore. "The Emerging Gay Presence," *The Advocate,* no. 245 (July 12, 1978): 7-8, and 43; no. 246 (July 26, 1978): 7-8; no. 247 (August 9, 1978): 17-18, 20.
Survey of the gay liberation movement from nineteenth-century Germany and England to the present, with emphasis on the United States. In the 1950s pioneer organizations like the Mattachine Society, One, Inc., and the Daughters of Bilitis emphasized social and educational goals. In the 1960s gay groups like the Society for Individual Rights and the Mattachine Societies of New York and Washington, D.C. turned to political action. The Stonewall riot of June 1969 ushered in a radical and militant phase led by the Gay Liberation Front and the Gay Activists Alliance. The success of the gay groups has aroused a strong, hostile reaction from the New Right; yet, barring an unexpected disaster, the prospect that gay people will "find their own place as equals in society" is excellent.

55. Licata, Salvatore. "Gay Power: A History of the American Gay Movement, 1908-1974." Ph.D. dissertation, History, University of Southern California, 1978.
Licata divides the American gay movement into four periods: 1908-1948, early attempts to form a civil rights organization; 1948-1960, the formation of such informational and educational organizations as the Mattachine Society, One, Inc., and the Daughters of Bilitis; 1961-1969, the shift of organizations to a stance of political and social activism; and 1969-1974, the formation of gay liberation groups concerned with openly confronting hostile social attitudes and institutions.

56. Lloyd, Robin. "The History of Boy Prostitution," in *For Money or Love: Boy Prostitution in America* (New York: Vanguard Press, 1976), pp. 63-77 (chap. 6). Also in paperback: New York: Ballantine.
Brief and superficial discussion of homosexual prostitution in ancient Greece, Rome, and China, and in twentieth-century Italy, Spain, Ceylon, India, the Middle East, China, Mexico, and the United States.

57. Marrou, Henri I. "Pederasty in Classical Education," in *A History of Education in Antiquity,* translated from the French by George Lamb (New York: New American

Library, 1956), pp. 50-62 (chap. 3). Mentor paperback original.

A distinguished French scholar argues that pederasty in ancient Greece was not only associated with the comradeship of warriors but also with an idealized educational relationship in which an older man served as model and guide to an adolescent youth. Sometimes, the author says, a sexual element may have been involved.

58. Martin, Del, and Lyon, Phyllis. *Lesbian/Woman.* San Francisco: Glide Foundation, 1972. 283 pp. Also in paperback: New York: Bantam.

Candid account of lesbians written by two self-accepting women who for the last twenty-five years have played a major role in the leadership of the American homosexual community. Well written and carefully organized, this book is filled with biographical, autobiographical, and historical data illustrating the triumphs and tragedies experienced by lesbians as they lead their lives in an often hostile society and as they seek to determine the proper relationship between gay liberation and the women's movement. What lesbians want, the authors say, is acceptance, not toleration.

59. Masters, Robert E. L. *The Homosexual Revolution: A Challenging Exposé of the Social and Political Directions of a Minority Group.* New York: Julian Press, 1962. 230 pp. Also in paperback: New York: Belmont.

Semihistorical work of fair quality on the homophile movement, especially in the United States. Separate chapters are devoted to the Mattachine Society, One, Inc., and the Daughters of Bilitis. Attention also is given to the political demands of these groups and the homosexual vote.

60. Murphy, John. *Homosexual Liberation: A Personal View.* New York: Praeger, 1971. 182 pp.

Seeing homosexuality as a powerful and creative force, Murphy argues that homosexual men and women should reject society's repression and proudly create their own freedom. The author discusses his own feelings and experiences—especially as they emerged during and after his association with New York City's Gay Liberation Front in 1970, which converted him into an angry homosexual radical demanding revolutionary change.

61. Olsen, Jack. *The Man with the Candy: The Story of the Houston Mass Murders.* New York: Simon and Schuster, 1974. 218 pp. Also in paperback: New York: Pocket Book.

The story of Dean Corll and his two teenage accomplices, Elmer W. Henley, Jr. and David Brooks, who murdered at least twenty-seven Houston boys between 1971 and 1973.

62. Onge, Jack. *The Gay Liberation Movement.* Chicago: Alliance Press, 1971. 90 pp. Paperback original.

Brief but useful survey of the homophile movement of the 1950s and 1960s. Fairly detailed treatment of the gay liberation movement (1969-1971) in New York City, Chicago, San Francisco, and Los Angeles. Extensive use of movement source materials. Some concern with the political philosophy and role of gay liberation.

63. Pacion, Stanley J. "Sparta: An Experiment in State-Fostered Homosexuality," *Medical Apsects of Human Sexuality* 4 (August 1970): 28-32.

Homosexuality, the author says, was an essential part of Spartan life. Male lovers were comrades-in-arms and were responsible for each other's actions. For reproduction, however, males also were expected to marry.

64. Plant, Richard. "The Men with the Pink Triangles," *Christopher Street,* Feb. 1978, pp. 4-10.

Using written materials and interviews with gay survivors, Plant relates Nazi Germany's treatment of homosexual males in concentration and work camps.

65. Ruggiero, Guido. "Sexual Criminality in the Early Renaissance: Venice, 1338-1358," *Journal of Social History* 8 (1975): 18-37.
The author says sodomy was the most serious sex crime of the time. In 1357, two men were burned for sodomy. Later, in 1406-1407, after discovery of a large group of homosexual men, sixteen or seventeen young nobles and clerics were burned to death.

66. Rule, Jane. *Lesbian Images*. Garden City, New York: Doubleday, 1975. 246 pp.
Discussion of some aspects of the lives and writings of Radclyffe Hall, Gertrude Stein, Willa Cather, Vita Sackville-West, Ivy Compton-Burnett, Elizabeth Bowen, Colette, Violette Leduc, Margaret Anderson, Dorothy Baker, May Sarton, and Maureen Duffy. Several chapters also discuss the women's movement and lesbianism as seen in both the political and literary arenas.

67. Russo, William. "Caravaggio," *In Touch,* no. 39 (January-February 1979): 74-75, 78-79.
Argues that the painter Caravaggio was homosexual and that many of his works were commissioned by and for homosexual clients. Interesting sketch of Caravaggio's brief life—he died in 1610 at age 36.

68. Russo, William. "Edward II, England's Gay King," *In Touch,* no. 43 (September-October, 1979): 61-63.
Discussion of Edward's relationship with Piers Gaveston and Hugh Despenser. Argues that Edward (d. 1327) was deposed and murdered for his homosexuality and that modern historians have judged him harshly for the same reason.

69. Russo, William. "Hart Crane," *In Tauch,* no. 41 (May-June, 1979): 69-72, 75.
Argues that sex, alcohol, and the hostility of the heterosexual world prevented Crane (d. 1932) from becoming a successful gay poet.

70. Russo, William. "Horatio," *In Touch,* no. 38 (November-December, 1978): 30-31.
Recent research reveals that Horatio Alger, who wrote over 100 novels about boys who went from rags to riches, and who for over thirty years was spiritual adviser at a home for orphan boys in New York City, was homosexual.

71. Russo, William. "Lawrence of Arabia," *In Touch,* no. 44 (November-December, 1979): 61-62, 64.
Discussion of Lawrence's personal life—especially his romantic association with several Arab boys—and his activities in Arabia before and during World War I.

72. Russo, William. "Leonardo: A Brush with Gayness," *In Touch,* no. 37 (September-October 1978): 39, 92-95.
The public records of Florence show that in 1474 a charge of sodomy, which was not prosecuted, was made against twenty-two-year-old Leonardo da Vinci. Later Leonardo took ten-year-old Salai into his household and Salai remained with Leonardo for over twenty years. During the last few years of Leonardo's life, a boy named Meizi was his constant and loyal companion.

73. Sagarin, Edward. "Historical Precedents" and "The Mattachine Society and Its Predecessors," in *Structure and Ideology in an Association of Deviants* (New York: Arno Press, 1975), pp. 17-39, 59-88 (chaps. 2 and 4). Reprint of Ph.D. dissertation, Sociology and Anthropology, New York University, 1966.

Brief survey of efforts to form gay organizations. Special attention is given to the Mattachine Society of New York and to the problems and issues its leaders and members had to deal with.

74. Simpson, Colin; Chester, Lewis; and Leitch, David. *The Cleveland Street Affair.* Boston: Little, Brown, 1976. 236 pp.

Using material recently released by the British government, the authors discuss the 1889 London scandal of a male brothel where postal boys consorted for money with patrons allegedly including aristocrats close to the Prince of Wales, who later became King Edward VII.

75. Smith, A. E. ''Peter Ilyich Tschaikovsky: His Life and Loves Re-examined,'' *Homophile Studies: ONE Institute Quarterly,* no. 12 (1961): 20-36.

Smith argues that Tschaikovsky was an active, vigorous, and creative homosexual man as well as a major composer; that he was as happy and well-adjusted as a homosexual person could be in late-nineteenth-century Russia; and that his life was not at all the tragedy some writers suggest.

76. Smith, Timothy d'A. *Love in Earnest: Some Notes on the Lives and Writings of English ''Uranian'' Poets from 1889 to 1930.* London: Routledge and Kegan Paul, 1970. 280 pp.

A sort of literary history discussing the lives and poems of a small group of obscure English poets of the late nineteenth and early twentieth centuries who wrote of the love of adolescent boys.

77. Steakley, James. ''Gays under Socialism: Male Homosexuality in the German Democratic Republic,'' *Body Politic,* no. 29 (December 1976-January 1977): 15-18.

Summary of conditions of gay people in East Germany since 1949. The author says that the sodomy law has been repealed (1968), gay bars are operated by state-appointed persons, and (since 1971) a gay liberation movement has been taking form.

78. Steakley, James. *The Homosexual Emancipation Movement in Germany.* New York: Arno Press, 1975. 121 pp.

This important and well-researched work traces the emergence of homosexuality as an issue of public concern in the Germany of the 1860s, the appearance of homophile groups and publications in the 1890s, the homosexual scandal and witch-hunt of 1903-10, the struggle to create a national homosexual movement after World War I, and the Nazi campaign against homosexual males which resulted in the deaths of over 200,000 gay persons.

79. Teal, Donn. *The Gay Militants.* New York: Stein and Day, 1971. 355 pp.

A detailed history of the gay liberation movement, primarily in the New York City area in the year from June 1969 to June 1970. Special attention is given to the Gay Liberation Front and the Gay Activists Alliance and their various activities. Incorporated into the text are hundreds of quotations from documents and from newspaper and magazine articles.

80. Tripp, Clarence A. ''The Politics of Homosexuality,'' in *The Homosexual Matrix* (New York: McGraw-Hill, 1975), pp. 202-42 (chap. 10). Also in paperback: New York: Signet.

Political considerations, the author says, have led to homosexual witch-hunts (as in Boise, Idaho; Washington, D.C.; and other places), to suppression or misrepresentation (as in certain Congressional investigations), and to the termination of public support for worthwhile projects (as happened to the Kinsey Institute).

81. Tyler, Parker. *Screening the Sexes: Homosexuality in the Movies.* New York: Holt, Rinehart and Winston. 1972. 367 pp. Also in paperback: Garden City, N.Y.: Doubleday & Anchor.

Detailed and comprehensive survey and commentary on the treatment of homosexuality in the movies—whether masculine or feminine, covert or explicit, serious or humorous, and sympathetic or hostile. Camp, nudity, stereotyping, transvestism, transsexualism, sadism, and masochism are discussed, often in psychoanalytic terms. Underground movies and pornographic films are treated as well as movies produced by the major American and European studios.

82. Weeks, Jeffrey. *Coming Out: Homosexual Politics in Britain from the Nineteenth Century to the Present.* London: Quartet Books, 1977. 278 pp.

During the late nineteenth century, under the influence of urbanism and industrial capitalism, society, Weeks argues, sought to limit and control homosexuality by redefining it in increasingly hostile terms. In response, homosexual people created their own subculture and, in time, undertook reform efforts. Weeks carefully analyzes the work of individual reformers (e.g., Havelock Ellis, John A. Symonds, and Edward Carpenter) and reform groups (especially the supporters of the Wolfenden Report). Special attention is given to the period before and after World War II and to the militant gay liberation movement in Britain in the early 1970s. Weeks feels that homosexual men and women and their supporters have no historical sense of the "deeply rooted but changing nature of homosexual oppression" that makes it so difficult to change existing hostile beliefs. This book merits careful study.

83. Winter, Alan D. *The Gay Press: A History of the Gay Community and Its Publications.* Austin, Tex.: self-published, typewritten script, [1977], 114 pp.

Survey of the gay press and its interrelationship with the gay community in America. The gay press in the 1950s was secret and conservative; in the 1960s it was open and moderate; and between 1969 and 1971 it was radical and militant. In recent years it has been seeking new directions. The author sees the gay press as the major source for people searching for the history, ideas, and values of the gay community. The homophobia of the American press also is discussed.

DOCUMENTARY MATERIALS

84. *A Gay News Chronology: January 1969-May 1975.* New York: Arno Press, 1975. 156 pp.

Abstracts, 562 in all, running from two to forty lines in length, of all articles appearing in the *New York Times* between January 1, 1969 and May 15, 1975 and dealing with homosexuality. Useful in documenting the nature and extent of the *Times'* coverage of a subject that heretofore had received little attention.

85. *Government versus Homosexuals.* New York: Arno Press, 1975. 124 pp.

Three official reports important for documenting government hostility toward homosexual citizens: the 1921 United States Senate Report on "Alleged immoral conditions at Newport (R.I.) Naval Training Station," the 1950 United States Senate Report on "Employment of homosexuals and other perverts in government," and the 1966 Report of the Florida Legislature on "Homosexuality and citizenship in Florida."

86. Hyde, H. Montgomery, ed. *The Three Trials of Oscar Wilde.* New York: University Books, 1956. 384 pp. Also in paperback: New York: Dover.

Transcript, with slight alterations, of Wilde's three trials in London in1895. Also includes a lengthy introduction and six appendices by Hyde. Especially useful is the section entitled "The Prevalence of Male Homosexuality in England."

87. Katz, Jonathan. *Coming Out: A Documentary Play about Gay Life and Liberation in the United States of America.* New York: Arno Press, 1975. 110 pp.

A seventy-page play, plus thirty-six pages of notes, reviews, and comments on the play. This play uses historical and literary materials to document the struggles of homosexual Americans from Colonial days to the present. Among the twenty-two incidents treated are the Boise witch hunt, the Stonewall resistance, the Snake Pit raid, and the Chicago conspiracy trial. Among persons dealt with are Willa Cather, Gertrude Stein, Horatio Alger, Allen Ginsberg, and Walt Whitman.

88. Katz, Jonathan. *Gay American History: Lesbians and Gay Men in the U.S.A.—A Documentary.* New York: Thomas Y. Crowell, 1976. 690 pp. Also in paperback: New York: Avon Discus.

An anthology of 186 documents, with brief analytical comments. The work is divided into the following sections: *I. Trouble—1566-1968:* forty-eight documents relating to the conflict of homosexual men and women with society and with themselves; *II. Treatment—1884-1974:* thirty-six documents relating to the treatment and mistreatment of homosexual patients by psychiatrists and psychologists; *III. Passing women—1782-1920:* eighteen documents relating to women who dressed, worked, and lived as men and associated with other women; *IV. Native Americans/Gay Americans—1528-1976:* forty-eight documents relating to homosexuality among the inhabitants of North America before Europeans arrived; *V. Resistance—1859-1972:* sixteen documents relating to individuals and groups who resisted oppression before the recent gay liberation movement; *VI. Love—1779-1932:* twenty documents indicating intimate relations between persons of the same sex. The documentary materials cited include letters, diaries, written and oral interviews, newspaper articles, government reports, articles in medical and scientific journals, law cases, and selections from biographies and autobiographies. Excellent and informative notes, together with the documentary materials, provide the basis for further research and, ultimately, the writing of a narrative history of homosexual men and women in America.

89. Reade, Brian, ed. *Sexual Heretics: Male Homosexuality in English Literature from 1850 to 1900.* New York: Coward-McCann, 1970. 459 pp.

An anthology of eighty-nine selections of English prose and poetry that are either directly or indirectly homosexual in tone. A fifty-six-page introductory essay discusses the homosexual subculture that the author sees in the English literary scene of this period.

BIOGRAPHY AND AUTOBIOGRAPHY

90. Ackerley, Joe R. *My Father and Myself.* New York: Coward-McCann, 1968. 219 pp. Also in paperback: New York: Harcourt Brace Jovanovich.

Ackerley tells of his search to learn about his father and also to find his own identity. Frank discussion of his own homosexual activity in London during the years between World Wars I and II. Witty and well-written.

91. Asprey, Robert. *The Panther's Feast.* New York: Putnam's Sons, 1959. 317 pp. Also in paperback: New York: Bantam.

Biography of Colonel Alfred Redl, one-time Deputy Chief of Intelligence of the Austro-Hungarian General Staff, whose homosexual involvements led him to commit treason by selling secret military defense documents to the Russians on the eve of World

War I. Carefully researched and well-written, this work resorts to the novelist's technique of creating scenes and words for which there is no documentation.

92. Boyd, Malcolm. *Take Off the Masks.* Garden City, N.Y.: Doubleday, 1978. 160 pp.
A well-known Episcopal priest and civil-rights activist tells of his homosexual feelings as a boy, his attempts to live without physical sex of any kind, and his decision to come out of the closet.

93. Brown, Howard. *Familiar Faces, Hidden Lives: The Story of Homosexual Men in America Today.* New York: Harcourt Brace Jovanovich, 1976. 246 pp.
Dr. Brown tells what it is like for himself and over a dozen others to be homosexual in the United States today. The picture he presents is one of men who make significant contributions to society despite the impediments they face.

94. Crisp, Quentin. *The Naked Civil Servant.* New York: Holt, Rinehart and Winston, 1968. 217 pp. Also in paperback: New York: Signet.
An effeminate, open, and flamboyantly homosexual man tells of his experiences as a social outcast in twentieth-century England.

95. Croft-Cooke, Rupert. *Bosie: The Story of Lord Alfred Douglas, His Friends, and Enemies.* London: W. H. Allen, 1963. 414 pp.
A sympathetic biography of Alfred Douglas based on letters, newspaper articles, eyewitness accounts, and the personal knowledge of the author. After sketching Bosie's family background and boyhood, the author treats in detail the relationship between Bosie and Oscar Wilde, Bosie's failure as a husband and father, his financial and legal problems, and his conversion to Catholicism. Bosie's conduct in his dealings with Wilde is presented as honorable and courageous, though ill-advised and impulsive.

96. Croft-Cooke, Rupert. *Feasting with Panthers.* New York: Holt, Rinehart and Winston, 1967. 309 pp.
Discussion of the lives of a number of Victorians—especially Algernon Swinburne, John A. Symonds, and Oscar Wilde, together with their friends and associates—and some of their works that reflect their homosexual interests.

97. Croft-Cooke, Rupert. *The Unrecorded Life of Oscar Wilde.* New York: David McKay, 1972. 289 pp.
The author discusses Wilde at Oxford, his tour of the United States, his marriage, his editorial work, his relationship with Alfred Douglas, the homosexual world of London in Wilde's time, his many homosexual encounters, his arrest and trial, the effect of punishment on him, and his last years.

98. Croft-Cooke, Rupert. *The Verdict of You All.* London: Secker and Warburg, 1965. 254 pp.
The author tells of his own arrest, trial, and conviction for homosexual offenses in England in 1953, and of his prison experiences.

99. Deford, Frank. *Big Bill Tilden: The Triumph and the Tragedy.* New York: Simon and Schuster, 1975. 286 pp.
Part I tells the story of Tilden's professional experiences as the outstanding tennis player of his time. Part II details Tilden's private life, which led finally to several convictions for sexual relations with young boys. The author claims there are "practically no homosexuals in big-time male sports."

100. Fryer, Jonathan. *Isherwood: A Biography.* Garden City, N.Y.: Doubleday, 1978. 303 pp.

Frank treatment of Christopher Isherwood's life as a writer and homosexual man, giving careful attention to his literary collaboration with W. H. Auden and to his romantic relations with lovers in Germany and the United States.

101. Goodman, Paul. "Memoirs of an Ancient Activist," in Joseph A. McCaffrey, ed., *The Homosexual Dialectic* (Englewood Cliffs, N.J.: Prentice-Hall, 1972), pp. 175-81. Also in paperback: New York: Spectrum.

A well-known writer and political activist comments on the role homosexuality has and has not played in his life.

102. Grier, Barbara, and Reid, Coletta, eds. *Lesbian Lives: Biographies of Women from the Ladder.* Oakland, Calif.: Diana Press, 1976. 432 pp. Paperback original.

Brief biographical sketches of over sixty women who were or may have been lesbians. Subdivided into eight sections, the work treats famous couples, adventurers, novelists, queens and their consorts, poets, artists, writers, and pathbreakers. Among the women included are: Amelia Earhart, Colette, Willa Cather, Marie Antoinette, Sarah Teasdale, Rosa Bonheur, Madame de Stael, Dorothy Thompson, Edith Hamilton, and Mary Wollstonecraft.

103. Hamilton, Wallace. *Christopher and Gay: A Partisan's View of the Greenwich Village Scene.* New York: Saturday Review Press, 1973. 216 pp.

The author discusses gay life in Greenwich Village, especially the lives of some twenty young men—from drag queens to leathermen—who have turned to him as a surrogate father in their time of troubles. Well-written and thoughtful.

104. Hansen, Waldemar. "Naked to His Enemies," in *The Peacock Throne* (New York: Holt, Rinehart and Winston, 1972), pp. 396-412 (chap. 24).

In Mogul India in the seventeenth century, Sarmad, a Persian Jewish homosexual convert to Islam, became a great scholar, prophet, teacher, and Sufi mystic poet. He was put to death for religious improprieties, especially for public nakedness.

105. Hyde, H. Montgomery. *Oscar Wilde: A Biography.* New York: Farrar, Straus, Giroux, 1975. 410 pp. Also in paperback: London: Magnum.

Utilizing information only recently brought to light, Hyde treats fully all aspects of Wilde's life, including his last years in exile, and ends with a discussion of Wilde's literary rehabilitation.

106. Isherwood, Christopher. *Christopher and His Kind, 1929-1939.* New York: Farrar, Straus, Giroux, 1976. 339 pp.

Isherwood describes the ten years of his life between his departure from England and his arrival in the United States, detailing his experiences in Germany until 1933 and his travels in seven other European countries thereafter.

107. Kantrowicz, Arnie. *Under the Rainbow: Growing Up Gay.* New York: William Morrow, 1977. 255 pp. Also in paperback: New York: Pocket Books.

The author writes of his experiences as a Jewish homosexual young man with his family and friends, of his professional associates, and of his participation in the gay liberation movement in New York City. Frank and well-written.

108. Kopay, David, and Young, Perry D. *The David Kopay Story: An Extraordinary Self-Revelation.* New York: Arbor House, 1977. 247 pp. Also in paperback: New York: Bantam.

Kopay describes his childhood, his early education at a Catholic seminary, his career as a professional football player, his unsuccessful marriage, his final recognition of his homosexuality, and especially the consequences of his public revelation of his sexual orientation. Twenty-seven pictorial illustrations are included.

109. Maugham, Robin. *Escape from the Shadows.* New York: McGraw-Hill, 1973. 273 pp.
A famous and talented English writer, who finally came to accept himself, reveals his thoughts and experiences regarding homosexuality and other matters.

110. Miller, Merle. *On Being Different: What It Means to Be a Homosexual.* New York: Random House, 1971. 65 pp. Also in paperback: New York: Popular Library.
A well-known novelist discusses his life and experiences as a homosexual man in the United States today. (Originally published in the *New York Times.*)

111. Myron, Nancy, and Bunch, Charlotte. *Women Remembered: A Collection of Biographies from the "Furies."* Baltimore: Diana Press, 1974. 89 pp. Paperback original.
Early sketches of such feminists—most of whom are believed to be lesbians—as Queen Christina of Sweden, Emily Dickinson, Dona Catalina de Erauso, Susan B. Anthony, Anne Bonny, and Mary Read.

112. Perry, Troy, and Lucas, Charles. *The Lord Is My Shepherd and He Knows I'm Gay.* Los Angeles: Nash Publishing Co., 1972. 232 pp. Also in paperback: New York: Bantam.
The founder of the Metropolitan Community Church tells of his personal experiences, how he came to found a church for homosexual people and the many difficulties involved in doing so, and how he has tried to protest against and do something about the discrimination that gay people face in this country.

113. Reid, John (pseud.). *The Best Little Boy in the World.* New York: Putnam's Sons, 1973. 247 pp. Also in paperback: New York: Ballantine.
A successful young businessman, indignant at society's attitudes toward homosexual persons, discusses his feelings and experiences as a homosexual man and describes gay life in New York City and Boston.

114. Swicegood, Thomas L. P. *Our God Too.* Pyramid Books, 1974. 379 pp. Paperback original.
Biographical account of Rev. Troy Perry and his friends and associates in Los Angeles who made possible the establishment of the Metropolitan Community Church, a church primarily for gay people. Most of the contents are historical, but some persons and conversations are at least in part fictional.

115. Tobin, Kay, and Wicker, Randy. *The Gay Crusaders.* New York: Paperback Library, 1972. 238 pp. Paperback original.
Sketches of eleven male and four female leaders of the gay liberation movement in the United States. Included are Troy Perry, Frank Kameny, Barbara Gittings, Jack Baker, and Jim Owles.

116. Wells, Anna M. *Miss Marks and Miss Woolley.* Boston: Houghton Mifflin, 1978. 268 pp.
Portrait of the life-long love of Mary Woolley, former president of Mount Holyoke College, and Jeanette Marks, a member of the English and Drama department.

117. Wildeblood, Peter. *Against the Law.* London: Weidenfeld and Nicolson, 1956. 189 pp. Also in paperback: Harmondsworth, England: Penguin.

First-hand account of one of the five homosexual men involved in the famous "Lord Montagu" case (1954) in England. Wildeblood tells of his arrest, conviction, and imprisonment.

118. Williams, Tennessee. *Memoirs.* Garden City, N.Y.: Doubleday, 1975. 264 pp. Also in paperback: New York: Bantam.

Williams discusses frankly both his personal and professional life. He tells about his family, childhood, friends, and relatives; his career and associates in the theater; and the ups and downs of his literary, social, sexual, and emotional lives.

BIBLIOGRAPHIES

119. Bullough, Vern L.; Legg, W. Dorr; Elcano, Barrett W.; and Kepner, James. *An Annotated Bibliography of Homosexuality,* 2 vols., New York: Garland Publishing Co., 1976. 873 pp.

Lists 434 references (vol. 1, pp. 37-66) under "history," 681 (vol. 2, pp. 1-41) under "biography and autobiography," and 818 (vol. 2, pp. 292-333) under "homophile movement." Many references are to materials in foreign languages.

120. Damon, Gene; Watson, Jan; and Jordan, Robin. *The Lesbian in Literature: A Bibliography,* 2nd ed. Reno, Nev.: The Ladder, 1975. 96 pp. Paperback original.

Lists sixty-six references under "biography" and fifty-six under "autobiography."

121. Parker, William. *Homosexuality Bibliography: Supplement, 1970-1975.* Metuchen, N.J.: Scarecrow Press, 1977. 337 pp.

Subject index lists twenty-nine references under "history, homosexuality in"; twenty-seven under "biography"; and thirty-nine under "autobiography."

122. Parker, William. *Homosexuality: A Selective Bibliography of over 3,000 Items.* Metuchen, N.J.: Scarecrow Press, 1971. 323 pp.

Subject index lists thirty-five references under "history, homosexuality in"; forty-five under "biography"; and sixteen under "autobiography."

123. Weinberg, Martin S., and Bell, Alan P. *Homosexuality: An Annotated Bibliography.* New York: Harper & Row, 1972. 550 pp.

Subject index lists sixty-six references under "history, homosexuality in."

BOOK REVIEWS

THE UNMENTIONABLE VICE: HOMOSEXUALITY IN THE LATER MEDIEVAL PERIOD, by Michael Goodich. *Santa Barbara, California: American Bibliographical Center-Clio Press, 1979. xvii + 164 pages.*

This is the kind of monograph that I hope will appear in greater numbers in the future. It deals with a limited time period, essentially from the eleventh through the thirteenth centuries; a limited geographical area, Catholic Europe; and is based upon the original source material. Goodich presents his material in the context of previous research on human sexuality. He does not change the basic outline of concepts that I proposed in my *Sexual Variance in Society and History,* but he does flesh them out in greater detail. He argues that there was a strong effort to impose the canons of Catholic sexual morality on the public in the eleventh and twelfth centuries, and that these attempts were systematized first in canon law and then, by the thirteenth century, in scholastic philosophy. Persecution, however, was episodic and actual prosecution for homosexual offenses did not take place until the fourteenth century.

Since Goodich originally became interested in the subject of homosexuality through his study of the Christian saints, his book is most valuable when it deals with the activities of the Cluniac and Hidebrandine reformers in the establishment of a strong opposition to homosexuality. This was accomplished first through written works about homosexuality and later through counciliar legislation. As befits a lecturer at the University of Haifa, Goodich also includes a brief discussion on Jewish attitudes during the same period, particularly as represented by Maimonides.

After tracing religious attitudes, Goodich turns to secular law in the thirteenth century. The book concludes with a translation of the record of the trial of Arnold the Catalan of Verniolle in 1323 on the charges of sodomy and heresy. The trial took place in the Albigensian area of Southern France and throws some light on the reasons why an individual would engage in homosexual activity. According to his own testimony, Arnold's first homosexual experiences occurred before he had reached puberty and took place in the bed which he shared with several fellow students at the grammar school. Once initiated, and in spite of his clerical status, Arnold continued to indulge in sexual activities with both men and women, apparently without much discrimination. In 1320 he suffered a skin disease he believed to be leprosy, which appeared shortly after having sex with a prostitute. Consequently, he decided to rely exclusively on sexual relations with boys. According to his own statements, he had sex with a large number of local youths at the rate of at least once every two weeks. Many of these youths engaged in homosexual activities with others and a whole network of contacts appeared in the area. After being found guilty, Arnold was stripped of his clerical orders, placed in iron chains, and ordered to be fed on a diet of bread and water for life.

The book is well documented and includes both a bibliography and an index. Goodich is careful not to go beyond his sources; in fact, my only negative criticism is that he is far too conservative. At this state of scholarship, however, that is probably an asset rather than a liaibility.

Vern L. Bullough, PhD
Dean, Faculty of Natural and Social Sciences
State University of New York, Buffalo

THE UNMENTIONABLE VICE: HOMOSEXUALITY IN THE LATER MEDIEVAL PERIOD, by Michael Goodich. *Santa Barbara, California: American Bibliographical Center-Clio Press, 1979. xvii + 164 pages.*

Michael Goodich, who is Senior Lecturer in Medieval History at the University of Haifa, must be commended for writing an objective and intelligent synthesis of scholarship on homosexuality in the Middle Ages. Although, for reasons that will be discussed later, his brief study is not definitive (as Kenneth Dover's recent and masterful book on Greek homosexuality is), it is nonetheless the best point of departure for anyone currently interested in the topic. His summations of the relevant original Latin sources are usually clear and accurate, and his bibliographical references to modern scholarship in German and French, as well as English, are reasonably complete.

Of the book's five chapters, the first is the least satisfactory, a diffuse commentary on various individuals and groups who lived between the tenth and fifteenth centuries and who were identified, if not accused, by contemporaries as being sexual deviants. Some, like King Edward II of England, have become notorious. Others, like Baudri de Bourgeuil, Archbishop of Dol, and Marbod, Bishop of Rennes, both of whom authored poems with homosexual themes or references in the early twelfth century, are known primarily to specialists in medieval literature. Still others, like Rolandinus Ronchaia, a transvestite ordered burned in 1354 for committing sodomy in Venice, or Nicola Campoli, condemned in 1412 for performing a similar act in one of the chapels of the church of San Petronio in Bologna, are familiar only to those scholars who have begun to investigate the court records stored in Italian municipal archives. Besides identifying homosexual suspects and other deviants, Goodich comments briefly on the reliability of the charges brought against King William II Rufus of England and Pope Boniface VIII, among others. He suggests that known centers of homosexual activity existed at the Anglo-Norman court in the early twelfth century, the University of Paris in the thirteenth century, and the Republics of Florence and Venice in the fourteenth and fifteenth centuries. He proposes reasons for both the presence of these centers and the absence of references to others. While Goodich's explanations for homosexual centers are plausible, his comments on the accuracy of some charges of homosexuality are overly cryptic, and his explanations for homosexual activity are frequently inadequate or unconvincing.

The nucleus of the book (chapters 2, 3, and 4) is successful. Here, Goodich describes more systematically the formulation of a coherent policy against homosexual activity between the eleventh and fourteenth centuries by the lawyers and theologians of the Roman Church. The eleventh century marked the beginning of the process, when clerics sympathetic to the views of Pope Gregory VII attempted to purify the clergy by imposing upon deacons and priests ascetic ideals previously associated only with monks: poverty and chastity. Gathering precedents from passages in the scriptures, from early Church council decisions, and from Roman imperial decrees, the Gregorian reformers published a variety of statements condemning concubinage, adultery, bestiality, and homosexual acts (sodomy). The most rigorous assault against same-sex relations was made by Peter Damian in the *Liber Gomorrhianus*. Peter, who was horrified by all sexuality, equated sodomy with murder and viewed even bestiality as less sinful than homosexuality because in bestiality only one soul, and not two, was damned. Although his specific theological judgments were not to be endorsed and his efforts to increase the traditional penances for deviant sexual acts failed to gain widespread contemporary acceptance, Church leaders in the next two centuries came to adopt Peter's negative attitudes and to find additional justifications for their condemnation.

During the twelfth century, at numerous local synods and at the ecumenical councils held at the Lateran in Rome (1179 and 1215), the offensive against clerical vice in general, and sodomy in particular, gained momentum: Stricter penalties were established, discretion in imposing penances was removed from parish priests and reserved for bishops, disciplinary actions were adopted for use against those bishops who failed to act vigorously, and lay authorities were called upon to assist in the enforcement of papal edicts. Moreover, laymen as well as clergy were forbidden to "sin against nature." In many respects, this restriction of sexual options paralleled a vigorous assault against heresy, with which sexual deviation came to be identified.

Led by the newly founded order of Dominican preachers, thirteenth-century clergy formulated new handbooks of penance that outlined in a clear, concise, and above all rational fashion, for clergy and laity alike, the Christian doctrine of sin. In these handbooks and in the contemporaneous books of theology and philosophy, sodomy was condemned as one of the most serious forms of lust because it violated the natural purpose of sexuality: procreation. While official criticism of homosexual acts spread and grew more severe, a contrary movement developed that prevented the establishment of a truly Puritan community: the use of dispensations and indulgences, which allowed many sinners, including sodomites, to avoid penalties by performing works of charity or offering gifts to the Church.

In the final narrative chapter of his book, Goodich examines the introduction of prohibitions against homosexuality into secular (as opposed to ecclesiastical) law. Prior to the twelfth century, tribal and community leaders rarely had concerned themselves officially with sodomy. This was a matter left to the Church and to individual families, for it did not affect property distribution or the peace of the community, as did adultery, theft, and murder. Between the twelfth and fourteenth centuries, kings and urban community leaders, especially the latter, came to legislate on a variety of moral issues, partly because they were persuaded by reformists and their converts that sodomy and other forms of deviant behavior were dangerous to the common safety, and partly because they had found a new model for lawmaking, that of Imperial Rome. As Christian Roman Emperors previously had legislated against heresy and sodomy, so did the medieval governments of Florence, Perugia, Siena, and many other states. The penalties stipulated were more severe than those in the eleventh-century books of penance. The Florentine statutes of 1325, for example, prescribed castration for a convicted pederast, a beating or a fifty-lire fine for a willing catamite under fourteen, and a 100-lire fine for the willing calamite between fourteen and eighteen. For "rogues," "imposters," and foreign criminals convicted of sodomy, punishments were even more stringent: They were subjected to beatings by the populace and then burned at the stake.

The Unmentionable Vice concludes with an appendix, which is in some respects the most interesting part of the entire book. It is a thirty-page selection translated from the Inquisitorial Record of Jacques Fournier, then Bishop of Pamiers (1317-1326) and subsequently elected as Pope Benedict XII (1334-1342). The selection reports on the trial of Arnold Verniolle, a subdeacon accused of sodomy and heresy, and includes the testimony of several students whom Arnold had seduced, as well as Arnold's own corroboration of the charges. What makes this so important is that it provides our only glimpse of the thoughts and actions of individuals who engaged in homosexual relations. From it we learn how different from official statements popular ideas and behavior could be. Arnold, for example, testified to his belief that sodomy was less serious than rape, deflowering a virgin, adultery, or incest. While most of Arnold's youthful partners denied sharing his ideas, they were willing enough to share his bed.

The vitality of Arnold Verniolle's trial record dramatizes the major limitation of Goodich's study: the absence of data to indicate the real social impact of the Church's campaign against sodomy. Did most people's sexual attitudes and behavior change substantially between the eleventh and fourteenth centuries? If so, did men and women conform to the stricter new laws or deviate increasingly from them? Were they more (or less) sexually free in the family-dominated and presumably conformist society of eleventh-century Europe, about which we know little, than in the individualist and heterodox society of the fourteenth century, about which we are better informed? These are questions that Goodich and other scholars have begun to ask but have not yet answered. *The Unmentionable Vice* usefully organizes what has been written about homosexuality in the Middle Ages and makes some important additions to the body of available knowledge. This is a good beginning.

William N. Bonds, PhD
Professor of History
San Francisco State University

COMING OUT: HOMOSEXUAL POLITICS IN BRITAIN, FROM THE NINETEENTH CENTURY TO THE PRESENT, by Jeffrey Weeks. *New York and London: Quartet Books, 1977. ix + 278 pages.*

The subject matter of *Coming Out* is broader than the subtitle suggests, for Jeffrey Weeks deals with more than homosexual politics. His book chronicles the legal, social, and even literary difficulties facing anyone involved with homosexuality until very recently, when toleration of sexual tastes that strayed from the norm expanded. Weeks is at his best when discussing events in his own lifetime. He knows the political and social movements of the 1960s and 1970s intimately; as a result, the last chapters of the book give the reader an interesting insight into attempts to raise gay consciousness and to reform British law. Unfortunately, Weeks is much less successful in earlier chapters.

The author begins, sensibly enough, by correctly identifying the profound differences between earlier attitudes toward sodomy and buggery and the late-nineteenth-century discovery of a group apart called "homosexuals." This is a distinction that has been made recently and elegantly by Michel Foucault in the first volume of *The History of Sexuality,* which appeared too late for Weeks to cite in *Coming Out.* Both writers argue that in earlier times the law punished sinners: men and women who had performed sexual *acts* that were contrary to accepted heterosexual norms. The nineteenth century witnessed the recognition of an entire deviant subculture and the invention of a new terminology (in particular, the word "homosexuality") to describe it. Weeks is to be congratulated for not reading the present into the past and for not proceeding, as have so many writers, on the assumption that Western society has conducted a relentless war on gay people since Biblical times. He understands that attitudes toward various sexual practices must be treated contextually and that these attitudes change from time to time.

Unfortunately, Weeks follows this promising beginning with a number of assertions about changing attitudes and practices that are probably incorrect and, at the very least, not proven by the evidence presented in this volume. Weeks' contention that the legal situation for homosexual males grew considerably worse in the late nineteenth century is central to his book. He contends that the change from sodomy as a sin to homosexuality as a crime brought in its wake more severe treatment of sexual dissenters. In support of this assertion, Weeks cites the tightening of the sodomy statutes in 1826, when courts no longer had to prove emission (as well as penetration) in cases of anal sex. Whether the motivation for this legal change was an attempt to convict more homosexual men is problematic. The emission requirement had only been on the books since 1771 and had created problems because of the difficulty of determining emission or the lack of it. The emission requirement was dropped, most likely, because it was difficult to prove or disprove. In any case, there is no evidence that this was the start of a vendetta against "homosexuals" in the nineteenth century, nor are there any studies to date that show that prosecutions and convictions increased dramatically after 1826. My own work on court records in the first part of the nineteenth century leads me to believe that, in fact, convictions may have decreased.

Weeks then cites the Labouchère Amendment of 1885, which made homosexual acts other than anal sex illegal; and the Vagrancy Act of 1898, which, while aimed primarily at prostitutes, also affected homosexual prostitution. Unfortunately, Weeks has looked at the law but not at its application. Before the 1885 Amendment (under which Oscar Wilde was tried and sentenced), men caught performing homosexual acts short of sodomy were regularly tried and convicted for attempted sodomy. This was a misdemeanor but conviction for it could result in a prison sentence of two years or longer. There is no evidence that the Labouchère Amendment brought about a substantial increase in prosecutions for homosexual activity. Indeed, since there was little discussion of it at the time, we know very little about the reasons why it was passed in the first place. The same point is relevant for the 1898 Vagrancy Act. Is there evidence that the Vagrancy Act resulted in increased pressure on homosexual solicitation? We have no studies that show this was the case. Previously, authorities dealt regularly with homosexual solicitation under the attempted sodomy statute.

Just as serious a flaw is the cavalier manner in which Weeks dismisses the well-known fact that in the eighteenth and early nineteenth centuries men were executed for sodomy. This was true not only in the Navy, as my own studies have shown, but in civilian society as well. The last execution of a civilian probably took place in 1836, and the last mariner executed for this crime was a man named Maxwell, in 1829. By 1861 the punishment for convicted sodomites had been reduced to life imprisonment. Rarely, if at all, was this harsh sentence imposed in English courts. To dismiss this very obvious softening of the law and then to claim that the 1885 Amendment represented a tougher attitude raises a serious question. Why is Weeks so intent on clinging to the hypothesis that persecution of homosexual males and sodomites grew in the nineteenth century? As far as I can determine, the answer lies in the author's ideological predilections: the conviction that persecution of homosexuality had something to do with the rise of capitalism in the nineteenth century and, in particular, the growth of what the author calls the "capitalist family." In his introduction, Weeks observes that "it is within the specific context of the capitalist family that modern concepts of homosexuality have developed" (p. 5). The author does not define "capitalist family," but presumably he is referring to the growth in importance of the family unit and, conversely, to the attitudes or practices that might threaten its centrality and stability. Many writers, of course, have noticed the significance of the family in the nineteenth century, and Weeks would have been on sound ground if he had simply argued that the nature of *fear* of homosexuality *changed* in the nineteenth century because of the importance of the family. Unfortunately, he tries to go beyond this in an attempt to blame capitalism and the family structure it spawned for the plight of homosexual men and women. As I have indicated, this is not supported by the evidence. Weeks' ideological biases seem to have overwhelmed his judgment.

We may be thankful that, after the first few chapters, Weeks pretty much ignores his central thesis and gets down to the business of telling about homosexual people in the late nineteenth and early twentieth centuries. There are chapters on John Addington Symonds and Havelock Ellis, though these contain little that is new, and a more interesting account of Edward Carpenter's career. On Carpenter, the author used primary materials from the collection in the Sheffield City Libraries. This source helps to make the chapter one of the better, more original ones in the book. There is a section on lesbianism, which is understandably short because of the difficulty of getting information on this subject, as well as some interesting chapters on sexual-law-reform societies in the interwar years. Since the author is more interested in homosexual pressure groups than in the political process that led to reform in 1967, the penultimate chapters seem unbalanced. We learn much more about the Homosexual Law Reform Society than we do about the Wolfenden Report or the politics of changing the law in the 1960s.

To sum up, *Coming Out* is, at its best, a straightforward narrative of the trials and successes of homosexual men and women over the past 100 years or so, but it fails to explain either the nature of or the reason for the changes that have occurred since the eighteenth century. Weeks has not taken the time and effort to understand thoroughly English society in the eighteenth and nineteenth centuries or, in particular, the meaning of the changes that have taken place in modern times.

Arthur N. Gilbert, PhD
Graduate School of International Studies
University of Denver

COMING OUT: HOMOSEXUAL POLITICS IN BRITAIN, FROM THE NINETEENTH CENTURY TO THE PRESENT, by Jeffrey Weeks. *New York and London: Quartet Books, 1977. ix + 278 pages.*

Jeffrey Weeks' *Coming Out* joins James Steakley's *The Homosexual Emancipation Movement in Germany* in a very select school of quality scholarly investigation into gay history. Weeks documents the emergence of gay society in Britain from the seventeenth century to the present day of gay liberation politics.

The highly readable account pulls together all currently known references to homosexual existence in Britain and introduces several previously unpublished texts that illuminate early homosexual social networks. In particular, Weeks makes good use of the long-suppressed diaries of John Addington Symonds and the letters of a mid-1890s secret homosexual society called the Order of Chaeronea. Various aspects of homosexual life are given comprehensive treatement: a history of legal persecution and reform, the "sickness" hysteria invented by the medical profession, and, most importantly, insights into how people with homosexual interests came to organize themselves into a new and exclusive subculture whence gay identity emerged. The descriptions of the first homosexual clubs and organized street cruising of the eighteenth and nineteenth centuries are invaluable.

Early exponents of gay awareness, such as John Addington Symonds, Edward Carpenter, and Radclyffe Hall, receive full biographies, as do sympathetic sexographers such as Havelock Ellis and Sir Richard Burton. Weeks points out the early popularity of the "third sex" theory, which relieved homosexuality of guilt by making it "involuntary." Much of early English homosexual thought was also shaped by the romance of upper-middle-class men with (an image of) working-class men. The issue of class-defined sexuality, as raised in this book, merits further attention by scholars.

Homosexuality tended to be spiritualized among the early gay writers, no doubt as part of the general Victorian spiritualization of all sexuality, but especially because homosexual people had so often been reduced in the public mind to sexual creatures without emotional lives. Same-sex *affection* seems even now to be a greater scandal than sexuality. Legal tolerance demands that homosexual be "private"; public affection risks prosecution as "indecent" or "lewd" conduct.

The book details the show trials and purges of the postwar period, when the United Kingdom experienced the equivalent of McCarthyism; the slow march from the Wolfenden Report to legal reform; the explosion of gay liberation/lesbian-feminism; and the reorganization in the Campaign for Homosexual Equality.

Though billed as "sociology" by the publisher, Weeks' book is history as a "sequence of events," with only passing reference to the deeper structural changes in society that opened the possibilities for such "events." The roots of homophobia, for example, are traced to the rise of capitalism and the development of the nuclear family in a very sketchy and brief discussion in the "Introduction." This theme merits a more thoroughgoing treatment.

Weeks' book is destined to become a classic in gay studies. It is hoped that it will inspire equally careful and comprehensive histories of gay communities in other nations.

Barry D. Adam, PhD
Department of Sociology
University of Windsor

COMING OUT: HOMOSEXUAL POLITICS IN BRITAIN, FROM THE NINETEENTH CENTURY TO THE PRESENT, by Jeffrey Weeks. *New York and London: Quartet Books, 1977. ix + 278 pages.*

Years before the onset of the gay liberation movement, when I was an adolescent struggling to come to terms with my sexual identity, I fastened upon history as a personal road to self-acceptance. The history books I read made no reference to homosexuals, nor did they mention much about related topics such as sexual mores, personal relationships, or family life. Each book, however, carried the same essential message. History is the story of *change,* and change seemed to be the one constant, the inevitable feature, of human society. To me, the implications were obvious: If empires rise and fall, if the economic life of society can be transformed, if social relationships undergo metamorphoses, then society's treatment of homosexual men and women also could change. Oppression was neither inevitable nor eternal.

One of the great achievements of the gay movement in the 1970s was the impetus it provided for uncovering a history of lesbianism and male homosexuality. Gay history is not merely a spinoff of the gay movement, however; it also feeds a growing stream of gay political activity through its impact on the consciousness of lesbians and gay men. A developing gay history calls into question the notion that homosexuality is an immutable, unchanging condition, a psychological aberration. History provides a social group with roots, with a tradition that empowers its members. For lesbians and gay men in particular, a history of our own demolishes the belief that each of us is the only one in the world, an isolated freak of nature.

The amount of historical work that has appeared in the last ten years is impressive, especially when one considers that homosexuality had virtually no written history until the last decade. Jonathan Katz' massive documentary collection, *Gay American History,* has done more, perhaps, than any other book to demonstrate the richness of gay history as a field of research and to encourage others to explore the subject. The number of articles appearing in scholarly journals and in lesbian and gay magazines is growing rapidly and covers a wide range of topics.

Jeffrey Weeks' excellent book, *Coming Out,* represents a major advance in the historiography of homosexuality. A monographic study of homosexual politics in Great Britain over the last 100 years, it attempts to construct a theoretical framework for understanding gay politics and gay identity. Weeks sharply distinguishes homosexual behavior, which is universal, from homosexual identity, which is historically specific. Concerning himself with the latter, he urges the reader to see "*Coming Out* . . . as a historical process, the gradual emergence and articulation of a homosexual identity and public presence." Weeks argues that in Britain (and, by implication, throughout European and North American capitalist societies) homosexual identity is a comparatively recent phenomenon. He sees it appearing in the wake of deepening hostility toward homosexuality, as "part of the restructuring of the family and sexual relations consequent upon the triumph of urbanization and industrial capitalism." His study of homosexual politics intertwines two themes: the social and ideological conditions that defined homosexual oppression and the efforts of reformers to unravel the web of oppression.

Weeks begins with a discussion of changing social attitudes in the late nineteenth century, when the state imposed more stringent legal penalties against homosexual behavior and a rising class of medical professionals labeled homosexuality as a sickness or biological anomaly. Out of this deepening hostility came a new self-definition among homosexual males, an inchoate group consciousness, and the beginnings of a gay male subculture. Major scandals, such as the Cleveland Street affair in the late 1880s and the Oscar Wilde trial in the mid 1890s, hastened this process.

Weeks places the emergence of a modern lesbian identity and subculture a generation later. The restricted social roles available to women and the prevailing definitions of female sexuality as passive and receptive narrowed the possibilities for leading a lesbian life; thus, the feminist movement was an essential precondition for the development of a lesbian identity. The obscenity trial of *The Well of Loneliness* in the late 1920s was a watershed in that it brought lesbianism into public view in a major way for the first time.

Most impressive is Weeks' reconstruction of a century of homosexual politics in Britain, much of it but dimly known until now. The book includes an excellent treatment of the work of three "pioneers," John Addington Symonds, Havelock Ellis, and Edward Carpenter, and moves on to discuss the different approaches to reform in the first half of the twentieth century. The description of the movement for law reform in the 1950s and 1960s suggests interesting parallels with the homophile movement in the United States. Throughout most of the book, Weeks maintains a critical attitude toward his reformers. While admitting the constraints placed on reform efforts by a hostile society and acknowledging the gains made, Weeks also analyzes the limits imposed by reformers themselves by virtue of their ideological perspectives and their strategic and tactical choices.

By far the most thorough and detailed section is the final one, which examines the gay liberation movement of the 1970s. Here Weeks can write as both participant and historian. While the details will be new to the North American reader, the contours are familiar: an initial radical impulse, growing out of the social upheavals of the 1960s, that placed gay oppression firmly within a critique of capitalist society; the waning of radicalism in the mid-1970s; and its replacement by a new brand of reform politics, new because radical gay liberation gave a visibility to lesbians and gay men that necessarily transformed the context in which reform could be pursued.

Coming Out has its flaws. There are times when Weeks, in his effort to document a continuing gay resistance to oppression, makes mountains out of molehills. His treatment of the secret Order of Chaeronea, for instance, left me unconvinced that the group was really much more than the projected fantasy of George Cecil Ives, its founder. From the evidence presented by Weeks, I thought Ives was more likely a crackpot than a courageous, farsighted, pioneering reformer.

More seriously flawed is Weeks' explanation of the emergence of a modern lesbian and gay identity. By interpreting it as a *response* to deepening hostility toward homosexuality, Weeks ironically perpetuates a notion of gay people as *re*-actors only, rather than as women and men making autonomous choices about their sexual identity. It is surprising that Weeks, a Marxist, has not looked for more direct, material explanations within the social relations of capitalism for the emergence of a gay identity. What impact, for instance, does the free-labor system of capitalism, which allows individuals to earn a living independently of the family, have in terms of increasing the options for men and women to pursue their sexual and emotional preferences for members of the same sex? What about the tendency of commodity production to expand until one can buy all the goods necessary for life, so that families are no longer necessary as producing units and individuals have greater freedom to *choose* the shape of their personal life, including their sexual orientation?

Still, Weeks' book is a major contribution toward uncovering a homosexual past. His argument that gay identity is historically specific will set the terms for further exploration into gay history, and his analysis of the different strands of homosexual politics should serve as a model for future efforts.

John D'Emilio
History Department
Columbia University

INDEX

$18.95